Piloting and Dead Reckoning

Second Edition

Piloting and Dead Reckoning

By H. H. Shufeldt, Captain, USNR (Retired) and G. D. Dunlap

Naval Institute Press
Annapolis, Maryland

Copyright © 1981, 1971
by the United States Naval Institute
Annapolis, Maryland

Fifth printing, 1989

Library of Congress Cataloging in Publication Data
Shufeldt, Henry H. 1898–1985
    Piloting and dead reckoning.

    Includes index.
    Supt. of Docs. no.: D 201.2:P64
    1. Navigation.   I. Dunlap, G. D., 1923–   joint
author.   II. Title.
VK555.S54   1981   623.89   80–606921
ISBN 0–87021–512–4 (flex. bdg.)

Printed in the United States of America

Contents

Preface

This text has been prepared to give the boatman the necessary knowledge for safe navigation under pilotage and dead reckoning conditions. It has often been said that "a little knowledge is dangerous," and this is applicable to the great mass of Americans who are turning to the sea for their recreation without a proper background in seamanship, navigation, rules of the road, weather, etc. With the dangerously crowded conditions on many of our inland waterways and the complete dependence of the crew on the skill of the navigator when operating offshore, the combination of knowledge and experience is a prerequisite for safe navigation. The satisfaction of accomplishment, at the conclusion of a successful voyage, is a rewarding experience.

Heretofore, the boatman was dependent on major textbooks, prepared primarily for military or large commercial users to obtain his navigational information. In this new text on piloting and dead reckoning, we have used a more informal approach and have eliminated data pertaining only to large vessels. The authors, who also prepared the twelfth edition of the basic textbook *Dutton's Navigation and Piloting*, have drawn freely from the subject matter used therein while using a simplified approach.

In this second edition, a new chapter has been added to provide data on the use of the pocket scientific calculator to provide a solution to many of the problems associated with piloting and dead reckoning.

We are especially grateful to the U.S. Coast Guard Auxiliary for their review of the manuscript and to the various government agencies and commercial firms that made available necessary material and illustrations for the preparation of the text.

H. H. SHUFELDT
G. D. DUNLAP

Piloting and Dead Reckoning

chapter one

The Earth and Its Coordinates

THE EARTH'S SHAPE

The earth is almost, but not quite, a perfect sphere. Its surface is covered with small wrinkles that form the mountains and the ocean deeps, but its lack of symmetry is greater than is indicated by these comparatively small irregularities. Since the earth is flattened somewhat at the poles and has a slight bulge at the equator, the polar diameter is about 6,864.57 nautical miles, while the equatorial diameter is approximately 6,887.91 nautical miles. This difference of 23.34 miles between the two diameters defines the ellipticity or compression of the earth, that is, its deviation from a true sphere.

The earth may therefore be termed a *spheroid*, in that it closely approximates the shape of a sphere. For most navigational purposes, it is considered to be a sphere, but in the preparation of charts, its actual shape is taken into consideration. As we all know, the earth rotates once each day from west to east about its *axis*. The terminals of the axis, where they reach the surface of the earth, are known as the North and South Poles. As we shall see, our method of determining position on the earth uses the axis as the basic reference.

GREAT CIRCLES

Before we can proceed with a discussion of the earth, we must familiarize ourselves with two types of circles on the earth's surface. The first of these is a *great circle*, which may be defined as a circle on the earth's surface described by a plane passing through the earth's center. The shortest distance between any two points on the earth lies along the shorter arc of the great circle passing through them. Figure 1-1 illustrates the great circle.

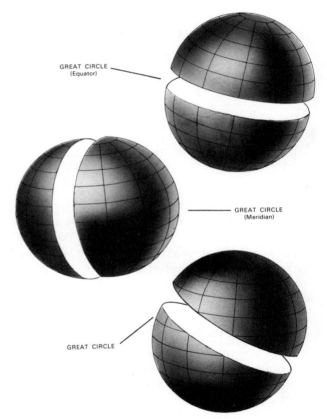

Figure 1-1. Great Circles

The second is a *small circle*, which is any circle on the earth's surface other than a great circle. That is to say that the plane of a small circle does not pass through the center of the earth, but divides the earth into two unequal parts. Small circles are illustrated in figure 1-2.

THE EARTH'S COORDINATES

More than two thousand years ago the Greeks realized that the earth was a sphere, and their

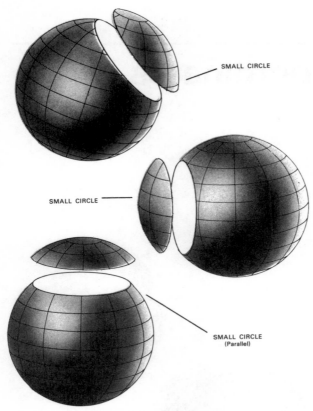

Figure 1-2.   Small Circles

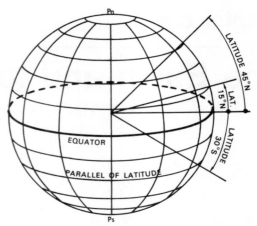

Figure 1-3.   Equator, Latitude, and Parallels of Latitude

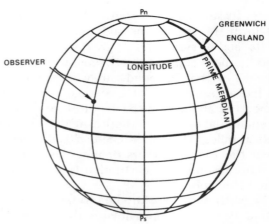

Figure 1-4.   Meridians, Prime Meridian, and Longitude

geographers felt the need to develop a system of *coordinates* so that any given spot could be located relative to another. A coordinate is defined as one of a set of magnitudes locating a point in space. The coordinates we are interested in are called *latitude* and *longitude*.

Parallels of Latitude

Parallels of latitude, often simply termed *parallels,* are so called because their planes are always parallel to the equator. The equator is a great circle, as its plane passes through the earth's center. All other parallels are small circles on the earth's surface, as illustrated in figure 1-3. The parallels form one magnitude of the earth's system of coordinates.

Meridians

The other magnitude is formed by great circles called *meridians.* Their planes pass through both the earth's center and its poles; the earth's axis lies within the plane of every meridian, and every meridian is therefore perpendicular to the equator. See figure 1-4. Every meridian lies in a true north and south direction.

Every spot on the earth's surface has a meridian passing through it. Two meridians may therefore be separated by only an infinitely small distance. For the sake of clarity, meridians are generally drawn on large-scale charts at intervals of a few minutes of arc.

As we have seen, every meridian is bisected by the earth's axis. The *upper branch* of a meridian is that half which passes through a given place; the *lower branch* is the half which lies on the opposite side of the axis. In common parlance, *meridian* is used to denote the upper branch.

The *prime meridian* is the upper branch of the meridian passing through the Royal Greenwich Observatory in England. The prime meridian, which is also called the *Greenwich Meridian,* is used as the origin for the measurement of longitude by the United States and most other nations. The lower branch of the prime meridian is called the 180th meridian.

Before passing on, let us stop to consider what we have learned of parallels and meridians. All parallels are, as their name implies, parallel throughout their circumference, and they are perpendicular to all meridians. The linear distance between any two parallels is the same at any longitude. Meridians differ from parallels, in that they converge as they approach the poles, where they intersect. The linear distance between two meridians therefore decreases as they approach the poles; that is to say, the linear distance decreases with an increase of latitude as shown in figure 1-4, but the angular measurement, called *arc* or difference of longitude, between the meridians remains constant.

The latitude of a place is thus established by the parallel passing through it, and its longitude by the meridian on which it lies. The measurement of latitude and longitude will be discussed in the succeeding section.

The Measurement of Latitude and Longitude

The *latitude (L)* of any point on the earth's surface is its distance north or south of the equator. This distance is measured in *arc,* that is to say in degrees, minutes, and seconds along the meridian passing through the place. In navigational practice, however, seconds of arc are not used, and the smallest unit of measurement employed is a tenth of a minute of arc. Latitude is measured from the equator, which has a latitude of 0°, north toward the North Pole, which has a latitude of 90°N, or south toward the South Pole, which has a latitude of 90°S. Remember that latitude, to be meaningful, must always be given the name *north* or *south;* usually symbols are used to describe latitude, as L 47°16.4′N. The measurement of latitude is illustrated in figure 1-3.

The *longitude (λ)* of any point is also a measure of angular distance expressed in degrees, minutes, and seconds of arc; it is the arc of the equator included between the prime meridian and the meridian of the point. Again, in navigation, the seconds of arc are omitted, and longitude is stated to the nearest tenth of a minute. Longitude is measured from 0° at the prime meridian to 180° west, and from 0° to 180° east. The measurement of longitude is illustrated in figure 1-4. Bear in mind that, as with latitude, longitude must be given a name, in this case, *east* or *west.* In navigation the Greek letter, λ (lambda), is ordinarily used as the symbol to denote longitude, as in λ 79°52.6′W. The designation *Lo* is also used by

some navigators. When both the latitude and longitude of a point are to be stated, the latitude is always given first. There are 60 minutes of arc in each degree of longitude regardless of the latitude of the measurement, but as pointed out previously, the linear distance in miles changes with latitude. This is illustrated in figure 1-5.

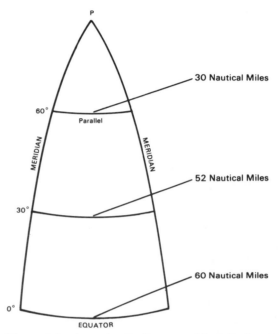

Figure 1-5.   Length of a Degree of Longitude at Various Latitudes

DIRECTION

We have now established how any spot on earth may be exactly located. The next consideration is the establishment of *true direction.* The navigator defines direction as the position of one point in space relative to another without reference to the distance between them.

The true direction of a line passing through a point is the inclination of that line to the point's meridian, measured clockwise from true north; as we have seen, all meridians lie in a true north-south direction. Direction is stated in degrees, starting from *true north.* A three-digit system is always employed, thus north is 000°, and direction is measured clockwise from 000° to 360°. Thus east is 090°, south is 180°, and west is 270°. With the three-digit system, a direction of 7° is written as 007°, and commonly spoken as "oh oh seven degrees," but in radio communication always given as "zero zero seven degrees." Figure 1-6

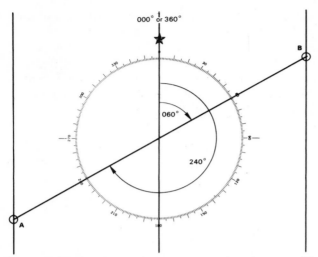

Figure 1-6.   Measurement of Direction *(course or track)* in Navigation

shows how direction is measured from the meridian.

Since a line extends in two directions, it does not indicate a single direction unless marked in some way. The two directions of a line are said to be reciprocals of each other. Thus, east or 090° is the reciprocal of west or 270°. To obtain the reciprocal of any number, subtract or add 180°. Lines must always be marked or labeled to indicate the proper direction. In figure 1-6 the course, *A* to *B*, is 060°. The reciprocal, *B* to *A*, is 240°.

Types of Direction in Navigation

The determination of direction is an important part of the navigator's work, particularly in piloting. Outlined below are some of the types of direction used by the navigator; they must be clearly understood. For the time being, we shall consider only true direction; later in this text we shall consider direction in reference to standards of measurement other than the true meridian.

Course (C) is a rhumb line direction. It is the horizontal direction of travel through still water, expressed in angular units from a reference direction, from 000° at the reference direction clockwise through 360°. The course is often designated as true, magnetic, or compass, when the reference direction is true north, magnetic north, or compass north, respectively. Course can be either an anticipated or an accomplished (course made good) direction of travel.

The *course line* is a graphic representation of the ship's course on a chart.

The *heading or ship's head (Hdg. or SH)* is the horizontal direction in which a ship points or heads at any instant, expressed in angular units, 000° clockwise through 360°, from a reference direction. Heading is a constantly changing value as a ship oscillates or yaws across the course because of effects of the sea and of steering error.

Track (TR), as used in navigation, is the rhumb line or lines describing the path a vessel desires to make good *relative to the earth* in proceeding from one location to another.

Bearing (B), in piloting, usually refers to the horizontal angular direction of one point from another. In figure 1-7, the direction of the light from the vessel is indicated by the line of sight, called a *visual* bearing. Such bearings are usually expressed in terms of either of two reference directions: (a) true north, and (b) the direction in which the vessel is headed.

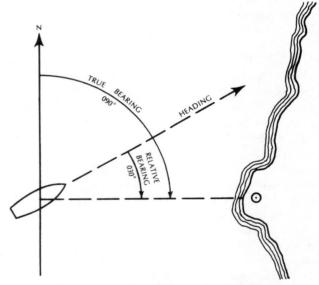

Figure 1-7.   True and Relative Bearings

If true north is the reference direction, the bearing is called a *true bearing (TB);* if the reference direction is the vessel's heading, the bearing is called a *relative bearing (RB).* A relative bearing is the angle between the vessel's fore-and-aft line and the line of sight to the object, measured clockwise from 000° at the vessel's head through 360°. As shown in figure 1-7 the true bearing of the light is 090°, and the relative bearing is 030°.

Bearing is also used to define the great circle direction of any place from a given point. In this instance, it is always measured from true north. Radio direction finder bearings, described in chapter 15, are bearings of this type.

DISTANCE

So far, we have mentioned distance only briefly. In a previous section, we stated that the shortest distance between any two points on earth lies along the shorter arc of the great circle passing through them. It is logical, therefore, that a unit of arc, the *minute,* on a great circle about the earth be used as the standard of measurement for most navigation. We have also stated that the earth is not a perfect sphere. This leads to slightly differing lengths for a minute of arc of a great circle, depending on how the circle is drawn about the earth. In the interests of obtaining a standard measurement, the International Hydrographic Bureau in 1929 proposed that the standard of measurement be one minute of arc of a great circle drawn on a perfect sphere having the approximate area of the earth and that this measurement be taken as being 1,852 meters, or 6076.1155 feet, in length. This length is the *nautical mile* and was adopted officially by the United States in 1954.

The nautical mile is the unit of distance most commonly used in navigation, although the *statute mile* of 5,280 feet is also used on the Great Lakes and by the Corps of Engineers on the Intracoastal Waterway. To convert from nautical miles to statute miles, multiply the nautical miles by 1.15; from statute to nautical, multiply statute miles by .87.

For all practical purposes, one minute of arc on a meridian of the earth, which is equivalent to one minute of latitude, is one nautical mile. Two thousand yards is also used as an equivalent to one nautical mile. This latter standard is used in naval tactics and should not be employed when the distance involved is long.

Differences of both latitude and longitude are usually expressed as units of arc, in degrees and minutes. Differences of latitude alone may be stated as nautical miles, as one minute of latitude closely approximates one nautical mile. Remember that meridians converge towards the poles as latitude increases; while the longitude, or angular measurement between them remains the same, the distance between them changes constantly as one moves away from the equator. *Never,* therefore, *use minutes of longitude for measuring distance.*

SPEED

In navigation, speed is usually expressed in *knots*. One knot (kn) is a speed of one nautical mile per hour. Note that the term *knots* includes both the time and distance relationship which is inherent in speed. The term *knots per hour* should therefore never be used except when referring to acceleration.

chapter two

Charts

Webster defines a map as a representation, usually flat, of the surface of the earth or of part of it; a *chart*, in the marine sense, is defined as a map for the use of navigators. A chart, therefore, is primarily concerned with the water and ordinarily shows only those features of the land which are of interest to the mariner, while a map devotes itself primarily to the land and its characteristics.

The chart is the most important adjunct available to the sailor. Inspection of a modern coastal chart will indicate the vast amount of both useful and essential information that is presented. Aids to navigation, as well as hazards such as shoals, are shown in their correct positions; the depths of water are indicated at frequent intervals, and notes and other pertinent data of interest to the navigator are printed within the outline of the land.

CHART PROJECTIONS

As stated in chapter 1, the earth is essentially a sphere. This presents a problem to the cartographer, as no part of a sphere can be presented as a flat surface without causing some distortion. This fact can be appreciated by anyone who has attempted to flatten out a portion of a hollow ball. The surface of a sphere or spheroid is termed *non-developable*, as no part of it can be spread flat without some distortion. The chartmaker gets around this problem by projecting or transferring points on the sphere onto a surface, such as a cone or cylinder, which can be readily unrolled to form a plane and is therefore said to be *developable*. On some special purpose charts, the projection is made directly onto a plane. This transfer of points from the sphere to a developable surface is called a *projection*. The projection is termed *geometric* or *perspective* if the points on the sphere are projected from a single point that may

be at the center of the earth, at infinity, or some other location; however, most map projections are derived mathematically, rather than geometrically.

A considerable number of projections are available in preparing maps and charts. Each projection offers distinctive advantages for certain uses; no single projection is best for all charting purposes. The differences in appearance between the various projections are most evident on charts depicting large areas, called *small scale* charts. On such a chart, the scale might be 1:8,000,000; that is, a unit of length on the chart represents 8,000,000 units on the earth. The projections appear to differ much less on *large scale* charts, such as harbor charts, where the scale may be 1:20,000. On such charts covering a small section of the earth, at low latitudes, the projections used in navigation become in appearance almost identical to each other. The desirable properties for a projection include:

1. True shape of physical features. ⎫ A projection offering these two characteristics is said to be *conformal*.
2. Correct angular relationship. ⎭
3. Equal area, that is, the representation of areas in their correct relative proportions.
4. True scale, which permits accurate measurement of distance.
5. Rhumb lines presented as straight lines. A *rhumb line* is a line on the surface of the earth that crosses all meridians at the same angle. (See the following section.)
6. Great circles represented as straight lines.

It is possible to preserve any one of these desirable properties in a projection; sometimes more than one property may be preserved. However, it is impossible to preserve them all. For example, it is impossible to prepare a chart on which both great circles and rhumb lines are represented by straight lines.

In coastal navigation, only two projections are in general use in this country; they are the *Mercator* and the *polyconic,* and it is with these that we will concern ourselves. The Mercator projection is used for all coastal charts covering the seaboard of the United States, while the polyconic projection is used for some charts of the Great Lakes.

Rhumb Lines

In the previous section, we defined a rhumb line as a line on the surface of the earth which crosses every meridian at the same angle. For short distance marine navigation, it is desirable for a chart projection to present rhumb lines as straight lines.

On a sphere, a rhumb line is not a straight line, but a curve spiraling towards the pole, as will be seen in figure 2-1. This spiral is called a *loxodromic curve* or *loxodrome.* On the earth's surface, the arc of a great circle connecting two points is shorter than the rhumb line. However, the difference is generally negligible for moderate distances or if the line approximates the equator or a meridian.

Rhumb lines are in general use in navigation for laying down courses, and as we shall see in the following section, they are represented by straight lines on a chart prepared on the Mercator projection.

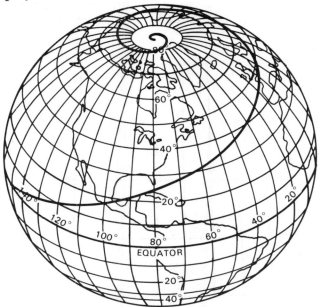

Figure 2-1. A Rhumb Line or Loxodrome

The Mercator Projection

The Mercator projection gets its name from a Flemish geographer, Gerardus Mercator, who invented it some four hundred years ago. It is the most widely used projection in marine navigation, as position, distance, and direction can be easily determined, and as rhumb lines plot as straight lines. It is also conformal; that is, all angles are presented correctly, and, for small areas, true shape of features is maintained. Conformality is one of the advantages of the Mercator projection, which makes it desirable for navigational use.

To envision the principle of the Mercator projection, imagine a cylinder rolled around the earth, tangent at the equator, and therefore parallel to the polar axis, as shown in figure 2-2. If we think of meridians as planes passed through the earth, the intersections of the planes and the cylinder are straight, vertical lines. If we imagine the cylinder to be a chart, when we unroll it, the meridians are all vertical straight lines, and all are perpendicular to the equator, which forms the horizontal axis of the chart.

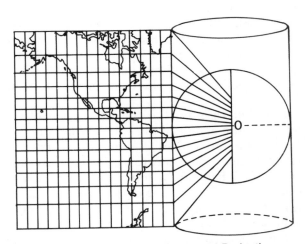

Figure 2-2. Mercator Conformal Projection

On the earth, meridians converge at the pole and therefore become progressively closer together as the pole is approached. Therefore, when meridians are presented as parallel vertical lines on a Mercator chart, the charted length of a degree of longitude remains constant despite any change of latitude. This is corrected by expanding the latitude scale mathematically to allow for the expansion of the longitude scale. For our purposes, we need not discuss the manner in which this expansion is achieved; the expansion of the latitude scale approximates the secant of the latitude.

Let us now take a look at the unrolled cylinder. The latitude scale has been expanded mathematically in accordance with the formulas for the Mercator projection. The *graticule* or *grid* of the Mercator projection appears as shown in figure 2-2. Note that the meridians are evenly spaced vertical lines and the parallels are straight horizontal lines, the spacing between them increasing with latitude. It is evident that the greater the distance from the equator, the greater is the distortion of this projection. The Mercator projection cannot be extended to the poles.

However, for the area it covers in charts used for piloting, the Mercator is satisfactory, and all meridians and parallels form rectangular areas with the lines crossing at 90-degree angles. A straight line drawn on the chart makes the same angle at each meridian, and is, therefore, a rhumb line. Incidentally, it also crosses each successive parallel at identical angles.

Polyconic Projection

The *polyconic projection,* as used for nautical charts of the Great Lakes, is actually compiled mathematically. It can be visualized as a projection on a series of cones tangent to the earth at different parallels of latitude. A conic projection can have the cone either tangent to the sphere or intersecting the sphere as shown in figure 2-3.

In either case, on the conic the point of projection is the center of the earth. When the cone is unrolled into a plane, the meridians appear as straight lines converging toward a point (the apex of the cone) beyond the top of the chart. Parallels of latitude will appear as equally spaced concentric circles crossing the meridians at 90-degree angles. Great circles are straight lines. The polyconic, as shown in figure 2-4, has one difference from a projection on a single cone, which is important to the navigator. The parallels of latitude are presented as curves, but they are equally spaced only along the central meridian of the chart and are not concentric but become farther apart toward the edges of the chart. This will be apparent only on a small-scale chart of a large area, and practically unnoticeable on a large scale chart used for piloting. As distance away from a central meridian is increased, distortion will be introduced. Figure 2-4 illustrates the arrangement of meridians and parallels on the polyconic projection. It is not a conformal chart but produces an excellent piloting chart, as radio signals that

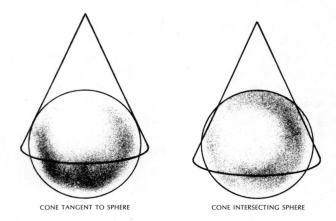

CONE TANGENT TO SPHERE   CONE INTERSECTING SPHERE

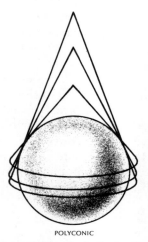

POLYCONIC

Figure 2-3.   Conic Projections

follow a great circle are plotted as straight lines, and for small areas, distances are uniform and plotting of both distance and direction is easily accomplished.

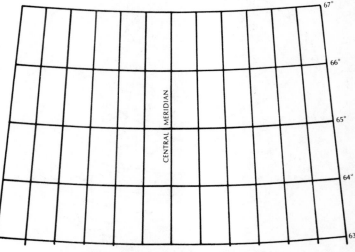

Figure 2-4.   Polyconic Projection

ACCURACY OF CHARTS

A chart is no more accurate than the survey on which it is based. In order to judge the accuracy and completeness of a survey, note its source and date, which are generally given in the title. Besides the changes that may have taken place since the date of the survey, the earlier surveys often were made under circumstances that precluded great accuracy of detail. Until a chart, based on such a survey, is tested, it should be regarded with caution. Except in well-frequented waters, few surveys have been so minute as to make certain that all dangers have been found. The fullness or scantiness of the soundings is another method of estimating the completeness of the survey, but it must be remembered that the chart seldom shows all soundings that were obtained. If the soundings are sparse or unevenly distributed, it should be taken for granted, as a precautionary measure, that the survey was not in great detail.

Dating of Charts

It is of the utmost importance that charts be up to date. Bottoms often shoal, wrecks may be a menace, and underwater structures, often invisible above the surface, may cause a hazard to navigation. Changes and hazards not shown on a chart may lead to serious damage.

Charts may be corrected from the regularly issued *Notices to Mariners* (see chapter 17). All charts published by the National Ocean Service are dated. A new edition of the chart is published when there are many corrections or when these corrections are so important to navigation as to make all previous printings obsolete. The number and date of the edition of the chart are printed in the lower left hand corner, as

6th Ed., July 12/81.

When the edition is revised and reprinted, the date of the revision appears to the right of the edition date, as

6th Ed., July 12/81; Revised 2/20/84.

A revised printing does not make prior printings of the same edition obsolete. A new edition does, however, cause an older edition to be obsolete.

Charts are distributed by government-approved chart agents in most coastal cities. These agents are not permitted to hand-correct the charts.

Consult the *Notices to Mariners* for additional corrections subsequent to the number and date given on the chart.

New editions of most harbor and coastal charts are generally scheduled for annual issue. All critical changes are published in the USCG *Local Notices to Mariners*. The edition date of these charts appears in the title and at the lower left-hand corner of each chart page.

Charts will be discussed further in chapter 3.

chapter three

Understanding the Chart

LARGE- AND SMALL-SCALE CHARTS

The terms *large scale* and *small scale* cause much confusion to many who are not accustomed to using charts. For example, if we speak of a chart at scale 1:5,000,000, the very "bigness" of the number erroneously makes it seem of a larger scale than one at 1:150,000. We need to remember that these scales can also be written as fractions, as $\frac{1}{5,000,000}$ or $\frac{1}{150,000}$, and the larger the denominator of a fraction, the smaller the scale. Probably everyone would rather have $\frac{1}{4}$ of a pie than $\frac{1}{10}$!

At a scale of 1:5,000,000, one mile is only 0.014 of an inch in length; at 1:150,000 it is 0.48 of an inch.

An expression such as 1:5,000,000 means that one inch on the chart represents 5,000,000 inches on the earth's surface; or one centimeter represents 5,000,000 centimeters; or one of any other unit represents 5,000,000 of the same units.

There is no firm definition for the terms *large-scale charts* and *small-scale charts*; the two terms are only relative. Thus, as compared with a chart at 1:150,000, the chart at 1:5,000,000 is a *small*-scale chart; it becomes a *large*-scale chart, however, when compared with one at 1:10,000,000. The chart that shows any particular feature (as an island or bay) at a larger size and in more detail is considered (comparatively, at least) as a *large-scale* chart.

A chart may also carry a statement of scale such as "one inch equals 16 miles"—that is, one inch on the chart represents 16 miles on the surface of the earth. On a Mercator chart, it may be stated that "one degree of longitude equals 1.25 inches." It is stated in this form because the spacing between meridians is the one constant on a Mercator projection.

Scales of Principal Chart Series

The scales of nautical charts range from 1:2,500 to about 1:5,000,000. Graphic scales are generally shown on charts of scale 1:80,000 and larger, and numerical scales are given in the upper right border for smaller scale charts. For convenient reference, charts may be classified according to scale as follows:

Sailing charts—scales 1:600,000 and smaller. These are planned for use in fixing the mariner's position as he approaches the coast from the open ocean, or for sailing between distant coastwise ports. On such charts the shoreline and topography are generalized and only offshore soundings, the principal lights, outer buoys, and landmarks visible at considerable distances are shown.

General charts—scales 1:150,000 to 1:600,000. These are planned for coastwise navigation outside of outlying reefs and shoals.

Coast charts—scales 1:50,000 to 1:150,000. These are planned for inshore navigation, for entering bays and harbors of considerable width, and for navigating large inland waterways.

Harbor charts—scales larger than 1:50,000. These are planned for harbors, anchorage areas, and the smaller waterways.

The entire Atlantic and Gulf Coasts of the United States are covered by a series of charts produced by the National Ocean Service at a scale of 1:80,000. They are similar to the training chart TR 1210. Individual harbors and other areas are also shown on larger scale charts in series that do not overlap to give complete coverage. The Pacific Coast is covered by charts generally numbered in the 18000 series at varying scales.

Intracoastal Waterway (inside route) charts are produced to a scale of 1:40,000, and have a 5-digit chart number. This is a special series of charts embracing the inside route in New Jersey and the route from Norfolk, Virginia, to Key West, Florida, on the Atlantic Coast and from Key West, Florida, to the Mexican Boundary on the Gulf Coast.

Small-craft charts. A considerable number of the harbor charts and those covering inland areas such as the Chesapeake Bay are designed to be especially helpful to the yachtsman. Tide tables for the local area, services available in local harbors, marine weather forecast data, etc. are given. The tide tables

are of course valid only for the year and dates shown on the tables. New editions are generally scheduled for annual issue.

Great Lakes charts. Great Lakes charts are printed at various scales. General charts of an entire lake are at 1:400,000 to 1:600,000. Coast charts are generally at 1:120,000, and small area, or harbor charts, vary from 1:5,000 to 1:80,000.

River charts. River charts are, in general, available from the U.S. Army Engineer Division. Cata-

Figure 3-1. Annapolis, Maryland, on Chart No. 12283 at a Scale of 1:10,000

logs covering, for example, the upper Mississippi River are available from the Engineer Division, Chicago, and those for the lower Mississippi are available from the Engineer Division, Vicksburg. Charts of the Ohio River and its tributaries are obtainable from the Engineer Division, Cincinnati, Ohio. Navigation on the Mississippi is almost entirely based on distance in terms of miles from a starting point. On the lower Mississippi mile zero is at Head of Passes, 95 miles below New Orleans, and mile 953.8 is at Cairo, Illinois. The upper Mississippi starts mile zero at Cairo, and extends to mile 857.6 at Minneapolis, Minnesota.

Mariners are urged to obtain and study thoroughly the largest scale charts available for a particular route even if a smaller scale is used for keeping track of position in passage.

As a comparison of detail that can be shown, figure 3-1 shows Annapolis, Maryland, on Chart No. 12283 at a scale of 1:10,000, while figure 3-2 shows a small section of Chart No. 12263 at a scale of 1:80,000 covering the same area.

Read carefully all notes appearing on the chart. Do not merely look at it as though it were a picture. Check the scale, determine the date of the survey on which it is based. Check to see whether soundings are in feet, fathoms, or meters. Check that the sounding coverage is complete and if not, note the areas where lack of information may indicate danger. Note the system of projection used, so that direction and distance can be measured

correctly. Check the tidal reference plane. Remember that a chart is a basic tool in the art of navigation. Learn to use it skillfully.

CHART SYMBOLS AND ABBREVIATIONS

Many symbols and abbreviations are used on charts. These constitute a kind of shorthand which tells the navigator the physical characteristics of the charted area and details of the available aids to navigation. The symbols used are quite standardized but are subject to some variation, depending on the scale of the particular chart or chart series. It simply is not possible on a small-scale chart to show all the details that can be shown on a large-scale chart.

Many pages of text would be needed to describe all the symbols and abbreviations employed to present the detailed information available on a modern chart. These symbols and abbreviations are shown in "Chart No. 1" of the National Ocean Service and are standard among the various government agencies producing charts.

The chart data are reproduced on the back of training chart TR 1210. This chart was "frozen" by NOS as a training chart and not further corrected, in order to have similar nautical charts available for students regardless of when the chart is purchased. TR 1210 should be procured and kept on hand for easy reference when studying the following material.

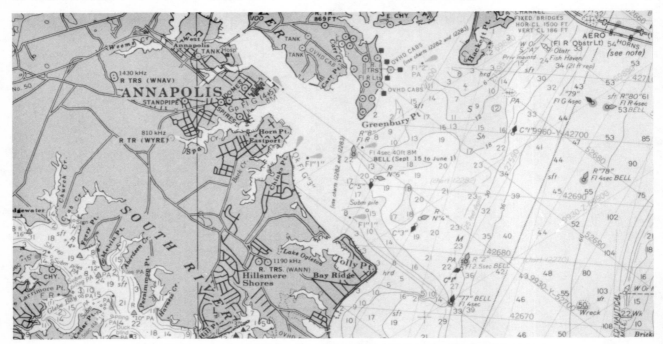

Figure 3-2.   Annapolis, Maryland, on Chart No. 12263 at a Scale of 1:80,000

Referring now to the reverse of TR 1210, read the general remarks contained thereon, as they give several important items of information not readily apparent from merely looking at the illustrations. It will be seen that even the type of lettering used on the chart conveys important information.

The man-made aids to navigation such as buoys, beacons, radio stations, etc., each have a distinct symbol assigned, which enables you to identify the location of the aid on the chart quickly and accurately. However, symbols indicating natural features of the land, the coastline, the quality of the bottom, etc., are equally important.

SUMMARY

In this and the previous chapter, we discussed chart projections and charts at some length.

The neophyte navigator, planning a cruise, often purchases only large-scale charts showing the various areas the cruise is to cover. This is a mistake, as it makes it impossible to plan the voyage intelligently—this must be done on a single chart.

For example, let us assume that a boat expects to cruise offshore from the Delaware Bay to Newport, that is, passing well south and east of New York and Long Island. It is not enough to have an NOS Chart showing Cape May, N.J., and the mouth of the Delaware, plus a chart showing the general area of Newport and Buzzard's Bay, together perhaps with some detail charts for the Newport area.

The boat's navigator should also carry NOS Chart No. 12300, which covers his whole offshore voyage with the exception of possibly the first ten miles. If he records his progress on this chart, he can, in the event of an emergency, select a suitable en route harbor and determine his course to reach it.

Of course, it will be helpful if he has a detail chart of this harbor or at least a 1:80,000-scale chart. This raises the point that it is better to have too many charts than too few. Charts not currently needed may be folded twice so that they are flat and not too large, and stowed under a berth mattress, where they will not take up valuable room.

Finally, ensure that charts are up to date and correct, and that the symbols used on the chart are thoroughly understood.

chapter four

Position, Distance, and Direction on Charts

POSITION ON A MERCATOR CHART

If we know the latitude and longitude of a position, we can readily plot it on a Mercator chart by using a straightedge and a pair of dividers. For example, suppose we want to locate a position in L41°09′ N, λ 70°44′ W. Referring to figure 4-1, which shows a latitude and longitude scale, we first locate the given latitude, 41°09′ N, on the latitude scale. We place a straightedge through this point aligning it parallel to any conveniently located parallel of latitude; alternately, it may be aligned perpendicular to a convenient meridian. The straightedge is now aligned in a true east-west direction. We next use the dividers to determine the longitude; as λ 70°44′ W. Without changing the setting of the dividers, we lay off this distance toward the east along the straightedge; this determines the desired position.

If this position is already located on the chart, and we desire to determine its latitude and longitude, we would place one leg of the dividers on the position and adjust the spread of the legs so that when rotated, the second leg would be tangent to the 71st meridian. The spread of the dividers now equals the difference of longitude from the reference meridian. The dividers are now transferred to the longitude scale and when one point is placed on the reference meridian, the desired longitude is read at the other point. A similar technique, measuring from the position

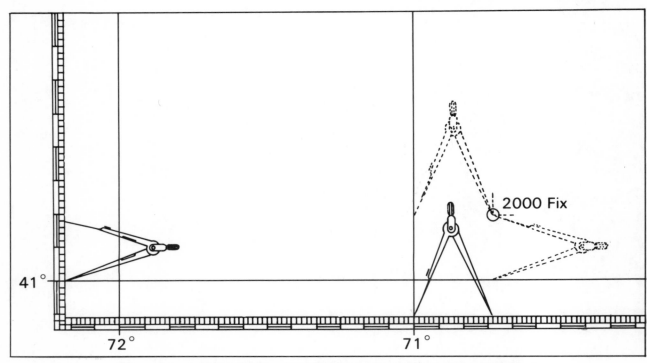

Figure 4-1.   Locating Position L 41°09′ N, λ 70°44′ W on a Mercator Chart

to a parallel of latitude, will provide the latitude.

Always be sure that the difference of latitude and longitude is measured in the proper direction from the reference parallel or meridian.

DISTANCE ON A MERCATOR CHART

For purposes of navigation, one degree of latitude may be considered to equal 60 nautical miles anywhere on the earth's surface, while the length of one degree of longitude varies with the latitude. The *latitude scale* must, therefore, always be used in *measuring distance*. While it is true that the latitude scale is expanded on a Mercator chart, this expansion is exactly equal to the expansion of distances at the same latitude. Therefore, when we measure distance on a Mercator chart covering a considerable north-south area, we must be careful to use that part of the latitude scale appropriate to the distance we are measuring. The scale at the mid latitude between the two points will give the best results. Distance is usually measured by placing one end of a pair of dividers at each end of the distance to be measured, and being careful not to change the setting, then transferring the dividers to the latitude scale located in the same area as the distance to be measured. Remember that one minute of latitude equals one nautical mile.

When the distance of a long line has to be mea-sured, it is often necessary to divide it into seg-ments, and then to measure each segment in the area of its own latitude, as in figure 4-2.

On large-scale charts, such as harbor charts, which cover a small area and therefore a small range of latitude, the Mercator length of a minute of latitude remains sufficiently constant for the entire area covered by the chart or a series of charts, so that for practical purposes it may be assumed to be constant. Such charts often have bar scales of miles and of yards, which may be used anywhere on the chart. Plotters or protrac-tors for use on these charts contain distance scales for measuring nautical miles in the same manner that you would use a ruler for measuring inches on a drawing. Place the 0 of the plotter's distance scale at point *A* and read the distance to point *B* on the scale as in figure 4-3.

DIRECTION ON A MERCATOR CHART

In chapter 2, we saw that a rhumb line is a line on the earth's surface that crosses each merid-ian at the same angle. Due to the construction of a Mercator chart, which shows all meridians parallel, a rhumb line will appear as a straight line. Its true direction can readily be measured with a protractor where it intersects any conve-nient meridian or by means of parallel rulers and the compass roses (see chapter 9) placed on Merca-

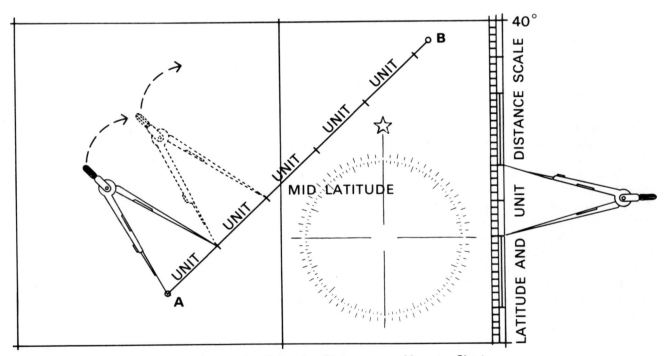

Figure 4-2. Measuring Distance on a Mercator Chart

Figure 4-3.   Measuring Distance on a Chart with a Paraline Plotter

tor charts. Figure 4-4 illustrates how direction may be measured on such a chart, using a Paraline plotter.

To measure the course between two points, place the plotter on the chart with the straightedge along the course to be measured (figure 4-4a). Then simply roll the plotter (generally only a few inches) to a position where the center point of the compass rose will be on any meridian (for predominately north and south courses) and read the course at the point on the compass rose that lies on the meridian. Both the course and its reciprocal are shown (figure 4-4b). For predominately east and west courses it will sometimes be much simpler to roll the plotter until the center point of one of the quarter circle compass roses on the plotter is located on a parallel of latitude. Read the course or its reciprocal on the parallel.

To lay down a known course or bearing toward or away from a point on the chart, you simply reverse the above process. Lay the plotter on the chart with both the center point of the compass rose and the desired bearing on the meridian. Roll the plotter until the straightedge passes through the bearing point and draw a line along the straightedge. The quarter circle compass roses on the ends of the plotter can be used for the same purpose when used with a parallel of latitude.

Always be sure to read the course in the right direction, and not its reciprocal.

Magnetic direction, when using parallel rules, may be determined by use of the magnetic compass rose placed inside the true rose on most charts. It may also be determined by applying the *variation* to the true direction. Variation is discussed in chapter 7.

Figure 4-5 shows a Mercator chart of the North Atlantic with a rhumb line drawn between Nor-

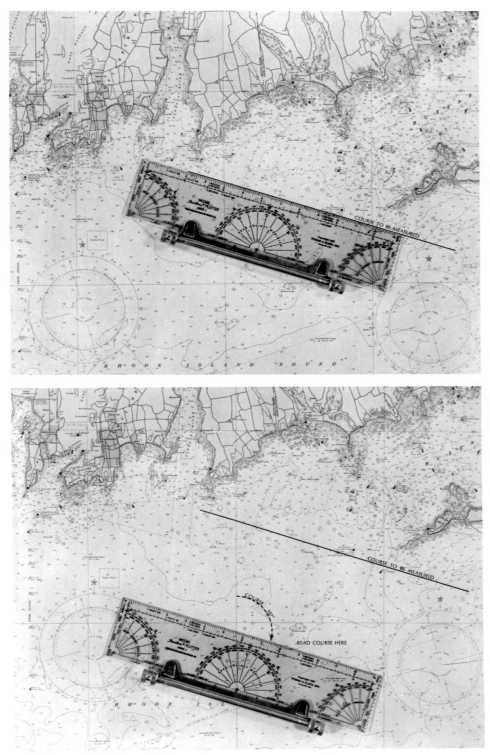

Figure 4-4. Measuring Direction on a Mercator Chart

folk and Brest; note that it crosses each meridian at the same angle. The great circle route between these two ports is also shown; it appears as a curve to the north of the rhumb line. Note that the curv-

ing great circle route appears to be longer than the straight rhumb line; actually it is 116 miles shorter. This seeming discrepancy is caused by the Mercator projection, on which a rhumb line,

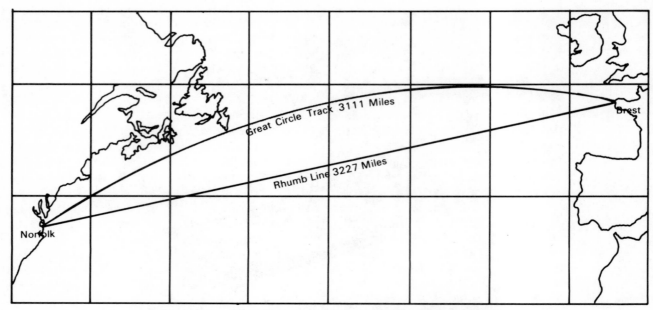

Figure 4-5.   Great Circle and Rhumb Line on a Mercator Chart

which is actually a portion of a spiral (see chapter 2), appears as a straight line, while the arc of a great circle, which is the shortest distance between two points on the surface of a sphere, appears as a curve. Figure 4-6 illustrates that on a globe, and therefore on the surface of the earth, the great circle is a straight line and the rhumb line is a curve covering a greater distance. We may note at this point that the great circle will always lie on the polar side of the rhumb line, i.e., it will lie to the north in north latitudes, and to the south in south latitudes.

In piloting, rhumb lines are invariably used, as for short distances the difference is negligible. However, on long ocean voyages, a great circle route can save a vessel much time.

The difference between rhumb line and great circle direction can be important in piloting when radio direction bearings are received from a distant station (to be discussed in chapter 15).

We should note two exceptions to the rule that a rhumb line drawn on the surface of a sphere is a spiral. One instance occurs when a rhumb line is drawn in a true north-south direction, in

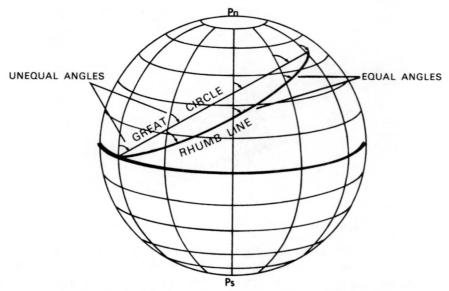

Figure 4-6.   Great Circle and Rhumb Line on the Earth's Surface

which case it falls on a meridian, which is a great circle. The other is when it is drawn along the equator, which is also a great circle.

POSITION ON A POLYCONIC CHART

Position may be determined by latitude and longitude on the polyconic projection charts used on the Great Lakes just as is done on a Mercator chart. A noticeable difference between the two projections, however, is that the latitude scale remains constant for the area covered by the chart; it is not expanded as the latitude increases. In addition, the parallels are slightly curved, rather than being straight lines, as on Mercator charts.

In high latitudes or on small-scale charts covering a large area, the convergence of the meridians on the chart will be quite noticeable. Position determination can be performed more accurately using the following procedures, which are illustrated on a Lambert chart (also a conic projection) of the North Atlantic.

Assume that an accurately determined position, a *fix*, has been obtained at 2000, as L 36°40′N,

λ 13°20′W, and is to be plotted on the chart. First, the longitude is plotted by laying a straight-edge through the appropriate subdivisions for 13°20′W, on the parallel for 35°N, and on the parallel for 40°N, and drawing at least a part of the line *AB* (figure 4-7). Plot the latitude by setting the dividers for the distance from the parallel for 35°N to the subdivision for 36°40′N, along any meridian, as at *C*; then lay off the same distance from the 35th parallel along the line *AB* (as at *C′*) to obtain the position of the fix.

The reverse problem of determining the geographic position of a fix obtained on the chart by graphic methods is arrived at quite easily by reversing the procedure just outlined.

On the small-scale charts, such as #14900, Lake Michigan, and #14960, Lake Superior, longitude is shown only in increments of five minutes on the border scales. Similarly, the border latitude scales show latitude increments of five minutes, except that at the approximate point of mid-latitude, single minutes are shown.

As the length of one degree of latitude, as represented on each of these charts, remains constant

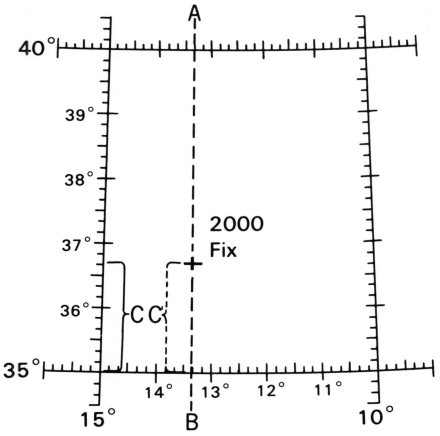

Figure 4-7. Position on a Conic Chart

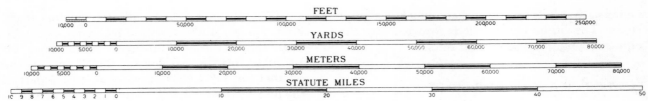

Figure 4-8. Bar Scale

for the whole area covered by the chart, latitude may be determined quite accurately by means of these scales.

Longitude to the nearest minute, however, must be interpolated by eye, since the smallest increment shown is five minutes. Also bear in mind that on the polyconic projection, the charted meridians are shown inclining in toward the elevated pole, which in this case is the North Pole. This inclination causes the meridians to lie closer together at the top of the chart than they do at the bottom. In the case of the Lake Michigan chart, the meridians are charted for every 30 minutes of longitude; these meridians are 26 statute miles apart at the bottom of the chart and only 24 statute miles apart at the top. Therefore, when taking off the longitude of a point, use the top or bottom scale, whichever is nearest.

Although small-scale charts covering a large area are best used to illustrate the differences in various projections, large-scale charts will normally be used in actual piloting. The small-scale charts are used chiefly for voyage planning.

DISTANCE ON A POLYCONIC CHART

Distance in nautical miles, even for very considerable distances in a generally north-south direction, can be taken off the latitude scales of polyconic charts with great accuracy. As we pointed out previously, the length of one minute of latitude appears as the same length on every part of the chart. In the polyconic projection, latitude is not expanded as it is in the Mercator projection; distance in nautical miles can therefore be determined both easily and accurately. Considerable distances extending in an east or west direction should, however, be determined in statute miles, using a bar scale (figure 4-8).

DIRECTION ON POLYCONIC CHARTS

A noteworthy difference between Mercator and polyconic charts is that a line drawn on the latter is not a rhumb line, although on large-scale charts it may, for practical purposes, be considered as such. Conventional compass roses, giving both true and magnetic direction, are conveniently lo-

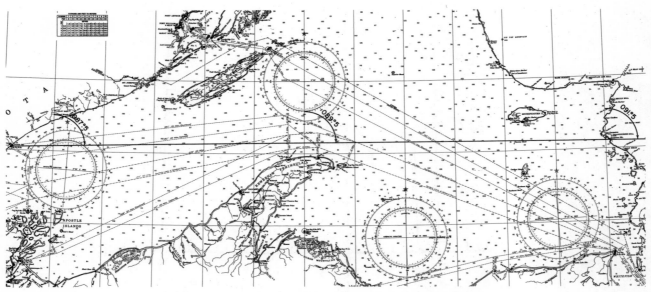

Figure 4-9. Measuring Direction on a Polyconic Chart

cated on the Great Lakes charts. Ordinarily, the rose lying nearest the line in question will serve to supply sufficiently accurate direction for ordinary navigation.

However, when the distance involved is considerable, and the direction of travel is in a generally easterly or westerly direction, it is best to draw in a course line between the point of departure and the destination, and measure the angle the course line makes at the charted meridian most nearly halfway between the two points.

For example, on the Lake Superior chart #14960, Gargantua Harbor, Ontario, lies some 277 statute miles almost due east of Taconite Harbor, Minnesota. If we draw in a course line from Taconite to Gargantua and measure the angle it makes with the first charted meridian (λ 90°30′ W) east of Taconite, the course appears to be 087.5°. However, if we measure the course line on the charted meridian (the 85th) directly west of Gargantua, the course proves to be 091.5°; there is thus a discrepancy of some four degrees. This discrepancy is resolved if we measure the angle where the course line crosses the 88th meridian, which is almost the halfway point between departure and destination, then the course proves to be 089.5° when measured, and this is the true course to steer. This is illustrated in figure 4-9.

In practice, segments of the entire distance would be used and the course for each area determined at the local meridian.

SUMMARY

The latitude of a place may be determined by measuring how far north or south it is of a charted parallel, using the latitude scales along the sides of the chart to determine the additional increments. Longitude is similarly obtained by measuring east or west from a charted meridian and then adding or subtracting the additional increments obtained from the longitude scale appearing along the north and south edges of the chart. The latitude scale makes a convenient scale for measuring distance, as one minute of latitude equals one nautical mile.

Straight lines on a Mercator chart are rhumb lines; they cross all meridians at the same angle. The direction of a line drawn on a Mercator chart may be measured at any meridian it crosses, or it may be referred to a compass rose. This holds good also for large-scale polyconic charts; however, on small-scale charts, when a line extends in a considerable east-west direction, it should be measured at the charted meridian nearest the midpoint of the line.

chapter five

Aids to Navigation— Buoys and Fog Signals *

AIDS TO NAVIGATION

The official definition of an aid to navigation is "any device external to a vessel or aircraft intended to assist a navigator to determine his position or safe course, or to warn him of dangers or obstructions to navigation." †

The aids to navigation with which we are primarily concerned are the ones local to each area and shown on the chart. These include buoys, lights, daybeacons, radio beacons, and sound signals, such as fog horns, bells, etc. There are over 40,000 such aids to marine navigation in the United States. The Coast Guard is responsible for their installation and maintenance.

Buoys

The primary function of buoys is to warn of some danger or to delineate channels. However, if we consider that a buoy marks a definite charted spot, we have a great advantage when we are alongside it, in that we know our precise position on the chart and can orient ourselves regarding the land and any possible hazards to navigation. The size, shape, coloring, signaling equipment, and numbering on a buoy all help us to identify it and its location. The location of each buoy is shown on the chart, which also shows some descriptive data. Full data on each buoy may be found in the appropriate *Light List*, described in chapter 6.

The various types of buoys are listed below:

1. *Can Buoys*—Buoys built of steel plates having the shape of a tin can.

* Portions of this chapter have been adapted from *Dutton's Navigation and Piloting*, 14th Ed. (Annapolis: Naval Institute Press, 1985).
† *Aids to Marine Navigation in the United States*, CG-193 (Washington, D.C.: U.S. Coast Guard, 1970).

2. *Nun Buoys*—Buoys built of steel plates, the above-water portion having the shape of a truncated cone.
3. *Bell Buoys*—Steel floats surmounted by short skeleton towers in which the bells are fixed. Most bell buoys are sounded by the motion of the buoy in the sea. In newer types, the bells are struck by compressed gas or electrically operated hammers.
4. *Gong Buoys*—Similar in construction to bell buoys, but sounding a distinctive note caused by sets of gongs, each gong having a different tone.
5. *Whistle Buoys*—These buoys provide a sound signal which is useful at night and also during fog and low visibility. As the whistle mechanism is operated by the motion of the buoy in the sea, these buoys are used principally in exposed locations. A type of sound buoy is also in use in which a horn is sounded at regular intervals by mechanical means.
6. *Lighted Buoys*—A metal float on which is mounted a short skeleton tower at the top of which the light is placed. Electric batteries, by which the light is operated, are placed in the body of the buoy below the water level.
7. *Combination Buoys*—These are buoys in which a light and a sound signal are combined, such as a lighted bell buoy, lighted gong buoy, or a lighted whistle buoy.
8. *Radar Reflector Buoys*—Radar reflectors, which return a strong echo to the radar screen, are fitted on many buoys of all types.

It should be noted that spar buoys are no longer used as aids to navigation in the federal system; some spar buoys remain in use for special purposes, such as marking fishnet areas.

All buoys serve as day aids; those having lights are also available for use at night, while those equipped with sound signals are more

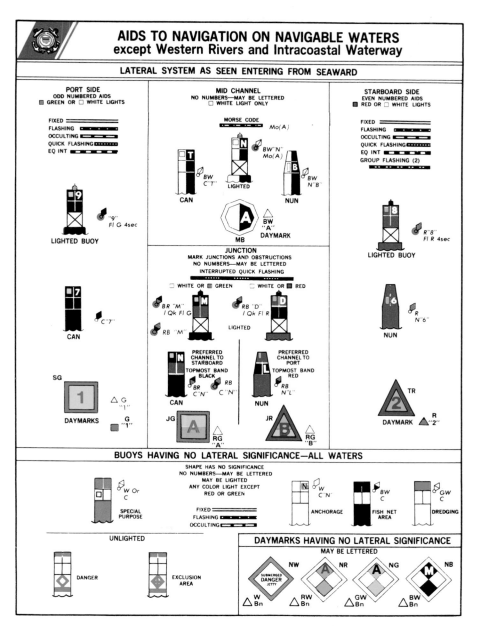

Figure 5-1.

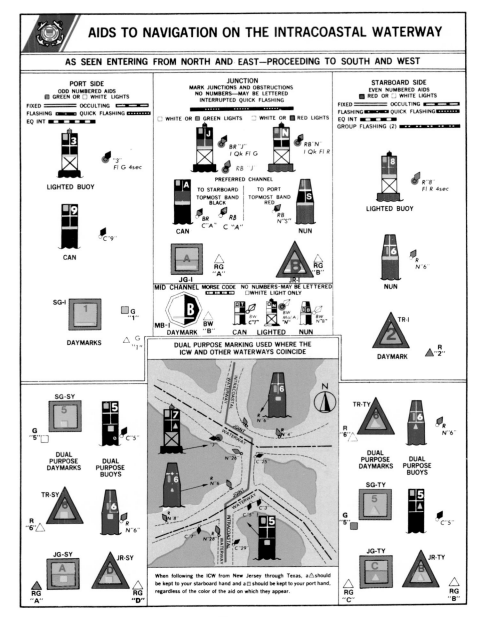

Figure 5-2.

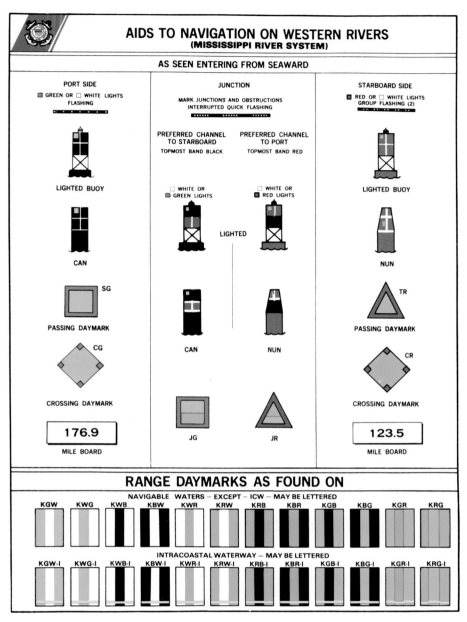

Figure 5-3.

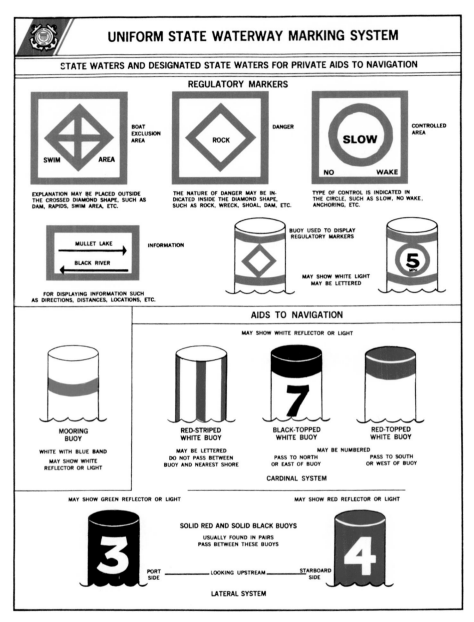

Figure 5-4.

The IALA Maritime Buoyage System "B"

In the spring of 1982, some eighty of the major maritime nations of the world, including the United States, signed an agreement to implement a relatively new system of buoyage called the International Association of Lighthouse Authorities (IALA) System. The IALA system uses a combination of lateral-type buoys and marks to delineate channels and cardinal-type buoys to draw attention to special features or to indicate the direction of safe water. There are two "regions" established in the system: Region A, encompassing most of Europe, Africa, and Asia, and Region B, covering North, Central, and South America, Korea, and the Philippines.

The major difference between the old U.S. Lateral System and the new IALA Region B system being implemented in U.S. waters is that the latter uses green vice black buoys to delineate the left side of channels when approaching from seaward. Other changes include: midchannel buoys going from vertically striped white and black to white and red with a topmark when lighted, and a new spherical shape when unlighted; junction buoys having their black horizontal bands changed to green and their light characteristic standardized as composite group flashing (2 + 1); a new red-and-black horizontally banded isolated danger mark; and new yellow special-purpose buoys. These changes are all illustrated in figure 5-5 on the following page.

Implementation of the system is scheduled to coincide with the established Coast Guard maintenance cycle for buoys, to be completed by 1989. It is not anticipated at this time that much use will be made of cardinal marks in U.S. waters, and Canada plans to use them only sparingly.

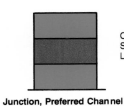

Color: Green
Shape: Cylindrical or pillar
Light (if fitted): Green,
        any characteristic

Port-side Channel Mark

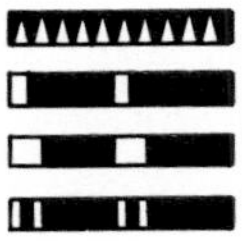

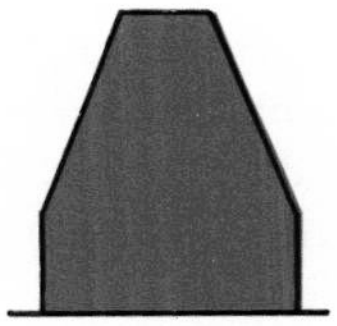

Color: Red
Shape: Conical or pillar
Light (if fitted): Red,
        any characteristic

Starboard-side Channel Mark

Color: Green with one red band
Shape: Cylindrical or pillar
Light (if fitted): Green,
        Comp. Gp. Fl (2 + 1)

Junction, Preferred Channel to Starboard

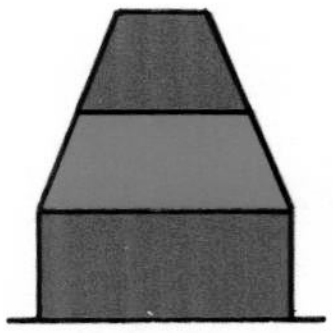

Color: Red with one green band
Shape: Conical or pillar
Light (if fitted): Red,
        Comp. Gp. Fl. (2 + 1)

Junction, Preferred Channel to Port

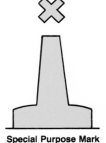

Color: Black with broad red band(s)
Shape: Optional, with 2 black spherical
        top marks
Light (if fitted): white,
        Gp. Fl. (2)

Isolated Danger Mark

Color: Yellow
Shape: Optional
Light (if fitted): Yellow,
        any characteristic

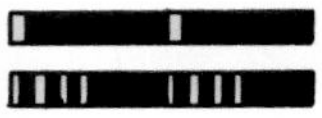

Special Purpose Mark

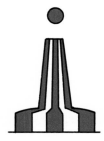

Lighted
Color: Red & white stripes
Shape: Pillar or spar with topmark
Light: White, Isophase,
        Occulting (10 sec), Mo. A.

Unlighted
Color: Red & white stripes
Shape: Spherical

Safe Water (Midchannel) Mark

Figure 5-5.

readily located in time of poor visibility, whether in darkness or fog.

THE LATERAL SYSTEM OF BUOYAGE

The *lateral system* of buoyage is used by the United States to permit maximum safety in navigation. This system employs an arrangement of colors, shapes, numbers, and light characteristics to show the side on which the buoy should be left when proceeding in a given direction. The characteristics of a buoy are determined by which side of a navigable channel it marks, when the channel is entered *from seaward*. However, all channels do not lead in from the sea; some arbitrary assumptions must therefore be made so that the lateral system will be consistent. The characteristics of the system are based on the assumption that proceeding in a southerly direction along the Atlantic Coast, in a northerly and then westerly direction along the Gulf Coast, in a northerly direction on the Pacific Coast, and in a northerly and westerly direction on the Great Lakes (southerly in Lake Michigan) is proceeding from seaward. How buoys and daymarks (channel markers on fixed structures) are placed according to shape, color, and number under this system is discussed below.

Note that this sytem does not apply on western rivers and on the Intracoastal Waterway. Aids to navigation along the latter are discussed in a subsequent section.

Color, Numbering, and Shape in the Lateral System

Under the lateral system of channel buoyage, the *color* and *number*, and if unlighted, the *shape*, all indicate on which side a mark should be passed. In the left-hand column of figure 5-1 are shown the marks to be kept on the *port* side when returning from sea. Note that they are painted *black* or *green* and carry *odd* numbers. Additionally, port side unlighted buoys are in the shape of *cans* or cylinders. The *starboard* side marks shown in the right-hand column are painted *red* and carry *even* numbers. Unlighted starboard side buoys are called *nuns*; in shape they are truncated cones.

Markers that might be encountered in midchan-

nel are shown in the center column of figure 5-1; they serve to indicate channel junctions or obstructions, as well as the midchannel or fairway. The *junction* and *obstruction* marks carry *red* and *black* or *green* horizontal bands. If the preferred channel, when entering from seaward, requires that the mark be left to *port*, the top band is *black* or *green*; conversely, if the preferred channel calls for leaving it to *starboard*, the top band is *red*.

Fairway or midchannel marks have vertical black and white or red and white stripes. They serve to mark the center of the traveled channel.

From the above outline, we can see that for channel marks, *color*, *shape*, and *number* can all serve to identify their position relative to the channel.

Color identification can be remembered by means of an old mnemonic involving the three Rs—*Red Right Returning*.

Shape often serves to help in identifying a buoy which is not lighted or fitted with sound equipment.

All right-hand buoys when returning from seaward are red nuns.

All left-hand buoys when returning from seaward are black or green cans.

Black or red and white vertically striped buoys may be either nuns or cans. In this instance, the shape has no significance.

Lighted or sound buoys, painted in the appropriate colors, may replace any of the above. No significance is attached to the shape of these buoys; their purpose is indicated by their coloring, numbering, or light characteristics.

In the matter of numbering, most marks are identified with numbers; additionally, some carry letters or a combination of letters and numbers. These markings facilitate identification and location of marks on the chart. Remember that odd numbers are used only on black or green marks, while even numbers are found only on solid red marks. Also remember that numbers increase from seaward. Numbers are kept in approximate sequence on both sides of a channel by omitting numbers as required; thus, we might find a channel marked with aids numbered 1, 3, and 5 on the left side, and 2 and then 6 on the right-hand side. Numbers followed by letters are used on solid-color marks when a letter is required so as not to disturb the sequence of numbering, and on important buoys, such as those marking isolated offshore dangers. Letters without numbers are applied in some cases to fairway or midchannel marks, junction marks, and other special purpose marks.

Lighted Buoys

In the U.S. lateral system, especially in the U.S. IALA Region B system, light colors are well standardized. *Red lights* are used only on red buoys and markers, and red and green (formerly black) horizontally banded buoys with the topmost band red. *Green lights* are used only on solid green (black) buoys, or red and green (black) banded buoys with the topmost band green. *White lights* are used only on safe water (formerly mid channel), isolated danger, and cardinal marks. *Yellow lights* are used only on special-purpose buoys.

Light phase characteristics, i.e., the pattern of flashes, also aid in identifying lighted markers. The various characteristics used on markers of the U.S. lateral system are illustrated in Figure 5-6. Certain of these characteristics are standardized on various classes of markers. *Fixed lights* and *flashing lights* (not more than 30 flashes per minute) may be used only on green or red channel markers, or yellow special purpose markers. *Quick flashing lights* (between 50–80 flashes per minute) are placed on channel markers and special markers requiring unusual caution, such as those indicating a sharp turn or dangerous obstruction that must be passed only on one side. *Composite group flashing (1 + 2) lights* are used only on preferred channel marks (formerly these were called junction or obstruction marks and carried *interrupted quick flashing lights*). *Morse (A) lights* (short-long flashes recurring at intervals of eight seconds) are used only on safe water markers. *Group flashing (2) lights* are fitted only on isolated danger marks.

Where there are a number of markers located in the same area, or where it is desired to call attention to a particular hazard, various other characteristics may be used for differentiation on channel, safe water, and special marks.

Lighted markers are symbolized on charts using standard purple light symbols plus abbreviations for their characteristics, as indicated in Figure 5-6. Their period (time in seconds required for a light to go through a complete cycle of changes) is also given in the case of lights not having fixed or quick flashing characteristics. Light colors are indicated by the abbreviations *R* for red, *G* for green, and *Y* for yellow; white lights are indicated by a purple light symbol with no color abbreviation.

Lighted buoys are fitted with batteries and are capable of operating for long periods of time. Most lighted buoys are fitted with a photoelectric cell, which turns the light off during daylight hours.

Unlighted channel marks are fitted with reflecting tape, which permits them to be located during the hours of darkness by means of a searchlight. Reflectors may be red, white, or green and have the same significance as lights of these colors.

Sound Buoys

Bell, gong, and whistle buoys were described previously. Note that these buoys may also be lighted.

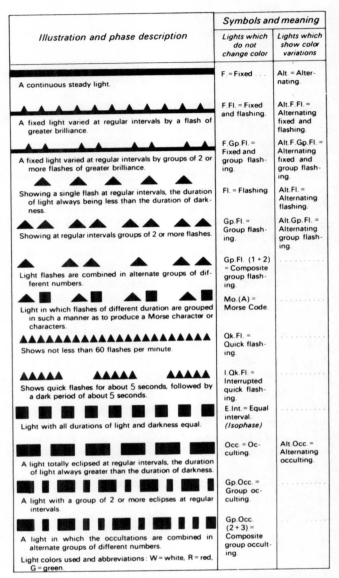

Illustration and phase description	Symbols and meaning	
	Lights which do not change color	Lights which show color variations
A continuous steady light.	F. = Fixed	Alt. = Alternating.
A fixed light varied at regular intervals by a flash of greater brilliance.	F.Fl. = Fixed and flashing.	Alt.F.Fl. = Alternating fixed and flashing.
A fixed light varied at regular intervals by groups of 2 or more flashes of greater brilliance.	F.Gp.Fl. = Fixed and group flashing.	Alt.F.Gp.Fl. = Alternating fixed and group flashing.
Showing a single flash at regular intervals, the duration of light always being less than the duration of darkness.	Fl. = Flashing.	Alt.Fl. = Alternating flashing.
Showing at regular intervals groups of 2 or more flashes.	Gp.Fl. = Group flashing.	Alt.Gp.Fl. = Alternating group flashing.
Light flashes are combined in alternate groups of different numbers.	Gp.Fl. (1 + 2) = Composite group flashing.	
Light in which flashes of different duration are grouped in such a manner as to produce a Morse character or characters.	Mo.(A) = Morse Code.	
Shows not less than 60 flashes per minute.	Qk.Fl. = Quick flashing.	
Shows quick flashes for about 5 seconds, followed by a dark period of about 5 seconds.	I.Qk.Fl. = Interrupted quick flashing.	
Light with all durations of light and darkness equal.	E.Int. = Equal interval. (Isophase)	
A light totally eclipsed at regular intervals, the duration of light always greater than the duration of darkness.	Occ. = Occulting.	Alt.Occ. = Alternating occulting.
A light with a group of 2 or more eclipses at regular intervals.	Gp.Occ. = Group occulting.	
A light in which the occultations are combined in alternate groups of different numbers.	Gp.Occ. (2 + 3) = Composite group occulting.	
Light colors used and abbreviations : W = white, R = red, G = green.		

Figure 5-6. Light Phase Characteristics

Almost all these sound buoys are operated by the action of the sea; a very small percentage are operated by internal power. At times, therefore, when it is very calm, it may not be possible to locate such a buoy by its sound signal. Sea-activated whistle buoys require a good deal of motion to generate their sound signal; they are therefore generally used in exposed positions.

It is possible to differentiate between bell and gong buoys, as the latter are fitted with a set of gongs, each of which has a different tone.

Special Purpose Buoys

The meaning of *special-purpose* buoys, which are not part of the lateral system, is indicated by their colors as follows:

1. *White buoys* mark anchorage areas.
2. *Yellow buoys* mark special areas or hazards not able to be marked by other colors.
3. *White buoys with green tops* are used in connection with dredging and survey operations.
4. *White and black horizontally banded buoys* mark fishnet areas.
5. *White and international orange buoys* alternately banded, either horizontally or vertically, are for special purposes to which neither the lateral-system colors nor the other special-purpose colors apply.
6. *Yellow and black vertically striped buoys* are used for seadrome markings and have no marine significance.

Daybeacons

There are many aids to navigation that are not lighted. Structures (not buoys) of this type are called *daybeacons.* They vary greatly in design and construction, depending upon their location and the distance from which they must be seen. A daybeacon may consist of a single pile with a *daymark* at the top, a spar with a *cask* at the top, a slatted tower, or a structure of masonry. Daymarks are colored, as are lighthouses, to distinguish them from their surroundings and to provide a means of identification. Daymarks marking the sides of channels are colored and numbered in the same manner as buoys and minor light structures—red indicating the right side entering, and green the left side entering. Daymarks are also fitted with reflecting tape and are identified by numbers or letters to facilitate locating them at night by means of a searchlight.

Notes on Buoyage

Whenever practicable, buoys, beacons, and all other aids to navigation are arranged in the *Light List* of the U.S. Coast Guard in regular order as they are passed by vessels entering from sea.

Keep in mind that the buoys in thoroughfares and passages between the islands along the coast of Maine are numbered and colored for entering *from eastward.*

Buoys do not always maintain exact positions; therefore, they should always be regarded as warnings and not as fixed navigational marks, especially during the winter months or when moored in exposed waters. A smaller nun or can buoy called a *station buoy* is sometimes placed in close proximity to a major aid, such as a sea buoy, to mark the station in case the regular aid is accidentally shifted from station. Station buoys are colored and numbered the same as the regular aid to navigation. Lightship station buoys bear the letters *"LS"* above the initials of the station.

A ship's position, when possible, should not be plotted using buoys exclusively, but by bearings or by horizontal angles of fixed objects on shore. Lighted buoys cannot always be relied on, because the light may become extinguished or, if periodic, the apparatus may fail to operate. Many whistle and bell buoys are sounded by the action of the sea; therefore, in calm weather they are less effective and at times may not sound.

Normally harbor buoys are shown only on the harbor chart. An approach chart will display sea buoys, approach buoys, and the beginning of buoyed channels. Smaller scale charts will show sea buoys only. The position of a buoy is indicated on the chart by a diamond symbol with a dot marking its location. A larger overprinted magenta dot indicates a lighted buoy, and the legend will include information as to the color of the light and its characteristics. Additional printed information is used to advise of warning features such as a sound signal (WHIS, BELL, GONG, etc.), or a radar reflector. The number or letter designation is given in quotation marks near the symbol for the buoy. For unlighted buoys, the letter *C* or *N* by the buoy indicates a can or nun. As a general rule, the amount of printed information given near a charted buoy symbol will depend upon the space available on the chart to print it. (See figure 5-1.)

Fog Signals

Any sound-producing instrument operated in time of reduced visibility (caused by fog, snow, haze, smoke, etc.) from a definite point shown on the charts, such as a lighthouse, lightship, or buoy, serves as a useful fog signal. To be effective as an aid to navigation, you must be able to identify it and to know from what point it originates. The simpler fog signals are bells and whistles on buoys, and bells at lighthouses. As signals on buoys which are operated by the action of the sea do not produce sounds on a regular time schedule, positive identification is not always possible.

At most lighthouses and lightships, fog signals are operated by mechanical means and are sounded on definite time schedules, providing the desirable feature of positive identification.

The various types of apparatus employed for sounding fog signals are of interest principally because each type produces distinctive sounds, familiarity with which assists in identification.

The various types of fog signals differ in tone, and this facilitates the recognition of the respective stations. The type of fog signal apparatus for each station is stated in the *Light List.*

Diaphones produce sound by means of a slotted reciprocating piston actuated by compressed air. Blasts may consist of two tones of different pitch, in which case the first part of the blast is high and the last part is low. These alternate-pitch signals are called *two-tone.*

Diaphragm horns produce sound by means of a disc diaphragm vibrated by compressed air, steam, or electricity. Duplex or triplex horn units of differing pitch produce a chime signal.

Gongs produce sounds of varying tones, activated by motion.

Sirens produce sound by means of either a disc or a cup-shaped rotor actuated by compressed air, steam, or electricity.

Whistles produce sound by compressed air or steam directed through a circumferential slot into a cylindrical bell chamber.

Bells are sounded by means of a hammer actuated by hand, a descending weight, compressed gas, or electricity.

Sound signals in fog are not always dependable. At times the signal may fade out entirely and may not be heard again until close aboard. Always take soundings in fog, and navigate with the utmost caution.

INTRACOASTAL BUOYS AND MARKERS

In order that vessels may readily follow the Intracoastal Waterway route where it coincides with another waterway such as an important river marked on the seacoast system, special markings are employed. These special markings are applied to the buoys or other aids which mark the river or waterway for other traffic. The special marks consist of a yellow square and a yellow triangle, painted on a conspicuous part of the dual-purpose aid. The yellow square, in outline similar to a can buoy, indicates that the aid on which it is placed should be kept on the left hand when following the Intracoastal Waterway *from New Jersey toward Mexico.* The yellow triangle, in outline similar to a nun buoy, indicates that the aid on which it is placed should be kept on the right hand when following the Intracoastal Waterway from New Jersey toward Mexico. By this marking, when approaching a body of water such as the Savannah River, and knowing that you must follow it for some distance before again entering a dredged cut of the Intracoastal Waterway, you know that your track lies along such buoys or other aids as are specially marked in yellow. You determine the side of your vessel on which these aids should be passed by the shape of the yellow marks, always bearing in mind the basic direction of your travel.

Where coincidental marking is employed, the navigator following the Intracoastal Waterway disregards the color and shape of the aid on which the mark is placed, being guided solely by the shape of the yellow mark. Can buoys of the seacoast system may have painted upon them yellow triangles or yellow squares, depending on whether the waterway which they mark is followed in the direction of the sea or in the direction of its headwaters, as the Intracoastal Waterway is followed in the direction of Mexico. Mariners not traversing the Intracoastal Waterway entirely disregard the special yellow markings.

The aids to navigation on the Intracoastal Waterway are illustrated in figure 5-2.

UNIFORM WATERWAY MARKING SYSTEM

In addition to material described heretofore, there is an additional system of marking that is employed by some states in their local waters and sometimes in navigable waters. These markings are illustrated in figure 5-4. In the upper section of the figure under Regulatory Markers, the borders on the signs and buoys are outlined in yellow.

Figure 5-3 illustrates the buoys and daymarks used on western rivers. They are similar to the lateral system.

chapter six

Aids to Navigation— Lighthouses and Lightships *

LIGHTHOUSES AND LIGHTSHIPS

Lighthouses are found along most of the world's navigable coastlines and many of the interior waterways of various countries. Such structures are so well known as to require little description. Lighthouses are placed where they will be of most use, on prominent headlands, at entrances, on isolated dangers, or at other points where it is necessary that mariners be warned or guided. Their principal purpose is to support a light at a considerable height above the water. The same structure may also house a fog signal and radio-beacon equipment, and also contain quarters for the keepers. However, in the majority of instances, the fog signal, the radio-beacon equipment, and the operating personnel are housed in separate buildings grouped around the tower. Such a group of buildings constitutes a *light station.*

The location of a lighthouse, whether in the water or on shore, the importance of the light, the kind of soil upon which it is to be built, and the prevalence of violent storms, have a direct bearing upon the type of structure erected and on the materials of which it will be built. Engineering problems will not be entered into here, but it is important to note that the materials used and types of construction differentiate one lighthouse from another and hence aid in identification.

Lighthouses vary markedly in their outward appearance (see figure 6-1) because of the points already mentioned and also because of the great difference in the distances at which their lights should be seen. Where the need for a powerful light is great and the importance and density of traffic warrants, a tall tower with a light of high candlepower is erected. Conversely, at points in-

termediate to the major lights, where the traffic is light, and where long range is not so necessary, a less expensive structure of more modest dimensions suffices.

The terms, *minor* lights, *secondary* lights, and *major* lights indicate in a general way a wide variety of lights, each class shading imperceptibly into the next. These lights may be displayed from towers resembling the important seacoast lighthouses, or may be shown from almost any type of inexpensive structure. The essentials of a light structure where keepers are not in residence, as for all lights, are: best possible location dependent on physical conditions of the site, sufficient height for the location, a rugged support for the lantern, and a housing for the tanks of compressed gas or electric batteries by which the light is operated. Meeting these essentials are many types of structures—small tank houses surmounted by a short skeleton tower, a cluster of piles supporting a battery box and the light, and countless other forms.

Color is applied to lighthouses and automatic light structures for the purpose of making them readily distinguishable from the background against which they are seen, and to distinguish one structure from others in the same vicinity. Solid colors, bands of color, and various other patterns are applied for these purposes.

Minor light structures are sometimes painted black or red, to indicate the sides of the channel that they mark, following the same lateral system used in the coloring of buoys. When so painted, red structures mark the right side of the channel, and black structures the left side of the channel, entering from seaward.

Lightships serve the same purpose as lighthouses, being equipped with lights, fog signals, and radio beacons. Ships are used only when it is impracticable or impossible to construct a lighthouse at the desired location. Lightships mark the

* Portions of this chapter have been adapted from *Dutton's Navigation and Piloting,* 13th Ed. (Annapolis: Naval Institute Press, 1978).

Official U.S. Coast Guard Photos

Figure 6-1.   Typical Light Structures

entrances to important harbors or estuaries, dangerous shoals lying in much frequented waters, and also serve as leading marks for both transoceanic and coastwise traffic.

The only remaining lightship on station in United States waters is the Nantucket Shoals Lightship (her relief lightship is in Boston), all others having been replaced by fixed structures. She is painted red with the name of the station on both sides in white.

Superstructures are white; masts, lantern galleries, ventilators, and stacks are painted buff. Her relief lightship is painted the same color, with the word "RELIEF" in white letters on the sides, and exhibits lights and sound signals having the characteristics of the station.

The masthead lights, the fog signals, and the radio-beacon signals of the lightship all have definite characteristics, so that the lightship may be distinguished from nearby lighthouses. As with lighthouses, details regarding these signals are shown briefly on charts and more completely in the *Light List*.

A lightship underway or off station will fly the International Code signal flags *"LO"*, signifying that the lightship is not at anchor on her station. It will not show or sound any of the signals of a lightship, but will display the lights prescribed by the International or Inland Rules for a vessel of its class. While on station a lightship shows only the authorized aid to navigation light, and an anchor light on the forestay, the latter serving to indicate the direction in which the ship is heading. By day whenever it appears that an approaching vessel does not recognize the lightship or requests the information, the lightship will display the International Code signal of the station. As lightships ride to a single anchor, the light on the forestay also indicates the direction from which the combined wind and current effect is acting.

All but this one lightship have been replaced by light towers or large navigational buoys, as the latter are far more economical to maintain. These light towers usually take the form of a square platform on four legs; they are somewhat similar in appearance to the offshore oil rigs called "Texas Towers." Such a light is shown in figure 6-1.

The characteristics of lights displayed by lighthouses, lightships, and lighted buoys are shown and described in figure 5-5, which also shows the description of each light, as printed in the *Light List*.

Identification of Lights

In order to obtain full benefit from lights we must understand their use and be able to intrepret all data concerning them given in the *Light List* and on charts. It is essential that the *Light List* be kept corrected to date.

One of the most frequent sources of groundings is the failure to identify lights correctly. When making a landfall, the charts and the *Light List* should be consulted to learn the exact characteristics of the light or lights that it is expected will be first seen. When a light is observed, its color is noted, and by means of a watch or clock with a second hand, a note is made of the time required for the light to perform its full cycle of changes. If color, cycle, and number of flashes per cycle agree with the information in the *Light List*, correct identification has been made. The *Light List* should be examined to ascertain if any other light in the general locality might be seen and mistaken for the desired light. If there is doubt, a careful timing of the length of all flashes and dark intervals, for comparison with the *Light List*, is usually conclusive.

In approaching a light of varying intensity, such as fixed varied by flashes, or alternating white and red, due allowance must be made for the inferior brightness of the less powerful color of the light. The first-named light may, on account of distance or haze, show flashes only, and the true characteristic will not develop until the observer comes within range of the fixed light; similarly, the second-named may show as occulting white until the observer comes within range of the red light. At short distances and in clear weather flashing lights may show a faint continuous light.

In the *Light List*, bearings are in degrees true, reading clockwise from 000° at north; bearings relating to visibility of lights are as observed *from a vessel*; distances are in nautical miles unless otherwise stated; heights are referred to mean high water; depths are referred to the plane of reference of the largest scale chart of the area. Lighthouses are not *watched* or manned, unless the *Light List* states "resident personnel." Lightships almost invariably are manned. Unwatched lights have a high degree of reliability; however, they may become irregular or extinguished. Latitudes and longitudes in the *Light List* are approximate and are intended only to facilitate reference to a chart.

Light Sectors

Sectors of colored glass are placed in the lanterns of certain lighted aids to navigation to mark shoals or to warn mariners off the nearby land. Lights so equipped show one color from most directions and a different color or colors over definite arcs of the horizon indicated in the *Light List* and upon the charts. A sector changes the color of a light, when viewed from certain directions, but *not* the characteristic. For example, a flashing white light having a red sector, when viewed from within the sector, will appear flashing red.

Sectors may be but a few degrees in width, marking an isolated rock or shoal, or of such width as to extend from the direction of the deep water toward shore. Bearings referring to sectors are expressed in degrees as observed from a vessel *toward* the light.

For example, the *Light List* describes a certain light as displaying a red sector from 045° clockwise to 120°. Both are true bearings as observed from seaward. Figure 6-2 is a sketch of this light indicating the limits through which the light would appear red as observed from aboard ship.

In the majority of cases, water areas covered by red sectors should be avoided, the exact extent of the danger being determined from an examination of the charts. In some cases a narrow sector may mark the best water across a shoal. A narrow sector may also mark a turning point in a channel.

In some conditions of the atmosphere white lights may have a reddish hue; the mariner therefore should not trust solely to color where there

are sectors, but should verify the position by taking a bearing of the light. On either side of the line of demarcation between white and a colored sector there is always a small sector of uncertain color, as the edges of a sector cannot be cut off sharply. Note here also that the bearings given on the lines of demarcation on the chart are true bearings of the light as seen from the ship.

When a light is cut off by adjoining land, and the arc of visibility is given, the bearing on which the light disappears may vary with the distance of the vessel from which the light is observed, and the height of eye.

Range Lights

Two lights, located some distance apart, visible usually in one direction only, are known as *range lights.* They are so located that the mariner, by bringing his ship into line with them when they will appear one over the other, places his ship on the axis of the channel. If he steers his ship so that the lights remain continuously in line, he will remain within the confines of the channel. Entrance channels are frequently marked by range lights. The Delaware River and the St. Johns River on the Atlantic coast, and the Columbia River on the Pacific coast are examples of successive straight reaches marked in this manner.

The lights of ranges may be any of the three standard colors, and may also be fixed, flashing, or occulting, the principal requirement being that they stand out distinctly from their surroundings. Most range lights lose brilliance rapidly as a ship diverges from the range line. Ranges should be used only after a careful examination of the charts, and *it is particularly important to determine for what distance the range line can be safely followed,* this information not being obtainable from the lights themselves in all cases.

The arc of visibility of the two lights forming a range may be extremely limited. For example, at Cape May, New Jersey, the front and rear range lights are visible only for two degrees on each side of the centerline of the channel.

LIGHT LIST

The *Light List* is compiled by the U.S. Coast Guard, and is an invaluable aid to mariners. Five volumes are issued. Volumes I and II cover the Atlantic and Gulf Coasts; data on Puerto Rico and the Virgin Islands are included in Volume II. Volume III covers the Pacific Coast of the continental

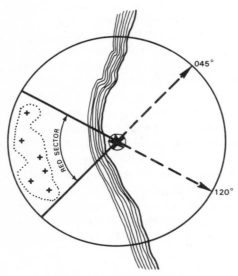

Figure 6-2.   A Red Sector

(1) No.	(2) Name Characteristic	(3) Location Lat. N. Long. W.	(4) Nominal Range	(5) Ht. above water	(6) Structure Ht. above ground Daymark	(7) Remarks Year
					RHODE ISLAND	FIRST DISTRICT
	SAKONNET RIVER					
	—Buoy 11A	In 22 feet, marks western end of remains of stone bridge.	....	....	Black can	Green reflector.
	— Buoy 12A	In 22 feet, marks eastern end of remains of stone bridge.	....	....	Red nun	Red reflector.
	— Buoy 13	In 21 feet	....	....	Black can	White reflector.
	— Buoy 15	In 42 feet	....	....	Black can	White reflector.
	(For Mount Hope Bay, see No. 766)					
	NARRAGANSETT BAY (Charts 236, 1210)					
	EASTERN APPROACH					
705	*Fish Trap Area Outer Lighted Buoy A.* **Fl. W., 3^s**	In 79 feet, marks outer end of fish traps southerly of Aquidneck Island. 41 26.0 71 16.9	....	....	Black and white horizontal bands; spar.	Private aid maintained from Apr. 25 to June 30.
705.11	*Dumping Ground Lighted Buoy DG–A.* **Fl. W., 4^s**	In 108 feet	6	....	Orange and white vertical stripes.	Ra ref.
705.31	*Fish Trap Lighted Buoy CC* .... **Fl. W., 4^s**	In 102 feet 41 25.7 71 18.6	....	....	Black and white horizontal bands; barrel.	Private aid maintained from Apr. 15 to July 25.
705.51	*Dumping Ground Lighted Buoy DG–B.* **Fl. W., 4^s**	In 102 feet	6	....	Orange and white vertical stripes.	Ra ref.
706	*Brenton Reef Light.* .... **Gp. Fl. W., 10^s** 0.2^{s}fl., 3.0^{s}ec. 0.2^{s}fl., 6.6^{s}ec. 2 flashes.	In 78 feet, at entrance to bay. 41 25.6 71 23.4	25	87	Red house on black square superstructure on four black piles; "BRENTON" on sides.	Light also displayed during daytime when sound signal is in operation. MARKER RADIOBEACON: Antenna on top of super-structure. See p. XIX for method of operation. HORN, 2 blasts ev 60^s (3^{s}bl-3^{s}si- 3^{s}bl-51^{s}si). Piles floodlighted from sunset to sunrise. 1962
	Seal Ledge Bell Buoy 2A.	In 30 feet, south of Seal Rock.	4	....	Red	White reflector.
707	*Brenton Point Lighted Whistle Buoy 2.* **Fl. R., 4^s**	In 57 feet, southwest of 21 foot shoal. 41 25.9 71 21.8	....	....	Red	Ra ref.
	SOUTHERN APPROACH					
708	*Torpedo Range Lighted Bell Buoy A.* **Fl. W., 4^s**	In 120 feet 41 16.6 71 24.0	7	....	Orange and white horizontal bands.	
	Torpedo Range Bell Buoy B	In 122 feet	....	....	Orange and white horizontal bands.	White reflector.
	Torpedo Range Bell Buoy C.	In 109 feet	....	....	Orange and white horizontal bands.	White reflector.
	Torpedo Range Bell Buoy D	In 107 feet	....	....	Orange and white horizontal bands.	White reflector.
	Torpedo Range Bell Buoy E	In 106 feet	....	....	Orange and white horizontal bands.	White reflector.

U.S. Coast Guard

Figure 6-3. A Page from the *Light List*

U.S., as well as Alaska and the Hawaiian Islands. Volume IV takes in the Great Lakes, while Volume V lists the data for the Mississippi River and its navigable tributaries.

The *Light List* gives much useful data in addition to describing lights. All buoys, whether lighted or unlighted, are listed and described, as are daybeacons. The depth of water in which each buoy is anchored is shown, as are its color, number, and other characteristics. Lighthouses and light towers are referred to in the *List* merely as "lights"; they operate automatically, and are unmanned, unless the *List* shows the entry "Resident Personnel." Under the heading "Characteristic," the operating cycle of each light is given in detail. For example, while the chart lists the operating cycle of the Brenton Reef light to be "Group Flash (2) 10 seconds," the *Light List* shows the characteristic to be a 0.2-second flash, followed by a 3.0-second dark period, then a 0.2-second flash followed by a 6.6-second dark period. In addition, while the chart merely shows that Brenton Reef has a horn for a fog signal, the *Light List* states that it gives a group of two blasts every 60 seconds, the cycle being a three-second blast, three-second silence, three-second blast, and 51-second silence.

The *List* also shows the location of radio beacons and gives the manner of operation.

The abbreviations used in the *Light List* are tabulated and defined in the introduction to each volume.

Visibility of Lights

Column 4 in each volume of the *Light List* states the *nominal range* of powerful lights. The nominal range is the distance in nautical miles at which the light may be seen in clear weather by an observer with an *unlimited height of eye*. However, visibility is limited by the curvature of the earth, and the distance at which a powerful light may be seen depends both on the height of the light and that of the observer's eye above the water, as can be seen in figure 6-4.

On charts edited after June 1973 the nominal range, rounded to the nearest whole nautical mile, is the range printed on the chart near the light symbol. This is known as the charted range.

The geographic range of a light is now defined, since 1973, as the maximum distance at which a light may be seen, in unlimited visibility, for an observer whose eye is at sea level. A Geographic Range Table is contained in the general introduction to each *Light List*. This table gives the approximate geographic range for a light due to its height above water, or any other object of a known height. It is necessary, therefore, to add to the geographic range a distance of visibility corresponding to the height of the observer's eye above sea level. This will give the distance at which you should pick up a light, providing the light is powerful enough to travel such a distance; i.e., the nominal range exceeds the geographic range plus your distance to the horizon. The following table gives the horizon distance in nautical and statute miles for heights of eye below 15 feet.

Table 6-1 Distances to Horizon

Height of Eye (Feet)	Distance (Nautical Miles)	Distance (Statute Miles)
3	2.0	2.3
4	2.3	2.6
5	2.6	2.9
6	2.8	3.2
7	3.0	3.5
8	3.2	3.7
9	3.4	4.0
10	3.6	4.2
11	3.8	4.4
12	4.0	4.6
13	4.1	4.7
14	4.3	4.9
15	4.4	5.1

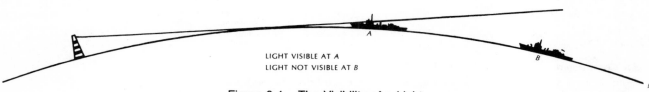

LIGHT VISIBLE AT *A*
LIGHT NOT VISIBLE AT *B*

Figure 6-4. The Visibility of a Light

Thus, if the elevation of a light is 15 feet, its geographic range is 4.4 nautical miles. If our height of eye is 7 feet, the distance to the horizon is 3.0 nautical miles. We would therefore add the two distances (7.4 nautical miles) to determine the distance at which we should pick up the light in clear weather.

These distances include a factor for *refraction*, which is the bending of light rays as they pass through the atmosphere. They are based on the formulas:

Distance to the horizon in nautical miles
$= 1.144\sqrt{\text{height of eye in feet}}$.

Distance to the horizon in statute miles
$= 1.317\sqrt{\text{height of eye in feet}}$.

Table 8 in the *American Practical Navigator* tabulates distances to the horizon in both nautical and statute miles for many heights of eye. This work is an encyclopedia of navigational knowledge, issued by the DMAHTC as *Pub. No. 9*. It is usually referred to simply as *Bowditch* after its original author.

PREDICTING THE TIME OF VISIBILITY OF A LIGHT

If we are fairly certain of the speed our boat is making good over the bottom, and if it is possible to hold a steady course, we can predict the time a given light should become visible. This is done by drawing an arc of a circle on the chart, centered on the lighthouse; the radius of the circle being equal to the visibility of the light, as determined above. The course line (discussed in chapter 10) is projected to where it cuts the arc. The distance from the last charted position to the arc is then measured along the course line and divided by the speed, to give the length of time of the run from the charted position to the point at

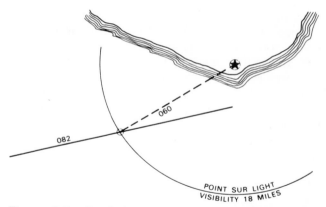

Figure 6-5. Predicting the Time and Approximate Bearing of the Sighting of a Light

which the light should be sighted. See figure 6-5.

Unusual Conditions of Visibility

When unusual conditions of refraction exist, the tabulated or calculated distances of visibility may be considerably exceeded; conversely, during periods of haze or rain, they may be reduced to almost zero. The *loom* or glow of a powerful light may often be seen just above the horizon well before the light itself comes into view. We may determine if a light is on the horizon by *bobbing* it; that is, reducing our height of eye by a few feet. If the light disappears when bobbed, it is on the horizon.

Multicolored Lights

Some lights of more than one color use different intensities of light. For example, Halfway Rock Light at one time operated on a 90-second cycle. See figure 6-6. It shows a fixed white light with a nominal range of 21 miles for 59 seconds; next

(1) No.	(2) Name Characteristic	(3) Location Lat. N. Long. W.	(4) Nominal Range	(5) Ht. above water	(6) Structure Ht. above ground Daymark	(7) Remarks Year
		MAINE				FIRST DISTRICT
320 6	HALFWAY ROCK LIGHT .... Alt. F. W., R., and Fl. R. 90ˢ (F. W., 59ˢ, F. R., 14ˢ, R. fl., 3ˢ (high intensity). F. R. 14ˢ).	On rock, midway between Cape Small Point and Cape Elizabeth. 43 39.4 70 02.2	21W 16FR 25 Fl. R.	76 77	White granite tower attached to dwelling.	RADIOBEACON: Antenna 30 feet 160° from light tower. Distance finding station. See p. XVIII for explanation. HORNˢ 2 blasts ev 60ˢ (3ˢbl-3ˢsi-3ˢbl-51ˢsi). 1871

Light List, U.S. Coast Guard

Figure 6-6.   Halfway Rock Light Characteristics

for 14 seconds, it shows a red light with a nominal range of 16 miles; this is followed by a 3-second high intensity red flash with a nominal range of 25 miles. The cycle is finished with another 14-second red light with a range of 16 miles. It is obvious, therefore, that the lookout on a big ship would first see only a 3-second red flash, occurring every 90 seconds.

Where a light employs a single power of intensity, but shows red or green in addition to a white light, the latter may become visible before the colored phase of the light cycle. It is essential that lights be most carefully identified when they first come into view; a stopwatch or watch with a second hand should always be used to detemine the light cycle in order that it may be properly identified.

chapter seven

The Theory of the Magnetic Compass *

The compass is one of the oldest tools used by the navigator, and probably the most important. No one knows when it first came into use; the Vikings apparently were familiar with it in the eleventh century, and it may well have been in use before then.

The first compass probably consisted of a magnetized iron needle thrust through a straw and floated in a dish of water. The needle had to be rubbed on a lodestone or a piece of magnetic iron ore from time to time, as it did not retain its magnetism for long.

The importance of the compass lies in the fact that it enables us to determine direction quite precisely, even under conditions of zero visibility, as in a heavy fog.

PRINCIPLES OF OPERATION

The earth itself is a magnet; its magnetic field lies roughly in a north-south direction. The magnetic North Pole lies in the vicinity of L 74°N, λ 101°W, while the magnetic South Pole lies near L 68°S, λ 144°W. Note that the magnetic field is not symmetrical; this is because the magnetic materials in the earth are not symmetrically distributed. The compass needle aligns itself in the earth's magnetic field, because magnetic materials of *opposite polarity attract* one another, while those of the same polarity repel one another. The compass needle, free to swing on its pivot, therefore aligns itself with the earth's field and indicates magnetic north and south. Remember that the earth's magnetic lines of force do not coincide with the true meridians, except in limited areas. Over most of the earth, the north end of the magnetic compass therefore points to the east or west

* Portions of this chapter have been adapted from *Dutton's Navigation and Piloting*, 13th Ed. (Annapolis: U.S. Naval Institute, 1978).

of true north; the angular amount by which it varies from true north we call *variation*. The concept of the earth's magnetic field is illustrated in figure 7-1.

Figure 7-2 is a chart of the world, showing in simplified form the distribution of *isogonic lines*, or lines connecting points of equal magnetic variation. The isogonic lines *do not* point in the direction of the line of magnetic force (magnetic meridian) with which the compass needle will be aligned. The chart merely indicates the amount of variation at any location.

Changes in the Earth's Magnetic Field

The earth's magnetic field is not constant either in intensity or direction. The changes in the field are *diurnal* or daily, *yearly*, and *secular* or over a long period of time. For our purposes, we need

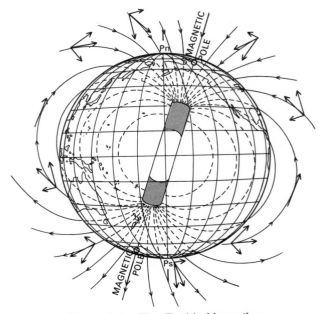

Figure 7-1.   The Earth's Magnetism

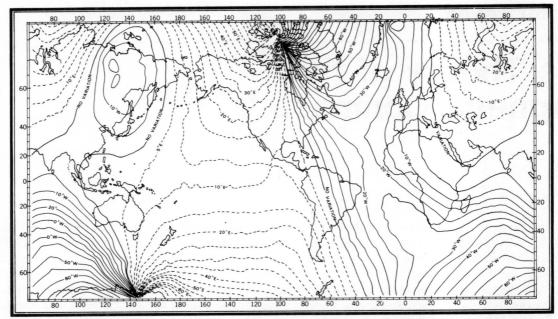

Figure 7-2.   Simplified Chart of Magnetic Variation of the World, from DMAHTC Chart No. 42. The lines shown are isogonic lines.

not concern ourselves with the diurnal or yearly changes in direction or with change in the intensity of the field. The secular change, however, is of importance to us. It has been under study for some 300 years, but the length of its period has not yet been established.

The secular change consists of a reasonably steady increase or decrease in the variation, or inclination of the magnetic meridian, to the true meridian at a given spot. The change in the varia-

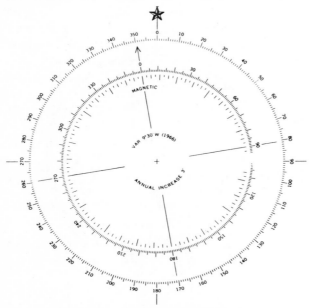

Figure 7-3.   A Compass Rose

tion at any location can be predicted accurately for a number of years into the future. This change is shown on the *compass roses* printed on the great majority of navigational charts. Figure 7-3 shows such a rose; the outer circle shows true direction in degrees. A third circle is sometimes added, showing magnetic direction in *points*, the formerly used system of dividing the circle into 32 points. Note that the variation for a stated year is given exactly, and the annual increase or decrease is also given.

Variation must always be given a name, either *east* (E) or *west* (W). It is called east if the compass needle points to the right, or east of the true meridian, and west if it points to the left.

Deviation

Life would be far simpler for the mariner if he could determine true north from his compass merely by applying the variation for the locality. Unfortunately, aboard the vast majority of vessels, both small and large, he must also contend with *deviation*.

We previously said that the compass needle, free to swing on its pivot, would indicate magnetic north. Unfortunately, aboard steel ships, or even aboard small craft that have some ferrous metal used in their construction, or that have an engine or electric and electronic gear, the needle is not completely free to point to the magnetic north.

Iron and steel, as well as much electric equipment, tend to have magnetic fields of their own, which often in some way affect the compass and tend to deflect it from the magnetic meridian. This type of deflection is called deviation.

Deviation is unlike variation, in that it differs on different headings, while variation is constant at any given time and location regardless of the heading of the vessel.

HOW DEVIATION AFFECTS THE COMPASS

On most vessels there will be numerous metal or electrical objects that can cause deviation of the compass. To visualize the manner in which these objects affect the compass, consider that in figure 7-4 the source of the deviation is a large metal object indicated by a square on the drawing with the center of magnetic attraction at *X* in the center of the square. The location of the compass is marked with a circle. With no deviation, the magnets on the compass card would be lined

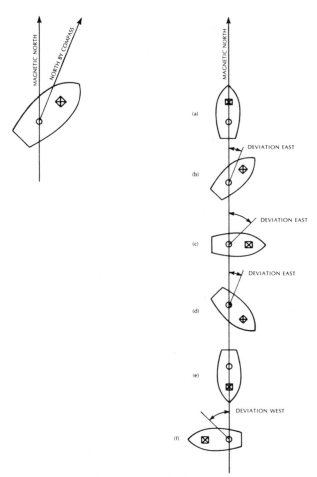

Figure 7-4. Effects of Deviation on the Compass

up with the magnetic meridian pointing to magnetic north. On various headings, the relative position of the metal object with respect to the alignment of the compass card produces a varying amount of error and also affects the direction of the error; that is, whether the magnets on the compass card are attracted toward the east or toward the west from the magnetic meridian determines the error and its direction.

In figure 7-4 at (a), the boat is headed magnetic north, and there is no deviation. At (b) she is headed about 30 degrees east of magnetic north, and a small amount of easterly deviation has arisen. When she heads magnetic east (c), the metal object's field pulls the compass off even more, and the easterly deviation is increased; it lessens as the boat swings towards the south (d), and there is no deviation when she comes to magnetic south (e). Conversely, the deviation becomes westerly as she swings towards the west, and it will reach its maximum when she is on a heading of magnetic west (f).

Bear in mind that this is an oversimplification of the actual problem; it is intended to show why deviation is not the same on different headings. In this illustration, deviation changed symmetrically as heading was changed. Unfortunately, this rarely occurs in boats.

From what we have said in the foregoing sections, it is apparent that direction can be expressed in three ways:

1. As *true,* when it is referred to the true meridian.
2. As *magnetic,* when it is referred to the local magnetic meridian; alternately, when the variation is applied to true direction, the resultant is magnetic.
3. As *compass,* when the axis of the compass card is the reference for measurement.

COMPASS ERROR

Compass error (CE) is the algebraic sum of the variation and deviation.

In the preceding section, we stated that direction could be stated as *true,* as *magnetic,* or as *compass;* any given direction can be expressed in all three ways if we understand that:

1. *True* differs from *magnetic* by the *variation.*
2. *Magnetic* differs from *compass* by the *deviation.*
3. *Compass* differs from *true* by the *compass error.*

Figure 7-5 outlines a vessel in which the com-

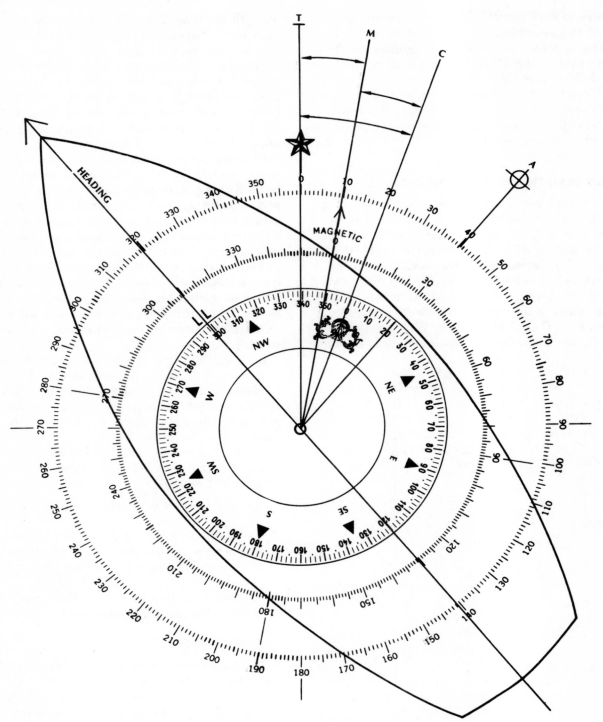

Figure 7-5.   Compass Errors

pass card is shown. *OC* is the axis of the compass needle, pointing toward compass north. The two outer circles, concentric with the compass, represent magnetic and true compass roses. *OM* is the magnetic meridian, and *OT* is the true meridian, indicating respectively magnetic and true direc-

tion. The magnetic meridian is 10 degrees to the right of the true meridian, therefore the local variation is 10 degrees east. By inspection, we note that to obtain the *true* direction of *M*, we must add 10 degrees, the easterly variation, to the magnetic direction of *M* (zero degrees on the magnetic rose) to obtain the *true* direction of *M* (10 degrees on the true rose). Now if we look at the compass needle, we note that it is 10 degrees eastward, or to the right, of the magnetic meridian; therefore the deviation is 10 degrees east on this heading of the vessel. Again, by inspection, we note that it is additive to the compass direction of *C* (zero degrees on the compass card) to obtain the magnetic direction of *C*, which is 10 degrees on the magnetic rose.

The compass error (CE) is the algebraic sum of the variation and deviation, so in this instance, CE = 10°E + 10°E or 20°E; we can thus obtain the true direction of *C* by adding the CE to the compass direction. The compass error is further illustrated in figure 7-5 by showing the bearing of an object on shore, which bears 20 degrees per compass, 30 degrees magnetic, and 40 degrees true; in practice, these bearings would be expressed by using three digits—020°, 030°, and 040°. The vessel's heading is 300 degrees by the compass, as is shown by the *lubber's line*, marked *LL* in the figure; the lubber's line is a mark on the compass bowl which denotes the ship's head. The magnetic heading is 310°, and the true heading is 320°.

The process of applying the deviation to the compass reading to obtain magnetic and/or applying the variation to magnetic to get the true reading, is called *correcting*. In the preceding paragraph, and from figure 7-5, we saw that easterly deviation is additive to compass in converting to magnetic, easterly variation is additive to magnetic in converting to true, and easterly compass error is additive to compass in converting to true. We can remember this by the short phrase: CORRECTING ADD EAST.

Memorize this phrase; it is much easier to have this rule firmly imbedded in your memory and to use it arbitrarily, than to try to reason out the correction in a moment of stress. It is obvious that if easterly error is additive in correcting, westerly error must be subtractive.

The reverse of correcting, that is converting a true direction to a magnetic or a compass direction, or a magnetic direction to a compass direction, is, for the lack of a better word, called *uncorrecting*. If easterly errors are additive in correcting, they must be subtractive in uncorrecting. Similarly, if westerly errors are subtractive in correcting, they must be additive in uncorrecting. By means of the one rule, *correcting add east*, we can therefore determine how to solve all four possible situations:

When correcting,	Easterly errors are additive
	Westerly errors are subtractive
When uncorrecting,	Easterly errors are subtractive
	Westerly errors are additive

CORRECTING

The process of correcting is one of starting with compass direction, applying deviation to obtain magnetic direction, and then applying variation to obtain true direction. Note the first letter of each key word in this process—COMPASS, DEVIATION, MAGNETIC, VARIATION, TRUE. The order of arrangement can be remembered by the sentence: CAN DEAD MEN VOTE TWICE? Write just the initial letters vertically down the page or horizontally across the page:

C _____   *C*   *D*   *M*   *V*   *T*

D _____   ____ ____ ____ ____ ____

M _____

V _____

T _____

Now by placing the given information in the corresponding blanks, the unknown values can easily be computed following the rule of the form.

Example 1

A ship is heading 127° per compass. For this heading, the deviation is 16°E and the variation is 4°W in the area.

Required: (1) The magnetic heading. (2) The true heading.

Solution: The problem is one of correcting. Since the deviation is easterly, it must be added. Hence, the magnetic heading is 127° + 16° = 143°. To find the true direction, we are again correcting, and since the variation is westerly, it is subtractive. Hence, the true heading is 143° − 4° = 139°. In this case, the compass error is 16°E − 4°W = 12°E. Applying this directly to the compass heading, we find the true heading is 127° + 12° = 139° as previously determined.

Answers: (1) MH 143°, (2) TH 139°.

Any compass with a deviation error this large should be adjusted by the use of correcting magnets. This procedure is discussed in the following chapter.

Example 2

A ship's course is 347° per compass. The deviation is 4°W and the variation is 12°E.

Required: (1) The magnetic course. (2) The true course.

Solution: Again we are correcting. The deviation is subtractive and the magnetic course is 347° − 4° = 343°. The variation is additive and the true course is 343° + 12° = 355°.

Answers: (1) MC 343°, (2) TC 355°.

Example 3

Two beacons are so placed ashore that when seen in line from seaward they mark the direction of a channel, 161°T. Seen in line from a ship heading up the channel, they bear 157.5° by compass. The chart shows the variation for the locality to be 2.5°E.

Required: (1) The compass error. (2) The deviation.

Solution: The compass error is 161° − 157.5° = 3.5°E. Since the true direction is greater than the compass direction, the error is easterly. The compass error is the algebraic sum of the variation and deviation. Hence, the deviation is the algebraic *difference* of 3.5° − 2.5° = 1.0°E.

Answers: (1) CE 3.5°E, (2) D 1.0°E.

It is obvious that these letters, C-D-M-V-T, can also be written horizontally across a page or on a homemade form and the values entered below the appropriate letter. For *uncorrecting*, covered in the following section, the above form can be used working from the bottom upwards, or if written horizontally, from right to left.

UNCORRECTING

Naval vessels and large merchantmen are equipped with gyro compasses, which usually indicate true north with an error of less than one degree. Almost all phases of their navigation are therefore based on true direction. For small craft using the magnetic compass, it is frequently desirable, however, to operate on the basis of magnetic or compass direction, and this often requires that true directions be *uncorrected.*

This can best be done by reversing the order of correction, and making it TRUE, VARIATION, MAGNETIC, DEVIATION, and COMPASS. This order of arrangement can be remembered by the sentence: TIMID VIRGINS MAKE DULL COMPANIONS. These would again be arranged in a column as shown, or written horizontally across a page. We would proceed in the same general manner as that described for correcting, except that we would bear in mind that in this case we were uncorrecting.

```
T _____          T    V    M    D    C
V _____         ___  ___  ___  ___  ___
M _____
D _____
C _____
```

Example

From a chart, the true course between two places is found to be 221°. The variation is 9°E and the deviation is 2°W.

Required: (1) The magnetic course. (2) The compass course.

Solution: For both requirements we are uncorrecting, so that the easterly variation is subtractive and the westerly deviation is additive. The magnetic course is 221° − 9° = 212°. The compass course is 212° + 2° = 214°.

Answers: (1) MC 212°, (2) CC 214°.

To use T V M D C for *correcting*, simply work from the bottom upwards or from right to left. From the discussion presented thus far, it should be obvious that once the theory is understood, the conversions from one value to another are quite simple and routine and can be accomplished using various forms or easy-to-remember phrases. Choose only one method and learn to use it automatically.

Additional practice for the student can be obtained by filling in the blanks in the following table. Correct answers are given in the lower section of the table.

	True	Variation	Magnetic	Deviation	Compass
1	045°	10°E	035°	___	040°
2	050°	10°E	040°	10°E	___
3	___	5°E	___	5°W	040°
4	080°	___	070°	___	060°
5	___	10°W	___	20°E	225°
6	300°	___	___	5°W	320°

Correct answers to above					
1	___	___	___	5°W	___
2	___	___	___	___	030°
3	040°	___	035°	___	___
4	___	10°E	___	10°E	___
5	235°	___	245°	___	___
6	___	15°W	315°	___	___

SUMMARY

It is absolutely essential that every boatman understand the effects of variation and deviation on his compass. Correcting and uncorrecting directions can be bothersome at first, but if the rule,

Correcting Add East, is borne in mind, any problem connected with compass directions can be solved. Computers with concentric dials are available to solve the problem mechanically.

Finally, remember that the needle always remains aligned in a north-south compass direction—the boat may turn, but the compass needle does not.

chapter eight

The Use of the Magnetic Compass

In chapter 7 we outlined briefly what is known of the history of the magnetic compass. Particularly over the past hundred years, much research has gone into a means of improving the performance of the compass; today it has reached a high state of accuracy and reliability. Metallic alloys have been intensively studied to produce magnets of improved strength and retentivity, and alloys containing nickel and cobalt, among other metals, have been found to be far superior in both respects to the simpler ferrous alloys previously employed.

Some larger craft carry two compasses—the *steering compass* and the *standard compass*. The former is used by the helmsman in steering; the latter is generally located on the weather deck, where it will be least affected by any magnetic field within the boat. This chapter is based on the assumption that only the steering compass is available; however, in general the matter in this chapter would apply equally to either compass.

COMPASS DESIGN

The compass used at sea differs in one very obvious respect from the majority of compasses intended for use ashore—it has a circular *compass card* instead of a needle. A typical modern compass card is shown in figure 8-1. Originally, the card was divided into thirty-two points, and each point was divided into quarters. This system, however, has largely been done away with and has been replaced by cards reading clockwise in degrees from 000° at North through 360°. The cardinal points, *north, east, south,* and *west* are also shown in letters. Graduations are generally by degrees, with every second or every fifth degree marked on yachting compass cards. In addition, some compasses have cards marked in degrees on their outer circumference with points shown inside them as illustrated in figure 8-2.

E.S. Ritchie and Sons

Figure 8-1. Typical Modern Compass Card

E.S. Ritchie and Sons

Figure 8-2. Compass Card with Both Degrees and Points

The types of compasses used aboard small craft fall into two general categories—*flat-topped* and *spherical* compasses. These will be discussed in the succeeding sections.

Compass Components

All magnetic compasses consist of a bowl made of nonmagnetic material, and are topped with glass or clear plastic. At the forward side of the bowl is the *lubber's line,* which indicates the direction of the vessel's bow or head. At the center of the bottom of the bowl is the *pivot,* a vertical pin upon which the card rests. The center of the card is usually fitted with a jewel, such as a synthetic ruby, which engages the pin. Two or more magnets aligned with the north-south axis of the card are usually attached to its underside; a few modern compasses use circular or ring magnets.

In order to damp vibration and reduce friction, almost all marine compasses use a bowl filled with clear liquid, such as alcohol and water, or compass oil, which will not freeze at low temperatures. A float is sometimes attached to the underside of the card, which supports all but a very small fraction of the weight of the card. Finally, the bowl contains an *expansion bellows,* which compensates for the expansion and contraction of the liquid with changes of temperature. The bowl can thus be kept full at all times without risk of damage to the compass.

The bowl of the flat-topped compass is supported in *gimbals;* these are double rings, hinged on both the fore and aft and the athwartships axes, which permit the bowl to remain horizontal, or nearly so, regardless of the vessel's motion. Figure 8-3 shows a flat-topped compass with outside gimbals.

The Spherical Compass

The *spherical compass* is so called because it is fitted with a transparent hemisphere instead of a flat top. This spherical construction offers two advantages—it greatly magnifies the size of the compass card, and it permits internal gimbaling; that is, the gimbaling system is contained entirely inside the bowl.

The marine compass has traditionally carried a flat card with the rose lettered on its upper surface. The lubber's line, which is located on the forward side of the bowl, is the reference point for reading the card; when changing course, the vessel, and therefore the lubber's line, is steered to the new course on the dial, which remains fixed in the magnetic field. The numerals on the dial increase in a clockwise direction; if steering 020°, the numerals 30 will therefore be to the right of the lubber's line.

E.S. Ritchie and Sons; Airguide Instrument Co.

Figure 8-4. Spherical Compass (top) and Front-Reading Compass (bottom)

E.S. Ritchie and Sons

Figure 8-3. Flat-Topped Compass

Aircraft compasses are designed to be mounted at eye level; their dials appear to be cylinders with the numerals printed on the vertical surface. The lubber's line is at the after end of the bowl in a transparent window. The numerals on the aircraft compass dials seem to increase in a counter-clockwise direction; if steering 020°, the numeral 30 is therefore to the left of the lubber's line. This fact is mentioned here as some spherical dome compasses are now appearing on the marine market with a flange or vertical surface on the card which carries the aircraft type of numbering. If steering a boat by a compass of this type, the helmsman might at first be confused and start his turn in the wrong direction, due to being accustomed to a topreading compass. Figure 8-4 illustrates a traditional spherical dome compass on the top and one with a front-reading card on the bottom.

The Binnacle

Many marine compasses are mounted in a *binnacle* or stand, which is made of nonferrous metal, plastic, or wood. This is not always the case, however, as the gimbaled compass may be set into the cabin trunk, the bridge deck, etc., and covered with a glass deadlight. A typical binnacle with a spherical compass intended for a sailing yacht is shown in figure 8-5. A much shorter version is shown in figure 8-6; this type is very popular aboard powerboats. Binnacles of both these types almost invariably make provision for holding *compensating magnets*. The position of these compensating magnets may be adjusted to reduce the deviation in the compass, principally on the cardinal points. Figure 8-7 shows a typical compensat-

Danforth
Figure 8-6.   Spherical Compass in Binnacle

ing magnet installation in the binnacle of a high quality compass designed for use aboard small craft. The use of these compensating magnets is discussed later in this chapter.

Aboard steel vessels, it is frequently desirable to use a binnacle fitted with *quadrantal spheres;* these assist in compensating for the deviation caused by the steel hull. A binnacle, fitted with these spheres, is shown in figure 8-8.

Arrangement for lighting the compass is also made in the binnacle. The compass may be *under-* or *over-lit;* that is, the card may be translucent, and lighted from below, or it may be lighted from above. Spherical compasses are almost invariably lighted from above.

Danforth
Figure 8-5.   Spherical Compass on Stand Binnacle

Danforth
Figure 8-7.   Binnacle with Compensating Magnets

E. S. Ritchie and Sons
Figure 8-8.   Binnacle with Spheres

NOTES ON COMPASSES

The spherical domed compass has one other great advantage over the flat-topped type—the center of the card generally has a high center pin. This pin greatly facilitates the obtaining of bearings across the compass and frequently makes it unnecessary to employ a pelorus (see chapter 9) for taking bearings.

When installing a compass aboard a boat, be sure that the lubber's line is aligned exactly parallel to the boat's fore and aft axis. If this is not the case, a constant error is introduced.

Certain items found in boats are highly magnetic and should be kept well away from the compass. Among the worst offenders are portable radios, camera lightmeters, and steel beverage cans. Always see to it that such items, as well as all steel and iron objects such as knives, spikes, etc., are kept well away from the compass.

One way of checking the mechanical condition of a compass, when the boat is not swinging, is to note the heading and then deflect the compass card horizontally with a magnet. When the magnet is removed, the card should return to the same heading. This deflection test should be made in both east and west directions.

Some inexpensive spherical compasses are only partially gimbaled; the card "hangs up" when the boat heels about fifteen degrees or more. Such compasses are entirely unsatisfactory for use aboard sailboats.

Always remember that the compass is the sailor's most important tool; protect it from mechanical damage. It is poor economy to purchase a low-quality compass, as your safety may depend on its accuracy and reliability.

FINDING THE DEVIATION OF THE COMPASS

Three methods of finding the deviation are widely used aboard small craft. The first of these is by means of comparing the magnetic azimuth, or bearing, of a celestial body, usually the sun, with its azimuth as observed by compass. This is the method frequently used by professional compass adjustors; however, the theory and methods of determining celestial azimuths are beyond the scope of this text.

The other methods of finding the deviation are by bearings of a distant object and by ranges.

Obtaining the Bearings

All three methods outlined above entail obtaining bearings every 15 or 30 degrees relative to the vessel's head, and this may be troublesome, due to the location of the compass. It may be difficult on some boats for the observer to obtain bearings abaft the beam, and on others, the superstructure may block off the view on certain relative bearings. In such cases, a pelorus (described in chapter 9) should be used.

For sailboats with a spherical compass installed in a fairly high binnacle, the problem is not too difficult, as bearings can usually be obtained quite easily except dead ahead, and in the case of a yawl, dead astern. With the spherical compass, the high center pin at the center of the compass card permits obtaining accurate bearings. The problem is more difficult aboard most powerboats, particularly if they have a flat compass. On any boat where a generally uninterrupted view across the compass and all around the horizon cannot be obtained, a pelorus should be employed. Great care must be used in order that it is exactly aligned with the fore-and-aft axis of the boat.

Compass bearings are obtained by setting the pelorus card to the vessel's compass heading. When the helmsman has steadied down on the desired compass course, have him sing out "Mark! Mark! Mark!" while the sighting vanes are lined up on the distant object or the range. If the helmsman holds steadily on the compass course, the desired compass bearing can be read directly off the pelorus.

FINDING DEVIATION BY BEARINGS OF A DISTANT OBJECT

If a vessel circles within a small area, say a circle with a diameter of about 100 yards, the bearings of a fixed object six miles or more away will not change materially during the swing. By observing the bearing of the object by compass as the vessel swings, the deviation can be obtained for each heading by comparing the observed bearing with the magnetic bearing, taken from the chart.

If the distant object is shown on the chart, its magnetic bearing is obtained by applying the charted variation to the true bearing, or more simply, by measuring the bearing directly on the magnetic compass rose. If the object is not charted, its magnetic bearing may be taken as the mean of a round of compass bearings observed on equidistant compass headings. This is on the assumption that if a vessel is swung through a circle, and deviations are obtained on equidistant headings, the sum of the easterly deviations will *theoretically* equal numerically the sum of the westerly deviations; the resulting net deviation for all headings therefore are zero. The error introduced is generally quite small unless there is a constant error. However, it is better practice to observe a distant object that can be identified on the chart, or a range, whenever possible. An example using bearings of a distant object is given later in this chapter. Even when maneuvering in a small area, remember to steady on each successive heading; never observe the bearing while the boat is turning.

Finding the Deviation by Ranges

Two fixed objects appearing in line constitute a range. Prepared ranges are placed in position to mark midchannels, turning points, measured mile limits, etc. Natural ranges will often be found. A position that will not interfere with normal ship traffic should be selected. The true direction of

the range selected is determined by measurement on the chart; magnetic direction is then determined by applying the variation of the locality. Alternately, the magnetic direction can be obtained directly from the magnetic rose. The deviation is found by crossing the range on the desired heading and observing the compass bearing at the instant the objects are in line.

Refer to figure 8-9. Beacons *A* and *B* form a range, the direction of which is 030° true. The local variation is 20°W. Hence, the magnetic direction of the range is 050°. If the observed bearing of the range is 045°, the deviation is 050° − 045° = 5°E.

Example

For determining the deviations of the compass, a vessel uses two ranges marking a measured mile. The true direction of the ranges is 091°, and the variation for the locality is 8°W, giving a magnetic direction of the range of 099°. As the vessel crosses a range on the headings shown in the first column of the following table, the navigator observes corresponding directions of the range as noted in the third column.

Required: The deviations of the compass.

Ship's Head per Compass	Magnetic Direction of Range	Direction of Range per Compass	Deviation
°	°	°	°
000	099	103	4W
015	099	103	4W
030	099	103	4W
045	099	102	3W
060	099	102	3W
075	099	102	3W
090	099	102	3W
105	099	101	2W
120	099	101	2W
135	099	101	2W
150	099	100	1W
165	099	097	2E
180	099	095	4E
195	099	093	6E
210	099	093	6E
225	099	093	6E
240	099	094	5E
255	099	095	4E
270	099	097	2E
285	099	099	0
330	099	100	1W
315	099	102	3W
330	099	103	4W
345	099	103	4W

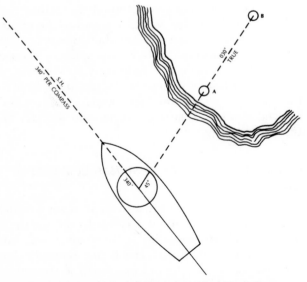

Figure 8-9.   Using a Range to Find Deviation

Preparing a Deviation Table

Small craft usually operate in well-charted waters. It is therefore almost always possible to make a swing near a charted buoy and observe a distant object, which is also charted; the *magnetic* bearing of the object can thus be determined from the chart.

Let us assume, therefore, that we departed New Bedford on a clear morning, heading to the south, and when we neared Michaum Ledge Lighted Gong Buoy 3A (41°28.9′N, 70°57.4′W), we sighted Buzzards Bay Entrance Light to the southwest. We decide that this is an excellent opportunity to swing ship to check the deviation. From NOS Chart No. 1210TR, we determine that Buzzards Light bears 229° magnetic from buoy 3A.

We next prepare the form shown in table 8-1 and write down the compass headings for every 30° in the first column, and then the magnetic bearing in the third column. Bearings will be taken to the nearest whole degree.

Table 8-1

Compass Heading	Bearing by Compass	Magnetic Bearing	Deviation
000°	222°	229°	7°E
030°	224°	229°	5°E
060°	226°	229°	3°E
090°	230°	229°	1°W
120°	233°	229°	4°W
150°	234°	229°	5°W
180°	234°	229°	5°W
210°	234°	229°	5°W
240°	230°	229°	1°W
270°	225°	229°	4°E
300°	223°	229°	6°E
330°	222°	229°	7°E

We are now ready to start the swing; while swinging, remember we must remain in the immediate vicinity of buoy 3A. When the boat steadies down exactly on the first heading, the helmsman sings out: "Mark! Mark! Mark!" While the helmsman maintains the heading, the observer notes the bearing by compass of Buzzards Light and enters it in the form.

Having completed the swing, we determine the deviation for each heading by taking the difference between the magnetic bearing and the bearing by compass. A useful memory aid in determining the name or direction of the deviation is "compass least, error east." The angular deviation and its name for each heading is now entered in the form as shown in table 8-1.

We now have the deviation for twelve compass headings; what we need primarily, however, is to determine the compass course to steer for a given magnetic course. To obtain this information, and also to check on the consistency of the observations obtained during the swing, it is wise to graph the deviation obtained on each heading. A graph based on the deviation table we prepared is shown in figure 8-10 in reduced size from the original. The latter was prepared on a scale of 1 inch equals 30 degrees of compass heading along the horizontal axis, and 1 inch equals 2 degrees of deviation along the vertical axis. In this example, easterly deviation is plotted above the horizontal axis, and westerly below it; the deviation recorded for each compass heading is shown as a circled dot.

A fair curve is drawn as far as possible through the dots; there must be no "doglegs" in the curve. The curve as drawn in figure 8-10 seems acceptably smooth, which means that the majority of our bearings were good. The notable exception to this is the one obtained on a heading of 210°, which shows about one degree too much westerly deviation. All other bearings seem valid to within one-half degree.

We next prepare a deviation card in tabular form, as shown in table 8-2. The first column lists the magnetic courses for every thirty degrees, and the second column gives the compass heading for each tabulated magnetic course. Having outlined the form and entered the magnetic courses, we turn to our graph and note the deviation—7°E for 000°, 5°E for 030°, 3°E for 060°, etc.—and apply each to the corresponding magnetic course, remembering "compass least, error east." We thus obtain the compass heading 353° for magnetic 000°, 025° for magnetic 030°, etc., and enter each compass heading in the appropriate space in the form.

Note that this is an approximate method of preparing a deviation card suitable only when deviations are relatively small. Obviously, when the deviation is sizable and changing rapidly, the deviations for x degrees compass heading cannot be the same as the deviation for x degrees magnetic heading. When large deviations are present or when maximum accuracy is desired, a Napier diagram, which will be discussed in the following section, should be prepared and the deviation table made up from this diagram.

Note that for a magnetic course of 210° we used a deviation of 4°W, as obtained from the smooth curve of the graph, rather than the observed value

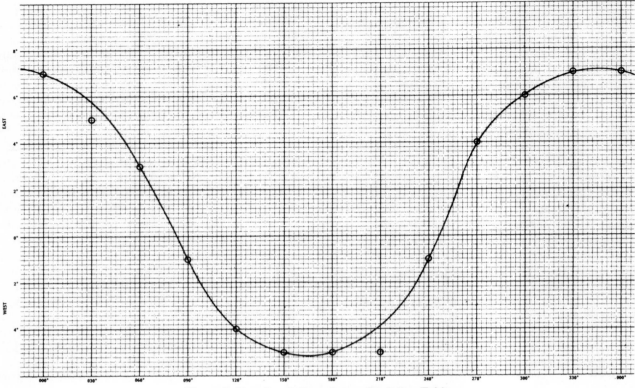

Figure 8-10.   Graph Based on a Deviation Table

Table 8-2

Magnetic Course	Compass Heading	Magnetic Course	Compass Heading
000°	353°	180°	185°
030°	025°	210°	214°
060°	057°	240°	241°
090°	091°	270°	266°
120°	124°	300°	294°
150°	155°	330°	323°
180°	185°	360°	353°

of 5°W. Ordinarily such a table, prepared for every 30 degrees, is sufficient to permit ready mental interpolation for courses intermediate to the tabulated ones. However, if it is deemed more convenient, a deviation card can be prepared every 10 or 15 degrees magnetic from the graph.

In concluding this section, it may be of interest to note that the values of deviation shown were actually obtained aboard a 41-foot fiber-glass sailboat, with an uncompensated compass.

The Napier Diagram

Where deviations are large, it is generally necessary to plot the deviation on a Napier diagram. This diagram gets its name from a British admiral, who devised it well over a hundred years ago. It serves both as a graph of the deviation and as an intermediate means of developing a deviation card for either compass or magnetic headings. A Napier diagram, with a deviation curve plotted on it, is shown in figure 8-11.

Assuming that we are beginning the swing on a heading of 000° per compass, we start at 0° on the diagram and move out along the dotted line, to the right and down if the deviation is east, and to the left and up if it is west. Each dot represents a deviation of one degree; in this case, the deviation on a heading of 000° is 21° east, so we move down and to the right, and circle the 21st dot.

This process is repeated until the deviation has been plotted for all the headings on which it was obtained. A finished curve is shown plotted in figure 8-11.

The use of the Napier diagram is summed up in a jingle, which may be helpful in remembering the correct method of use:

From compass course, magnetic course to gain
Depart by dotted, and return by plain.

From magnetic course, to steer the course alloted,
Depart by plain, and then return by dotted.

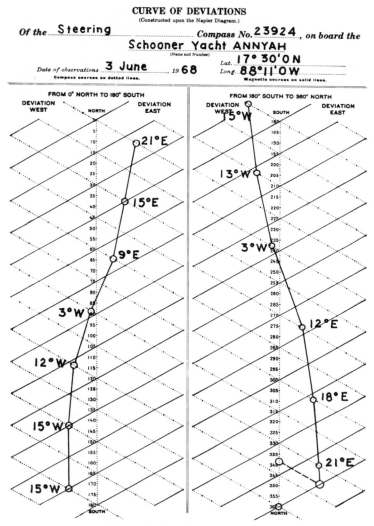

Figure 8-11. Napier Diagram

So, if we are to steer 000° magnetic, we find the north point (360°) on the baseline of the diagram and move out along the plain, or solid line, until it cuts the deviation curve. From that point we draw a line, parallel to the dotted lines, back to the baseline. The point where this line we have drawn intersects the baseline establishes the compass course equivalent to 000° magnetic; in this case, 339° per compass. Note that we have formed an equilateral triangle, 21-degree units of length on each side. This equilateral triangle is the basis of the Napier diagram.

ADJUSTING THE COMPASS

Adjusting or compensating the compass entails swinging the boat in much the same way as when preparing a deviation table, and similarly, a range

or distant object may be used as the visual reference during the process.

In this section, however, we will discuss compass adjustment while using the sun as a reference, but without calculating the azimuth, as this is usually the most convenient method and can ordinarily be completed in sheltered waters, close to the boat's home berth. We will assume that the compass to be adjusted has four compensating magnets installed in the binnacle, just below the compass bowl. For compasses that are not so equipped, it is best to obtain the services of a professional compass adjuster.

Certain preparations are necessary before getting underway. The first step is to make sure that the lubber's line is properly aligned; in other words, if a line were projected forward from the center of the compass card through the lubber's line, it would be exactly parallel to the boat's keel. If this is not the case, there will be a constant error in the compass reading. In some binnacles, the whole compass can be turned within the binnacle to achieve this alignment.

The next step is to obtain an unpainted board about 12 inches square, or a piece of plywood of this size, and drive a thin, long nail into the center just far enough so that the nail is firmly supported. *This nail must be vertical.*

When these preparations are completed, consider the adjusting magnets in the binnacle. These are mounted directly below the compass bowl and are placed as shown in figure 8-12. Two rods, one along the fore-and-aft axis and one along the athwartships axis, have a magnet placed near each end. Note that the ends of same polarity of the magnets in each pair point in opposite direction. These magnets may be turned about their horizontal axes by turning the rods.

When all magnets are in a horizontal position, they do not affect the compass reading. However, if a rod is turned by means of a nonmagnetic screwdriver inserted in its slotted end, either the red or the blue ends of the two magnets attached to that rod will draw nearer the compass card depending on the direction of rotation and will tend to turn the card relative to the lubber's line. The direction of the deflection—east or west— will depend on which ends of the magnets are elevated. The compass is adjusted to compensate for normal deviation by elevating or depressing the appropriate pairs of magnets. Before starting

out to compensate, put the magnets in a horizontal position and be sure that no loose material having magnetic properties is near the compass.

On most small-craft binnacles, the adjusting magnets cannot actually be seen, only the slotted head of the adjusting screw. If this slot is horizontal, the magnets are in a horizontal position. If built-in adjusting magnets are not included in the compass binnacle or if a flush-mount compass is used, then external bar magnets are used for compensating the compass. These can be taped down in position when adjusting the compass, then fastened down with tacks or other permanent means when the job is completed. For athwartship adjusting, a magnet is placed to the left or right of the compass and aligned in a fore-and-aft direction. To make adjustments this magnet is moved toward or away from the compass rather than being rotated. The fore-and-aft adjusting magnet is normally placed forward of the compass with the ends of the magnets aligned in an athwartship direction. This is illustrated in figure 8-12.

We will assume that these preparations are completed and that we are ready to swing for compensating the compass. We need a day when the sun is strong enough to cast a shadow and is low in the sky, so that the shadow will be long. Early morning and evening near sunset are the best times for this; the shadows will be long then, and as a bonus, there is also usually less wind at these times. The boat is now taken to an area suitable for swinging, where there will be no traffic to interfere while each heading is maintained. She is

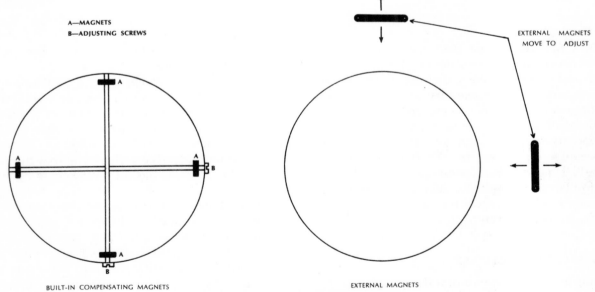

Figure 8-12.   Compensating Magnets

brought to cruising speed, and the same speed must be maintained on each heading, as acceleration can cause an error in the compass reading. The board with the nail is next secured in a spot where it is in the sun, with the nail vertical.

First bring the boat to a course of 000° by compass. When she has steadied down on this heading, take a straightedge and draw in the reciprocal of the sun's shadow, radiating out from the shadow pin. When this is done, have the helmsman make a 180-degree turn and adjust the heading until the sun's shadow falls along the pencilled line. If the compass does not read 180°, *remove half the error* by turning an *athwartships* screw. The direction in which to turn the screw is determined by trial and error. Thus, with the shadow now aligned with the pencilled line, if the compass reads 170°, adjust the athwartships screw until it reads 175°.

Next, come to a heading of 090°, and when steady on the heading, again draw the reciprocal of the shadow. Another 180-degree turn is then made, and the heading is adjusted until the shadow is aligned with the second pencilled line. If the compass does not read 270°, one-half of the error is again removed by turning a *fore-and-aft* screw.

Now the boat is turned toward 000° until the shadow and the reciprocal line, drawn on the first leg, form a straight line. If the compass does not read 000°, by means of an *athwartships* screw remove *half the error,* if the error exceeded about two degrees. It is not good practice to reduce the error further, since observational errors make further precision unrealistic. The same procedure is next followed on a heading of 090°, with the same proviso regarding an error of two degrees or less.

All that remains is to check her on the intercardinal headings of 045° and 225°, and 135° and 315°; however, the arrangement of the magnets we have discussed makes no provision for removing error on these headings. Intercardinal error is usually due to electronic equipment being installed too near the compass. If this equipment cannot be moved to a new location and the intercardinal error is considerable, try raising the level of the compass about six inches; this often helps to minimize the deviation. The other alternate is to enlist the assistance of a professional compass adjuster who is equipped to cope with special problems.

The above system is the most elementary and requires no special equipment. A pelorus with a shadow pin in the center can be used more satisfactorily, as it is gimbaled and more accurate. Small, relatively inexpensive models are available which can be used for this purpose. Another simplified method, similar to the board and nail method, is to place a 360-degree protractor on the board with the nail in the center being used as a shadow pin. In effect, this is a homemade pelorus, although not gimbaled. Instead of drawing a line on the board, for example, when heading east or west, the board is rotated until the shadow falls on the east or west point of the compass rose, and it is secured in place. Suppose this had been done on an east heading; the boat would be swung and run on a reciprocal course west by compass. If the shadow then fell on 278° rather than 270°, the total deviation would be eight degrees, and as described above half of it would be removed by adjusting the magnets. The same procedure is then followed on the north-south courses. The only real difference between these two systems is that when using the compass rose as a pelorus, the cardinal headings of north, east, south, and west are actually steered by compass. When using only the shadow pin on the board, it is necessary to steer a course almost on the cardinal headings, which will cause the shadow to be aligned with the pencilled line.

After the adjustment has been completed, swing ship and prepare a deviation table as outlined in the preceding sections.

One final word—do not adjust the compass directly after a boat has been laid up at about 90 degrees to the magnetic meridian for a considerable time, as some temporary magnetism will then be induced in the boat's ferrous metal. Run her for a few days before adjusting, so that this induced magnetism will have time to fade out.

SUMMARY

The compass is a vital piece of equipment aboard every boat, and it deserves the best of care. See that no loose gear that might affect it is left in its vicinity; portable radios, camera light meters, and beverage cans are among the worst offenders.

When cruising, make periodic checks of the deviation by one of the methods outlined in this chapter. By night, Polaris, the pole star, can be used for a quick check; it will always bear within two degrees of true north.

chapter nine

The Navigator's Tools

In this chapter, we will discuss the tools which have been found useful for navigation in small craft. They may be classified in various ways; we will group them as follows: 1: instruments for measuring direction both of courses and bearings; 2: instruments for measuring distance and for determining speed; 3: instruments for measuring depth of water; 4: plotting instruments; and 5: miscellaneous equipment.

The choice of which instruments to use in each category is a personal one depending on many factors including vessel size and use. In preparing this chapter, we have attempted to give the reader enough information on the various items, so that he may make an intelligent choice as to what will best meet his personal requirements.

Certain navigational equipment, such as the compass, charts, the *Light List*, the *Tide and Current Tables*, and the *radio direction finder* require lengthy treatment; they are therefore covered in separate chapters under the appropriate headings.

DIRECTION AND BEARINGS

The Pelorus

Aboard most boats, it is impossible to get an unobstructed view in all directions from the compass. In such a case, it is convenient to have a portable pelorus (also called a dumb compass), which can be mounted at one or more convenient points, so that bearings may be taken in any direction relative to the boat's heading. Such a pelorus is shown in figure 9-1.

A pelorus consists of a flat, nonmagnetic metallic or plastic ring mounted in gimbals. The inner edge of the ring has an index mark called a lubber's line to indicate the fore-and-aft line. On some models, a nonrotating pointer is affixed to the center pivot and this pointer serves as a lub-

Figure 9-1.   A Yacht Pelorus

ber's line. This arrangement is shown in figure 9-1. This ring encloses a graduated compass card called a *pelorus card*, which is flush with the ring. The card is rotatable, so that any degree of its graduation may be set to the lubber's line; some peloruses are fitted so that the card can be temporarily locked in place. A pair of sighting vanes are mounted on the card; they can be rotated about the card independently of the card itself and can be clamped at any desired setting.

True or *magnetic* bearings may be obtained with the pelorus. The pelorus card is set to the boat's heading (true or magnetic, as the case may be) by turning it until the graduation on the card coincides with the lubber's line; the card is then locked in that position. The sighting vanes are next turned until they are approximately aligned with the object to be observed. The helmsman is now directed to sing out "Mark! Mark! Mark!" when he is steady on the selected compass heading that represents the desired true or magnetic course. When he does so, take the bearing exactly by adjusting the position of the sighting vanes.

Relative bearings may be obtained with the pelorus by locking the zero-degree graduation of the card at the lubber's line.

The Hand Bearing Compass

The hand bearing compass is an extremely useful instrument for obtaining magnetic bearings; a typical instrument is shown in figure 9-2. It consists of a small, flat-topped compass bowl, containing a compass card, usually graduated for every two degrees. A sighting vane is attached to the compass at the far side from the observer. This vane may be rotated about a horizontal axis by means of thumb screws. To the vane is attached a magnifying prism, on which a vertical hairline is engraved. A flashlight battery case, with a switch, serves as the handle for the compass. Bat-

Figure 9-2.   A Hand Bearing Compass

teries contained in the handle supply electricity to light the compass card from below for night use.

To obtain a bearing, the compass is held at arm's length, so that the object to be observed is seen centered in the sighting vane. The angle of the vane and prism are then adjusted by means of the thumbscrew so that the section of the compass card directly below is seen reflected in the prism. Because of the magnifying power of the prism, this section of the card will appear greatly enlarged, and the bearing can be read with an accuracy of better than one degree at the hairline.

Aboard most boats, bearings taken with such a compass will ordinarily not be affected by deviation if the observer stands clear of wire rigging and away from the engine; they will, therefore, be magnetic bearings.

A hand bearing compass also makes a good emergency steering compass if it is secured in front of the helmsman and aligned so that the hairline represents the lubber's line.

Marine Sextant

The sextant is normally thought of as the precision instrument for celestial navigation. In that usage, angles with an accuracy of a few tenths of minutes of arc are required and a good brass or aluminum frame sextant is recommended. The sextant is also useful in piloting to measure horizontal angles. For this purpose it is generally not practical to plot the angles on the chart with an accuracy of better then approximately $\frac{1}{2}$ degree. The less-expensive plastic sextants are quite adequate for this and are often used by the small boat operator who is not going offshore.

A position, or fix, can be determined by measuring the angles between three objects that can be identified from your location and that are also shown on the nautical chart. The three-armed protractor (figure 9-13) is used for plotting the position. Danger angles, both vertical and horizontal (chapter 12) are best measured with the sextant. The distance from a lighthouse or other structure of known height can be determined by measuring the angle subtended by the object. This same principle is used to calculate the distance from another vessel if her mast height is known. The stadimeter is more easily used for this latter problem as it gives a direct readout of distance off, but the sextant is more versatile if only one instrument is to be purchased.

Figure 9-3.   The Marine Sextant

DISTANCE AND SPEED

Aboard large vessels, the term *log* is used to describe an instrument that indicates both speed and distance run. Aboard smaller craft, the term *log* is ordinarily used to describe an instrument that indicates the distance run, while *speedometer* is used for an instrument that gives a speed readout. There are, however, some speedometers that integrate speed and time to give a readout of distance run in addition to the speed reading.

Taffrail Logs

The *taffrail log* is the instrument most widely used aboard boats to indicate distance run. It gets

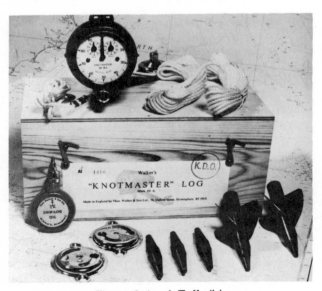

Figure 9-4.   A Taffrail Log

its name from the fact that in sailing ships the readout portion of the log was secured to the taffrail at the ship's poop.

Readout on most taffrail logs is by means of two dials, each with its own revolving pointer, which is located on the face of the instrument. The larger dial reads nautical miles, while the smaller dial reads tenths of a nautical mile. A typical taffrail log is shown in figure 9-4. To this is attached the *log line,* at the end of which is the *rotor.* Some logs use a cylindrical weight, which is attached around the log line forward of the rotor.

The rotor is, in effect, a streamlined propeller, which revolves as it is towed through the water. These revolutions are passed on to the log by means of the log line, where they actuate the two pointers through a gear train. The length of the log line depends both on the boat's speed and the height above the water of the log. The manufacturer's recommendations should be consulted as to the length of the line for each boat, and also as to how frequently the log should be oiled.

On most logs, it is possible to move the pointers to the zero setting at the beginning of a run.

In general, taffrail logs tend to under-read somewhat with a following sea and to over-read with a head sea. However, they can be invaluable in foggy weather or when making a passage out of sight of land. It is a wise precaution when at sea to carry a spare rotor and log line, as large fish sometimes mistake the rotor for a tasty morsel.

There is another important item in regard to the use of taffrail logs. The log line ordinarily hooks into a hole in the axis of the log flywheel. To get the log aboard, unhook the line from the fly wheel and pay out the hook end of the line as the rotor is pulled in. When the rotor is in hand, start hauling in the hook end and make the line up in a coil. If this method of securing the log line is not used, a truly incredibly snarled line will result.

Knotmeters

Knotmeters are usually actuated by a small free-turning paddlewheel mounted on the exterior of the hull beneath the waterline, whose revolutions are counted electronically. This electric type of transmission is advantageous in that the speed readout is not as compressed at the lower end of the scale as is the hydraulic type. This is a particularly desirable feature for use aboard sailboats. A typical knotmeter is shown in figure 9-5.

Figure 9-5.   Knotmeter readout

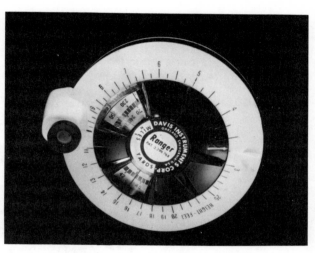

Figure 9-6.   Yacht Stadimeter

Knotmeters ordinarily require little or no attention. Most permit calibration of the speed readout, which should be checked from time to time over a course of known length, when there is no current or appreciable wind or sea. Should maintenance become necessary, most installations permit access without hauling the boat.

Some knotmeters are equipped to integrate speed and time for a readout of distance run.

Revolution Tables

It is most desirable to prepare a table showing the speed obtained at various engine revolutions. Such a table should be prepared on a calm day in an area where there is no current by timing the boat over a known distance at various throttle settings. However, bear in mind that headwinds and seas may tend to slow boat speed down very considerably at any given engine speed. The method of producing a speed curve is discussed in chapter 10.

Stadimeters

The stadimeter is an instrument for measuring the distance away of objects of known heights between 50 and 200 feet; on most stadimeters, the *ranges* or distances covered are from 200 to 10,000 yards. Other ranges may be measured by using a scale factor for the graduations. The stadimeter is used aboard all Coast Guard and naval vessels and in some yachts.

Stadimeters come in different forms, but all work on the same principle (figures 9-6, 9-7). Essentially, they consist of a frame on which is

mounted a telescope. A movable arm rotates an index mirror through a small arc, permitting alignment of the direct and reflected images as seen through the telescope. The arm is moved by rotating a micrometer drum. The instrument is initially set to the known height of the object; the stadimeter measures the angle subtended by the object and converts it into range, which is read directly from the micrometer drum.

Small optical range finders reading to 1,500 yards are also in use.

A sextant, if available, may also be used to measure the distance of objects of known height. The subtended angle may readily be converted into distance by means of table 9 in *Bowditch*.

DEPTH

Three methods of determining depth are commonly used in boats; these consist of the *sounding pole*, the *leadline*, and the *depth finder* (also called an *echo sounder* or *Fathometer*).

The Sounding Pole

The *sounding pole* is a most useful device on board boats of fairly shoal draft, particularly those used for "gunkholing." One method of marking the pole, which has proven satisfactory, is to put a readily visible ring around the pole to indicate a depth of one foot more than the boat's draft. Another ring can then be marked two feet above this. A boat drawing 2 feet 6 inches would thus have the lower ring 3 feet 6 inches above the rod's lower end and the second ring 5 feet 6 inches from the end. A boathook, if it is long enough, may be used for this purpose.

Figure 9-7.   Fiske Stadimeter

The Leadline

The *leadline* is probably one of the oldest tools used by the navigator. Two types of leads were and, in some instances, still are used. These are the *hand lead* and the *deep-sea lead*. The former weighs between 7 and 14 pounds and the latter, which is intended for sounding depths up to 70 or 80 fathoms, weighs between 50 and 100 pounds. The deep-sea lead is mentioned here only as a matter of interest, as its use would undoubtedly make confirmed farmers out of most modern sailors.

Leadlines may be marked in the traditional manner, as follows; a fathom, incidentally, equals six feet.

Fathoms	Marking
2	2 leather strips
3	3 leather strips
5	white rag
7	red rag
10	leather strip with a hole
13	3 leather strips
15	white rag
17	red rag
20	line with 2 knots
25	line with 1 knot
30	line with 3 knots
35	line with 1 knot
40	line with 4 knots

Alternately, each individual may put knots in the leadline according to a system of his own devising. However, the most satisfactory method is to purchase flexible waterproof markers, which can be inserted through the strands of the line. These markers are available at most ship and yacht chandlers.

To *heave the lead*, the boat must be traveling at low speed. The line is laid out in an open coil so that it can pay out freely; be sure not to stand in a bight of the line! Hold the line about eight feet above the lead and then start swinging it in an arc parallel to the boat's side. When the line is horizontal, or nearly so, and the lead is at the forward end of its swing, release the line but keep it running through your fingers. If the lead hits bottom, raise the slack, so that the line will be vertical as the boat passes the position of the lead. Note where the water surface is on the line; this will mark the depth.

While a light lead is more convenient to use, it is hard to get bottom with it in any but shoal waters. A seven-pound lead will generally be the most satisfactory one for depths to 25 fathoms.

Most leads have a concave bottom. This hollow can be *armed* or filled with tallow or yellow laundry soap to bring up a sampling of the bottom. Knowledge of the type of bottom can sometimes be helpful in determining the general location.

Depth Finders

The *depth finder* gives a continuous readout of the depth by measuring the time interval between the transmission of a sound signal and the return of the echo. Since the approximate speed of sound in water is known, the depth equals the speed multiplied by one-half the interval between sound and echo. The speed of sound in water varies with temperature, pressure, and salinity; however, an average value of 4,800 feet per second is sufficiently accurate for navigation.

The signal may be sonic or ultrasonic; it is generated electrically in a device called a *transducer* and is transmitted downward in the shape of a cone. The transducer also serves as a microphone and detects the returning echo, which is transmitted as an electrical impulse to the depth indicator.

Some depth indicators show the depth by means of a pointer, which reads out against a depth scale. Others have a circular scale, calibrated in depth readings; the outgoing signal appears as a flash of light at the zero mark, and the echo appears as a second flash opposite the appropriate depth marking on the scale. The scale may read in feet or in fathoms; some depth finders have a switching device, permitting readout in feet in shoal water, as from 0 to 50 feet, or in fathoms from 0 to 50 in deeper water. The readout arrangements described above are gradually being replaced by the use of a digital lighted readout. The instrument shown in figure 9-8 is so equipped. The three-digit display will provide readouts to 999-foot depths. For some models, a graphic readout is available, which traces on paper the depth against time. Such a device is called a *recorder;* recorders are very popular with fishermen, as a school of fish will appear as a lighter trace at the appropriate depth above the bottom, which will be a darker trace.

Hard bottoms act as better reflectors than soft and return a sharper echo; at times it is difficult to get a reading from an echo sounder near the limit of its readout if the bottom is soft mud.

Depth finders are widely used aboard small craft because of their low price, reliability, and capability of providing a continuous readout of depth.

PLOTTING EQUIPMENT

Pencils and Erasers

A medium-soft pencil, such as a No. 2, is best for general plotting, as work done with a very hard pencil is difficult to erase, and a very soft pencil tends to leave smudges. Several pencils should be available and, if there is room for it, a pencil sharpener. Draw light lines and avoid drawing them longer than necessary. Label all lines and points as soon as drawn; standard labeling is described in chapter 10. An art gum eraser is convenient for cleaning a considerable area, while a chisel-pointed eraser serves to make small erasures.

Dividers and Compasses

Dividers are an essential tool, primarily for measuring distance. Their legs should be at least six inches in length, and they should be tight enough to hold a setting. Protect the points from damage and also from rust.

Compasses are convenient for drawing distance circles, such as the computed visibility circle of lights. What was said about the size and protection of dividers applies equally to compasses. Navigator's sets that include a set of dividers and a compass in a storage case are popular.

Parallel Rulers

Parallel rulers are the navigator's traditional tool for determining the direction of any line on a chart by moving the rulers to a compass rose, while they are maintained parallel to the reference line. The most commonly used parallel rulers consist of a pair of rulers of equal length joined near each end by metal strips, which permit one ruler to be moved relative to the other while remaining parallel to it. Another type consists essentially of a straightedge fitted with rollers knurled to prevent slipping. The ruler retains its original alignment while being rolled across the chart.

Parallel rulers render satisfactory service when used on an absolutely flat surface and if they themselves are not warped. With one rule held firmly

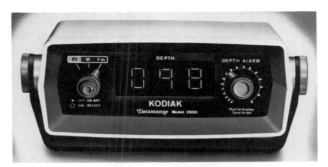

Figure 9-8.   A Typical Depth Finder

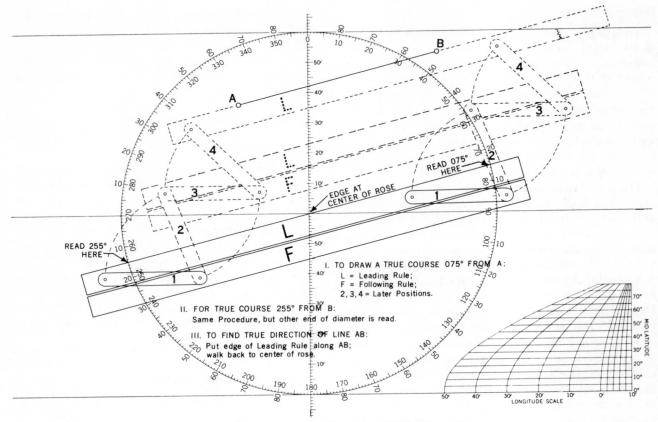

I. TO DRAW A TRUE COURSE 075° FROM A:
   L = Leading Rule;
   F = Following Rule;
   2, 3, 4 = Later Positions.

II. FOR TRUE COURSE 255° FROM B:
   Same Procedure, but other end of diameter is read.

III. TO FIND TRUE DIRECTION OF LINE AB:
   Put edge of Leading Rule along AB;
   walk back to center of rose.

Figure 9-9.   Use of Parallel Rulers

along a line of desired direction, a whole series of lines paralleling it may be drawn by simply moving the other rule to different positions.

When used for drawing courses, bearings, etc., on a chart, the instrument is "walked" by laying one rule into position, moving the other away from it, then holding the latter while moving the first one up to it, and repeating as often as necessary. (See figure 9-9.) Thus, a course or bearing line may be referred to a compass rose to determine its true direction; or in reverse, a direction selected on a compass rose may be transferred to a chosen point and from it a course or bearing line drawn in that direction. Warped rules, inaccurately placed pivots, and lost motion cause errors. If a rule slips, as frequently happens if the chart surface is not flat, a fresh start must be made. On small craft it is difficult to find space for the unfolded chart, which is necessary for successful use of parallel rulers. A plotter in this situation is more practical.

Parallel rulers are particularly useful for moving lines parallel to themselves, as in advancing a line of position. However, they are of limited value when no compass rose is shown on the chart, as in the Lambert conformal projection. Good paral-

lel rulers have small circles of cork on the underside to help reduce the ever-present problem of slipping.

Plotters and Protractors

An extremely useful device has been produced that combines the advantages of a rolling parallel ruler with those of a plotter; it is the *Paraline plotter* and is shown in figure 9-10. It is never necessary to roll the Paraline plotter far on the chart to determine true direction, as protractors are included, which permit reading direction either from a meridian or a parallel of latitude. The rollers may be temporarily removed from the plotter if desired. The device is scaled to permit direct reading of distance on chart scales of 1:80,000, 1:40,000, and 1:20,000, which are used for the majority of the National Ocean Service coast & harbor charts. This instrument has been adopted by the Coast Guard and has been assigned Federal Stock Number 6605-G 00-2320.

Plotters have been designed in many forms, and they are becoming increasingly popular with marine navigators.

Typical of many plotters used afloat is the *No.*

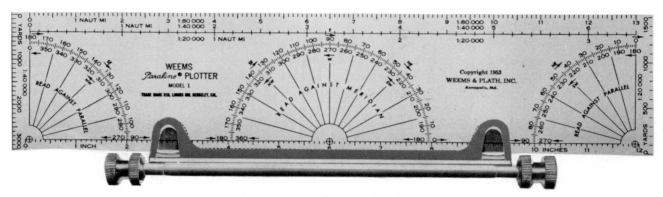

Figure 9-10.   The Paraline Plotter

641 *Navy Plotter,* shown in figure 9-11. This type of instrument was originally designed for aircraft navigation; however, its simplicity and convenience has brought it into wide favor afloat. The scale of 20 miles to the inch fits the DMA's Universal Plotting Charts.

Another type of plotter that is often found aboard small craft is illustrated in figure 9-12. It consists of a protractor that has a long plotting arm pivoted at its center. This arm carries the distance scales commonly used on National Ocean Service charts.

Draftsman's triangles can also be used in plotting; when two are employed, the direction of a line can be measured at a compass rose by sliding the triangles across the chart, while keeping the edge of one triangle parallel to the line. However, they are subject to some of the same drawbacks as parallel rulers on small craft.

The *Courser* is a transparent plastic sheet with parallel lines printed on it. If the sheet is laid on the chart and oriented so that one printed line passes through two charted points, direction may be read at the compass rose by means of another printed line. As the latter may not pass exactly through the center of the rose, it may be necessary to interpolate visually to read the direction. The Courser cannot be used conveniently for drawing lines. Its virtue is that the chart need not be laid on a flat surface; it can even be used with the chart in one's lap. *Do not use the Courser when exact results are required.*

The *three-armed protractor* (figure 9-13) is extremely useful for plotting an exact position using bearings obtained by sextant from fixed objects ashore. The fixed center arm is the reference; the angle between the left-hand and the center object is set on the protractor, and then the angle between the center and the right-hand object is set. The protractor is then placed on the chart and oriented so that the index lines on the three arms pass through the three charted objects. The vessel's position is then marked on the chart by placing the point of a pencil in the small hole at the center of the protractor.

Drafting Machines

Aboard most large ships, all chart plotting is done by means of a drafting machine. Essentially,

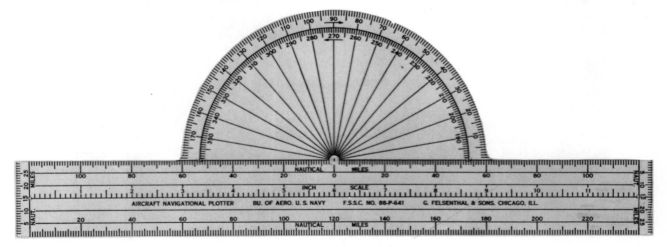

Figure 9-11.   Navy Plotter No. 641

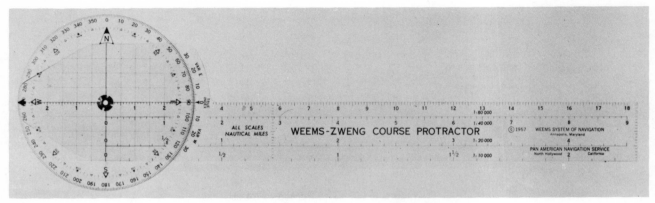

Figure 9-12.   One-Armed Course Protractor

it consists of a protractor with a straightedge attached; the protractor is carried by a parallel-motion system secured to the upper left-hand corner of the chart desk. The chart is securely fastened to the desk with masking tape, and the protractor is then oriented to the chart and clamped in this position. The straightedge can now be moved to any position on the chart, and the direction in which it is aligned is read from the protractor.

Plotting Boards

The navigator is frequently faced with problems in relative motion, such as determining the direction and force of the true wind when underway, or selecting the course to steer in order to offset a current of known set and drift. (See chapter 13.) Such problems can be solved mathematically or graphically by means of a vector diagram. In these problems the lengths of the sides represent speed. Given the lengths of two sides, and the angle between them, determined by the difference in directions, the length, and therefore the speed of the third side—as well as its direction—can be determined.

The *Vectormaster* is a plastic device that permits the rapid solution of these problems in relative motion by plotting; it is a smaller version of the maneuvering board used aboard U.S. Navy and Coast Guard ships. See figure 9-14.

Problems such as determining the course to steer to offset the effect of a current of known set and drift, or determining the direction and

Figure 9-13.   Three-Armed Plotter

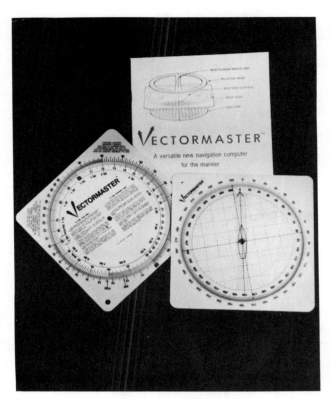

Figure 9-14.   The Vectormaster

speed of the true wind aboard a vessel underway can be solved rapidly with the Vectormaster.

The instrument consists of a fixed outer compass rose, which represents true direction; within it is mounted a second rotatable compass rose, representing relative direction. This latter rose is bisected by an index line representing the boat's head. A fixed transparent plotting surface is mounted within the fixed rose on which vectors can be drawn with a pencil. Below this surface is a rotatable disc, on which is printed a grid in black lines and concentric red circles; these patterns permit the accurate measurement of speed and distance vectors.

On the reverse of the Vectormaster is mounted a circular slide rule, which facilitates the solution of problems involving time, speed and distance, fuel consumption, etc.

The Anemometer

The anemometer is an instrument that measures wind speed; it is of particular importance aboard sailboats. Two types of anemometers are in general use: one type is hand-held and gives a direct reading; the other type is mounted on the truck of the mast, with a readout in the cockpit. They are shown in figure 9-15.

It must be borne in mind that when underway, the wind speed as read from the instrument is apparent wind speed; that is, the speed of the true wind as affected by the vessel's course and speed.

The direction and speed of the true wind may be determined from the direction and speed of the apparent wind, as noted aboard the boat, either by a graphic solution, or mathematically, as discussed in the section on the scientific electronic calculator.

The Scientific Calculator

Since *Piloting and Dead Reckoning* was first published, an extremely powerful tool has become

Figure 9-15.   Hand-held and Masthead-mounted Anemometer (Courtesy R. A. Simerl)

available to the navigator. This tool is the electronic scientific calculator; it differs from the ordinary calculator primarily in that it is designed to handle trigonometric functions—sines, cosines, tangents, and cotangents—in addition to performing the ordinary arithmetical functions of addition, multiplication, subtraction, and division. This trigonometric capability permits the accurate and extremely rapid solution of not only the majority of problems encountered in piloting, but also the problems in celestial navigation.

A simple scientific calculator, capable of solving all the examples in the section on the use of the calculator, can be purchased inexpensively from one of the many discount houses. More advanced models offer features that speed the solution of problems. Two of the most desirable features are the capability to convert polar to rectangular coordinates and vice versa at the touch of a key, and the several addressable memory storage compartments, in which intermediate answers may be stored for future recall. See figure 9-16.

The most sophisticated of these calculators are the programmable models; these permit the repeated solution of the same type of problem. Only the new basic data need be keyed in. Many of this latter type also have decision-making capability—if x is greater than y they follow one routine, while if y is the greater a different routine is automatically followed. These latter models are extremely well suited to the solution of problems encountered in celestial navigation.

As the manuals supplied by the manufacturers ordinarily do not devote much space to the use of the calculator aboard ship, examples illustrating the calculator solution of typical problems encountered in piloting are included in chapter 16. The *Calculator Afloat*, published by the Naval Institute Press, will be of interest to those who desire further information on the many ways the calculator can be used aboard any vessel.

Slide Rules

A slide rule can be of assistance in solving problems involving mathematics. It may be in the form of the nautical slide rule, shown in figure 10-4, which solves time, speed, and distance problems. If any two factors are known, the third may be determined. A conventional slide rule will, of course, solve the same problems and is also useful for other purposes, such as determining fuel consumption at various speeds, etc.

A logarithmic scale is shown on many charts; one appears on NOS Chart No. TR 1210. This scale may be used in conjunction with a pair of dividers to solve time, speed, and distance problems. The simple directions required to use the scale are printed directly below it.

Flashlight

A flashlight of the two-cell type is invaluable for night work. It should be equipped with a red bulb, or at least modified with a piece of red cellophane inside the lens. Red light does not adversely affect dark-adapted vision. This is most important to remember when underway at night.

Weather Information

Weather must be taken into consideration by the boatman, as it can make navigation hazardous. An *aneroid barometer* can at times be of assistance in determining whether strong winds are to be expected, and it is wise to have some knowledge of elementary marine meteorology. The federal government has embarked on a program of installing FM radio stations to cover widely used boating areas. These stations broadcast continuous-voice weather information on 162.40, 162.475, and 162.55 MHz (megahertz). This information can be of the utmost help. Small transistorized radio receivers, capable of receiving signals

Figure 9-16.   HewLett Packard 32E

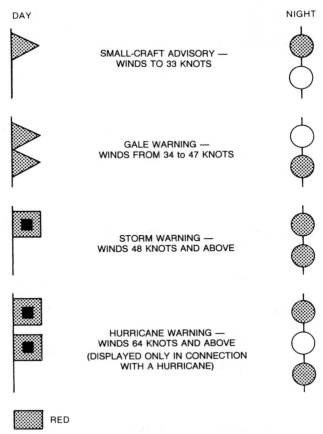

DAY   NIGHT

SMALL-CRAFT ADVISORY —
WINDS TO 33 KNOTS

GALE WARNING —
WINDS FROM 34 to 47 KNOTS

STORM WARNING —
WINDS 48 KNOTS AND ABOVE

HURRICANE WARNING —
WINDS 64 KNOTS AND ABOVE
(DISPLAYED ONLY IN CONNECTION
WITH A HURRICANE)

RED

Figure 9-17.   Day and Night Visual Storm Warnings

on this wavelength and equipped with self-contained telescoping antennas, can be purchased inexpensively.

The Department of Commerce publishes *Marine Weather Services Charts;* they are quite small in size and inexpensive. They list the call letters, locations, and frequencies of radio stations broadcasting marine weather forecasts, together with the time of these broadcasts.

Also shown are the locations where visual day and/or night storm warning signals are displayed. This latter information also appears on many NOS charts; on Chart No. TR 1210, it will be found near the left-hand edge.

The day and night storm warning signals are shown in figure 9-17.

SUMMARY

In this chapter, we have discussed many of the navigational instruments that can be useful to the small craft navigator. These have been considered under the following headings: instruments for determining direction; instruments for measuring speed and distance; instruments for measuring the depth of water; plotting instruments; and miscellaneous equipment that can be of assistance to the navigator.

In addition, we have listed briefly information on how marine weather forecasts and warnings can be obtained. Never risk your safety in weather than may overtax your boat.

chapter ten

Dead Reckoning*

Dead reckoning (DR) is one of the basic parts of navigation; it is used in connection with every form of navigation, and its importance cannot be overemphasized.

During the eighteenth and nineteenth centuries, charts were both scarce and expensive, and shipmasters did not use them to plot the courses and distances they had sailed. Instead, they calculated a current position mathematically, using the courses and speeds sailed from a previous position. This was called "deduced reckoning," which abbreviated to "ded reckoning," and eventually became "dead reckoning."

DEFINITION

The Navy and Coast Guard define dead reckoning as the process of determining a ship's approximate position by applying to the last well-determined position a vector or a series of consecutive vectors representing the run that has since been made, using only the *true courses* steered and the distance steamed as determined by the ordered engine speed, without considering current or leeway. However, in the case of sailboats, it would be necessary to substitute estimated speed.

The process of dead reckoning also permits the position to be run ahead and the vessel's position to be predicted at any desired time. The key elements of dead reckoning may be summarized as follows:

Only the true courses steered are used to determine a DR position.

The distance run used in obtaining a DR position is obtained by multiplying the ordered engine speed by the time it has acted or will act.

An intended DR plot is always plotted from a known position, that is, a fix or running fix.

The effects of current are not considered in determining a DR position.

This definition and these principles of dead reckoning are satisfactory for use aboard ships equipped with gyrocompasses, which permit ready determination of true direction, and where engine speeds can be adjusted to give quite precise speeds through the water.

For small craft using magnetic compasses and particularly for sailboats, it is sometimes more satisfactory to modify this definition somewhat. Instead of true courses, *magnetic courses* may be substituted, and the best estimate of speed may be employed, whether derived from a log, a speedometer, or engine revolutions. Again, for sailboats under sail, it is often difficult to run a position ahead to give a predicted position considerably in the future.

In this chapter, we will concentrate on dead reckoning based on true courses, as once the principle and techniques are mastered, you will have no problem shifting to the use of a DR based on magnetic directions, should you so desire.

ELEMENTS OF DEAD RECKONING

We have said that the importance of dead reckoning cannot be overemphasized. No vessel can always be in a position to determine its position exactly; at such times the navigator must rely on his dead reckoning to aid in determining his most probable position. How such a position is determined by applying various factors to a DR position will be discussed in this chapter, as will be the approved terminology and method of plotting the DR course line.

---

* Portions of this chapter have been adapted from *Dutton's Navigation and Piloting*, 13th Ed. (Annapolis: Naval Institute Press, 1978).

Plotting the DR course lines on a chart is vastly superior to the old method of calculating position. The danger of making a mathematical blunder is greatly reduced, and in coastwise navigation, the location of the vessel's DR position relative to hazards to navigation, such as shoals, is readily discernable.

DR Terms Defined

Definitions of terms used in dead reckoning vary greatly in different texts and have thus far not been standardized. Various adjectives can be used to clarify specific uses of basic terms, but confusion in terminology can be avoided by remembering that in marine navigation *course* is always used as a direction with reference to the path of the vessel through the water, while *track* is used with reference to the desired future path with respect to the earth. This usage is standard in this text.

A *line of position* (*LOP*) is a line on some point of which the vessel is presumed to be located. An LOP may be obtained in a number of ways, such as by taking a visual bearing on a charted object or by using an accurate radio direction finder bearing.

A *fix* (*FIX*) is an accurate position determined without reference to any former position. It is commonly obtained by crossing two or more LOPs obtained almost simultaneously.

A *running fix* (*R FIX*) is a position determined by crossing LOPs obtained at considerably different times. One or more lines may be advanced or retired along the DR plot to a common time.

Heading (*Hdg.* or *SH*) is the horizontal direction in which a ship points or heads at any instant, expressed in angular units, clockwise from 000° through 360° from a reference direction (see figure 10-1). The heading of a ship is called *ship's head*. Heading is a constantly changing value as a ship oscillates or yaws across the course because of the effects of the sea and of steering error.

Course (*C*) is a rhumb line direction, and is the horizontal direction of travel through still water, expressed in angular units from a reference direction, from 000° at the reference direction clockwise through 360°. The course is often designated as true, magnetic, compass, or grid as the reference direction is true, magnetic, compass, or grid north, respectively. The course is assumed to be a true course, unless another reference is stated. In such a case, the reference must be given as *magnetic* (*M*) or *compass* (*C*).

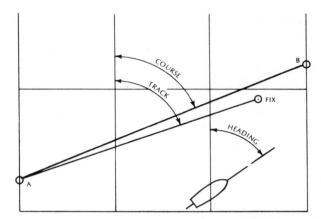

Figure 10-1.   Heading, Course, and Track

Course line, in marine navigation, is the graphic representation of a ship's course, normally used in the construction of a dead reckoning plot.

Course made good (*COG*), as used in navigation, is the rhumb line or lines describing the path a vessel actually made good relative to the earth.

Intended track (*TR*) is the anticipated path of a vessel relative to the earth. When used in constructing vector diagrams, the direction of the resultant side after drawing the vectors for course and speed, and estimated current set and drift, is termed the intended track.

Speed (*S*) is the rate of travel of a ship through the water, in knots. It is used in conjunction with time to establish a distance run on each of the consecutive segments or vectors of the DR plot.

Speed made good (*SMG*) is the speed along the track, representing the *speed made good* over the surface of the earth. It differs from the ship's speed (*S*) through the water by a vector of the current velocity. It is sometimes called *speed over the ground* (*SOG*).

Speed of advance (*SOA*) is the average speed in knots which must be maintained on a voyage to arrive at a destination at an appointed time.

DR position is a position determined by plotting a vector or series of consecutive vectors using only the true course and distance determined by speed through the water without consideration of current.

Estimated position (*EP*) is the most probable position of a ship, determined from incomplete data or data of questionable accuracy. In practical usage, it is often the DR position as modified by the best information available.

Dead reckoning plot is commonly called the DR plot. In marine navigation, it is the graphical representation on the nautical chart of the line or series of lines representing the vectors of the ordered true courses, and distance run on these courses at the ordered speeds, while proceeding from a fixed point. The DR plot originates at a fix or running fix; it is suitably labeled as to courses, speeds, and times of various dead reckoning positions, usually at hourly time intervals or at times of change of course or speed. The DR plot may represent courses and speeds to be used or those that have been used.

Estimated time of departure (ETD) is the estimate of the time of departure from a specified location in accordance with a scheduled movement.

Estimated time of arrival (ETA) is the best estimate of the time of arrival at a specified location in accordance with a scheduled movement.

Distance is a linear measurement between two points on the surface of the earth, represented in navigation by two points on the chart. The common unit of distance in navigation is the nautical mile, which is equal to 6,076.1 feet or one minute of arc of a great circle on the earth. A statute mile is an arbitrary unit of distance, 5,280 feet in length.

Labeling a DR Plot

It is most important that all lines and points on a DR plot be properly labeled. A standard method of labeling allows anyone to understand the plot, and no confusion will arise. The principal rules in labeling a DR plot are as follows:

1. Immediately after drawing a line or plotting a point, label it clearly and neatly.

2. The label for any point on a line should not be along the line but at an angle to be clear of the line.

3. The label indicating the direction of a course line (*C*) should lie along the line and above it, followed by three numerals indicating the true course in degrees. If a magnetic course is being used, print the letter *M* just after the direction; if the reference is to a compass course, add *C* after the direction.

4. The label indicating speed (*S*) should appear along the bottom of the line, beneath the direction, followed by numerals indicating the speed in knots. If statute miles are used in lieu of knots, the numerals indicating the speed should be followed by the letters *MPH*.

5. The label of any point on a DR plot consists of two parts: (a) a semi-circle around a dot which

locates the point, and (b) the time. A fix is shown by a circled dot which locates the intersection of LOPs (see chapter 11) and the time.

Note that in all navigation, the 24-hour method of recording time is used, and hours and minutes are always stated as four figures. Thus 9 hours 35 minutes AM is written as 0935, and 10 hours 27 minutes PM is written as 2227. When it is necessary to state hours, minutes, and seconds, time is stated as six figures, i.e., 032539.

Figure 10-2 illustrates the proper labeling of points and course lines in a DR plot.

The Navy and Coast Guard rules regarding the maintaining of a DR plot are given below. These are also the rules to which we will adhere in this text. A DR position shall be plotted:

1. Every hour on the hour.
2. At the time of every course change.
3. At the time of every speed change.
4. At the time of obtaining a fix or running fix.
5. At the time of obtaining a single line of position.

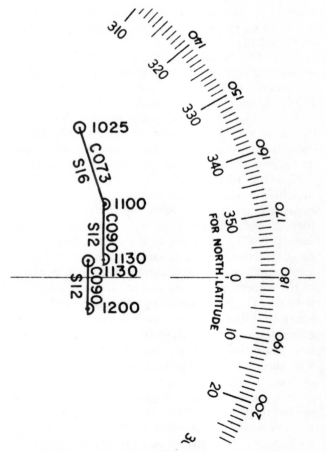

Figure 10-2.   Proper Labeling on a DR Plot

In addition, a new course line shall be plotted from each fix or running fix as it has been determined and plotted on the chart.

These rules are considered adequate to meet the requirements of navigation in open waters. When navigating in restricted waters, such as channels, a more frequent plot of the vessel's position is essential. Knowledge of when to plot more frequent fixes and DR positions will come with experience. The application of these rules is illustrated in the following section.

Example of a DR Plot

The following example outlines a typical dead reckoning problem; its solution is shown in figure 10-3. It is based on the log, which, in part, reads as follows:

> At *1015* with Brenton Reef Lt. bearing 000°, distant 200 yards, took departure for Buzzards Lt. on course 096° True, speed 10 knots. At *1100* slowed to 6 knots to adjust water circulating pump, as engine is overheating. At *1115* resumed speed of 10 knots. At *1125* changed course to 176° and speed to 12KT to check a small boat which appears to be in trouble, distant about 2 miles. At *1137* came alongside boat, named *Daisy*, of Newport, R.I. Assisted in cleaning distributor; at *1147 Daisy's* engine running well. Departed *Daisy*, and set course 075°, speed 8KT for Buzzards Lt. which is not visible, due to thick haze. At 1210 sighted

> Buzzards Lt. bearing 034°, distant about 2 miles. Changed course to 034°. At 1224 Buzzards Lt. bearing 033° distant 300 yards.

This illustrates the application of the rules outlined in the previous section. Note that the 1210 plot on the chart is an *estimated position* (*EP*) as we could not establish the distance exactly; we estimated it by eye to be about two miles. The EP is marked with a box ⊡ on the chart. If we had had a radar set to give an exact distance, this with the visual bearing would have made an excellent fix. On the other hand, it is assumed that distances not exceeding roughly 300 yards can be established visually so that, when combined with a bearing, they do supply a fix.

Ordinarily a new course line is drawn only from a fix or a running fix; however, in this instance we obtained a line of position when we sighted Buzzards Light and could thus run along that line to our destination.

THE DEAD RECKONING PLOT AND NAVIGATIONAL PLANNING

Navy and Coast Guard ships prepare a tentative DR plot before getting underway. This is based on a careful study of all available information, including the *Coast Pilot* (see chapter 17), the *Tide Tables* (see chapter 14), the *Current Tables* (see

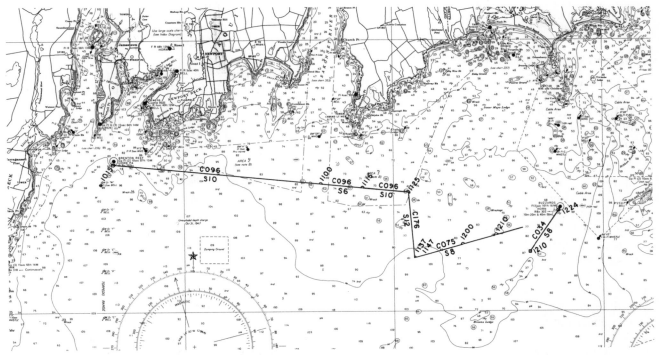

Figure 10-3. A Dead Reckoning Plot

chapter 14), and the *Light List* (see chapter 6). This preparatory work is known as *navigational planning*, which is a fundamental principle of safe navigation for every voyage.

From these sources, much information pertinent to the voyage is obtained. It includes navigational aids expected to be sighted, depths of water in port, tidal and ocean currents, charts of the area to be traversed, contour of the bottom, and any electronic aids to navigation that will be available, such as radio beacons (see chapter 15) and Loran coverage. The weather that may be expected on the cruise and unusually high winds that may be encountered

This detailed planning is somewhat simplified for the services, in that the time of departure and of arrival are usually known well in advance. Even in pleasure craft in the interests of safety, some navigational planning should be carried out in advance of any but the shortest trip. This should include laying down the intended track on the chart to see that it passes clear of any shoals or other dangers and noting its direction; and distances along the track should be marked off. When course changes are to be made, note where possible the bearing of some prominent object at the point where each such change is to be made. In addition, in harbors and inlets, the direction and strength of the tidal current must be taken into consideration. Lastly, in navigational planning, *always consider the weather*. Never embark on a cruise if it may be hazardous.

PLOTTING TECHNIQUES AND METHODS

Experience has shown that the mechanics of plotting presents many difficulties for the beginner. Below are listed certain helpful hints that, if followed, will increase both accuracy and speed of plotting:

1. If the chart is too large to fit on the desk used, determine the extent of the chart which must be used, then fold under the portions of the chart which will not be required to be exposed. Be sure to leave one latitude scale and one longitude scale available for measurement.
2. Use a *sharp* No. 2 pencil. A harder pencil will not erase well, and a softer pencil will smear.
3. Draw lines heavy enough to be seen readily, but light enough so that they do not indent the chart paper.
4. Avoid drawing unnecessary lines, and erase any lines used only for the purpose of measure-

ment. Do not extend lines excessively beyond the point at which their direction is to be changed.
5. Hold the pencil against the straightedge in a vertical position throughout the entire length of a line when drawing it.
6. Measure all directions and distances carefully. Accuracy is the mark of good navigation. On Mercator charts, measure distance on the latitude scale using the portion of the scale that is opposite the line that is being measured.
7. Be neat and exact in plotting work. Use standard symbols, and print all labels neatly.
8. Learn to use dividers with one hand and with either hand if possible.
9. Lay down a new DR track from each new fix or running fix. Plot a DR position at every change of course, at every change of speed, at the time of obtaining a fix, a running fix, or a single line of position, and on the whole hour.

SPEED-TIME-DISTANCE SOLUTIONS

The formulas for solving for the interrelated values of speed, time, and distance involve simple cases of multiplication and division:

$$\text{Distance} = \text{speed} \times \text{time}$$
$$\text{Speed} = \frac{\text{distance}}{\text{time}}$$
$$\text{Time} = \frac{\text{distance}}{\text{speed}}$$

In these formulas, if distance is expressed in nautical miles, speed must be in knots. If statute miles are used for distance, then speed must be in statute miles per hour (mph). Time is in hours and decimals of an hour. In navigation, however, we are more accustomed to using minutes of time than fractions or decimals of an hour. The formulas can therefore be altered to use time stated in minutes as follows:

$$\text{Distance} = \frac{\text{speed} \times \text{time (in minutes)}}{60}$$
$$\text{Speed} = \frac{\text{distance} \times 60}{\text{time (minutes)}}$$
$$\text{Time (minutes)} = \frac{\text{distance} \times 60}{\text{speed}}$$

Multiplication and division can be accomplished with greater speed and less chance of error by using a slide rule. The nautical slide rule has been designed for this particular purpose with the three scales clearly labeled. By setting any two of the three values, the third value is read from its appropriate index. As shown in figure 10-4, at a speed of 10 knots, it will take 120 minutes or 2 hours to cruise a distance of 20 nautical miles. The nautical slide rule illustrated is a standard Navy item and is also widely used by yachtsmen; a number of similar devices are available. The instrument consists of two dials on a base plate. The dials will turn together or independently. Pocket-sized circular computers designed for air navigation can also be used; they generally have only one dial and a base. The scales used are the traditional C

and D scales of any slide rule. When speed is set on the base opposite 60 on the dial, any distance traveled is automatically positioned on the base opposite minutes of time on the dial.

The printed scales on any slide rule used for multiplication and division are logarithmic scales. Multiplication is performed by adding numbers, and therefore, in reality, sections of the log scales are added. Division is performed by subtracting numbers or sections of the scale. This is basic to the use of logarithms. It follows, therefore, that these functions can be performed on any printed log scale without having a scale mounted on a mechanical slide rule or computer. Figure 10-5 illustrates the use of a pair of dividers with a loga-

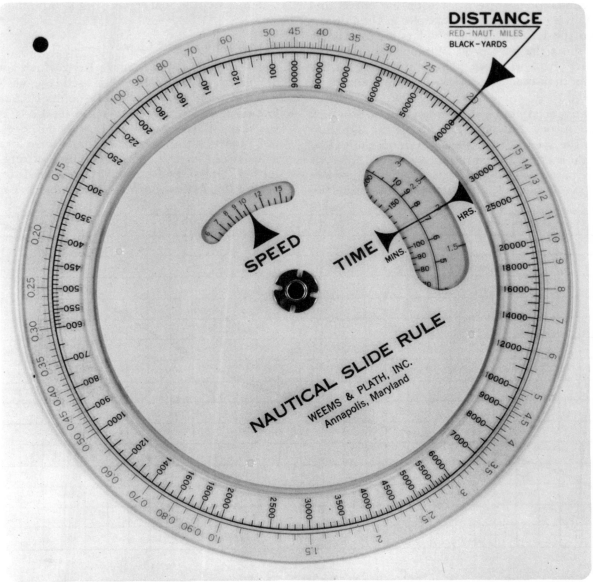

Figure 10-4.   Nautical Slide Rule

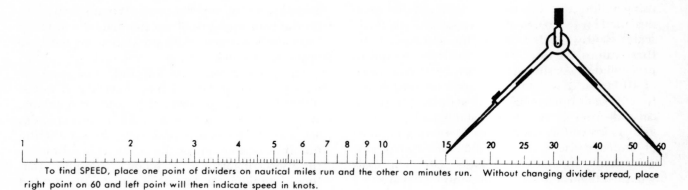

To find SPEED, place one point of dividers on nautical miles run and the other on minutes run. Without changing divider spread, place right point on 60 and left point will then indicate speed in knots.

Figure 10-5.   Logarithmic Speed Scale

rithmic scale to solve speed-time-distance. Instructions for use are printed on the charts that contain these scales. For example, to obtain time, place the left leg of the dividers on the speed, and the right leg on 60. Without changing the spread of the dividers, place the left leg on the required distance and read time in minutes at the right leg.

Two special short-cut rules can be used for quick solutions of a DR plot. The first is the 3-minute rule: the speed of the vessel in knots multiplied by 100 is equal to the distance traveled in yards in 3 minutes. The second is the 6-minute rule: the travel of a vessel in 6 minutes is equal to the

speed in knots divided by 10; thus at a speed of 7 knots, a vessel will travel .7 miles in 6 minutes.

Preparing a Speed Curve

To prepare a speed curve from which speeds at various rpm can later be used, the vessel is run between two identifiable points that are a known distance apart. At some locations, measured miles are established for this purpose with two objects set up ashore in line to form a range at each end of the measured mile. Lacking this facility, any sets of natural ranges consisting of geographic features or man-made objects can be

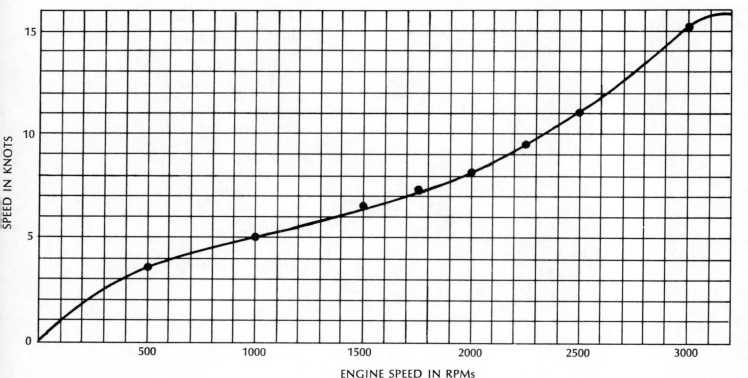

Figure 10-6.   Speed Curve

used if the points are identifiable on the chart so that the distance can be established. It is also possible to run between buoys and note the time when passing close aboard, but care should be exercised to be sure the buoys are in their charted position and have not drifted. At each rpm setting being checked, a run should be made in both directions and the speeds averaged to eliminate the effect of current and wind. The times should not be averaged, but the speed computed for each run individually; the speeds are then averaged. Speed-time-distance formulas, as discussed in the preceding section, are used. In the following example of preparing a speed curve, the distance between two buoys was measured on the chart as .85 miles. Elapsed time was recorded for each run up and down the course. Note that the time

in minutes and seconds was converted to minutes and decimals of a minute for solving the formula. If a decimal timer is used as a stopwatch, this value is read directly.

SUMMARY

In this chapter, we have presented the material essential to an understanding of the elementary dead reckoning process and have described the manner of labeling a DR plot in accordance with Coast Guard and Navy practice. The definitions given are also in agreement with those used by the services; it is essential that you be thoroughly familiar with them.

The DR plot, like all chart work, should be neat and legible. Avoid drawing lines that are not actually required, and also avoid drawing lines that are longer than necessary. The DR plot should be readily intelligible to anyone who studies it; therefore, use the standard labelings described in this chapter.

Many pleasure craft operators who cruise principally in a familiar local area will not keep a good DR plot, but will run from buoy to buoy. The Coast Guard receives thousands of calls each year from boats that are lost, stranded, wrecked, or out of fuel because of poor navigational practices. Even in familiar waters, as a bare minimum, the time of passing each buoy should be noted on the chart. Occasional bearings should be observed and plotted on the chart and properly labeled. Without this approximate knowledge of position it is impossible to set a compass course towards home or to safe waters when fog closes in or a severe squall suddenly develops. Without dead reckoning and piloting (which will be discussed in subsequent chapters) the chances of becoming another statistic are greatly multiplied.

Table 10-1

RPM	Time Down	Speed Down	Time Up	Speed Up	Speed Over the Bottom (In Knots)
500	13m48s		15m30s		
	13.8m	3.7	15.5m	3.3	3.5
1000	9m39s		10m48s		
	9.65m	5.3	10.8m	4.7	5.0
1500	7m24s		8m21s		
	7.4m	6.9	8.35m	6.1	6.5
1750	6m48s		7m36s		
	6.8m	7.5	7.6m	6.7	7.1
2000	6m00s		6m40s		
	6.0m	8.5	6.66m	7.65	8.1
2250	5m10s		5m44s		
	5.17m	9.9	5.73m	8.9	9.4
2500	4m21s		4m50s		
	4.35	11.7	4.83m	10.5	11.1
2750	3m44s		4m09s		
	3.73m	13.7	4.15m	12.3	13.0
3000	3m12s		3m37s		
	3.2m	15.9	3.62m	14.1	15.0

chapter eleven

Piloting I

Piloting is the directing of a vessel by reference to landmarks, aids to navigation such as lighthouses and buoys, soundings, and electronic navigational systems such as radio beacons and Loran. The latter method is somewhat specialzied; we will, therefore, discuss it in a separate chapter.

Good piloting requires both judgment and experience. Constant vigilance, mental alertness, and a sound knowledge of the principles involved are essential, as there is often little or no opportunity to correct errors. Momentary inattention may result in putting the vessel hard aground, often resulting in serious damage and perhaps hazarding the safety of those aboard. The principles of piloting are simple in their application—master them!

Always bear in mind that piloting deals with both the present and the future; the present situation must be constantly analyzed to plan successfully for the future. Use every means available to obtain warnings of any danger and to fix the position of your vessel both accurately and frequently; always be prepared to determine immediately the proper course of action, should some problem arise.

Finally, do not neglect the tenets of good seamanship; know the *rules of the road*, and avoid any risk of collision when in congested waters.

LINE OF POSITION (LOP)

In piloting, as in all methods of navigation, we constantly deal with lines of position. The LOP was briefly defined in chapter 10; we will consider it further at this point. A single, visual observation does not provide a position; it merely enables us to plot a line of position and to know that we are located somewhere along that line. Remember that an LOP obtained from a bearing by magnetic compass must be corrected for variation and deviation before it is plotted on the chart as a true direction.

In chapter 7 the relationship of true, magnetic, and compass direction was covered in detail. Deviation varies with the heading of the boat. The correction to be applied must therefore be for the amount of deviation on the heading that is being maintained at the instant a bearing is taken and never the value of deviation for the direction of the bearing.

Relative bearings are bearings measured relative to the vessel's head. They are measured clockwise from 000° at the vessel's head through 360°. Such bearings are usually obtained with a pelorus when 000° on the pelorus card is set to the lubber's line. Each relative bearing is *added* to the true heading, which is noted at the exact time the bearing is taken. If this value exceeds 360°, subtract 360° from the answer. This true bearing is then plotted on the chart. Relative bearings are illustrated in figure 11-1.

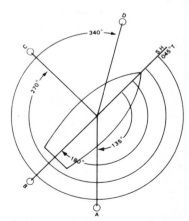

Figure 11-1. Relative Bearings

OBTAINING AN LOP

Bearings are obtained by means of sighting either across a pelorus, the compass, or a hand bearing compass and then reading the direction of the object. Using the hand bearing compass to take two quick bearings represents the simplest method for piloting aboard a small craft. Normally the steering compass is not conveniently placed for bearing taking and the use of a pelorus requires two persons—one for reading the pelorus and one for simultaneously reading the steering compass. The values are then combined, and the chance for error increases. Do not use the hand bearing compass on a steel boat. On a fiberglass, wood, or aluminum craft, simply stand up several feet away from the engine, or other large metal object, and use the compass, ignoring deviation.

Draw a line on the chart *from the observed object as the reciprocal of the bearing; this constitutes the LOP*. Remember, when labeling, to use the four-digit method of noting time, described in chapter 10.

For example, see figure 11-2. At 0930, Gay Head Light bears 086° true. Plot the reciprocal of this bearing from Gay Head Light; your position lies somewhere along this line.
Draw light lines on the chart and make them no longer than necessary. Particularly avoid drawing them through the chart symbols for aids to navigation, which may be rendered indistinct by erasures. In this chapter, broken lines extend from the symbols on the chart to illustrate principles. *The solid segment of the line of position is all that is normally plotted on the chart.* Note the correct method of labeling, *with time above the line.*

A more accurate way of obtaining an LOP is to observe a *range.* If two known fixed objects are in line, at that moment your position must lie along the line extended between them. Any two such objects, when in line, constitute a range.

For example, see figure 11-3. At 1410, Brenton Reef Light and Beavertail Light are in range, bearing 340° true.

Distance

If the distance to an object is known, your position lies somewhere on a circle having the object at its center and a radius equal to the known distance. This circle is called a *distance circle of position.*

Distance aboard small craft is usually found by means of a stadimeter (chapter 9) or a sextant, when the object is of a known height. If the object is a lighthouse, note carefully from the *Light List* whether the known height is "height above water" or "height of structure," and measure the angle accordingly. If the sextant is used, table 9 in *Bowditch* permits a quick solution for distance. If radar is available, distance can usually be determined very accurately. A distance circle is shown in figure 11-4.

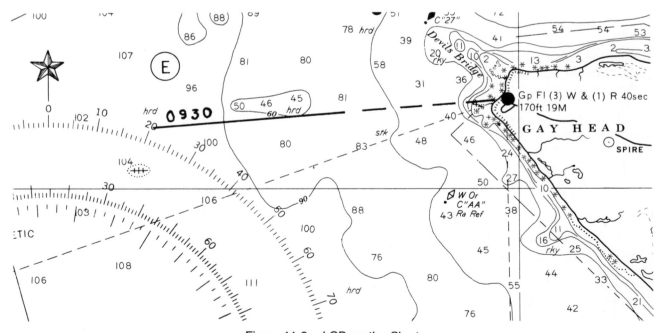

Figure 11-2.   LOP on the Chart

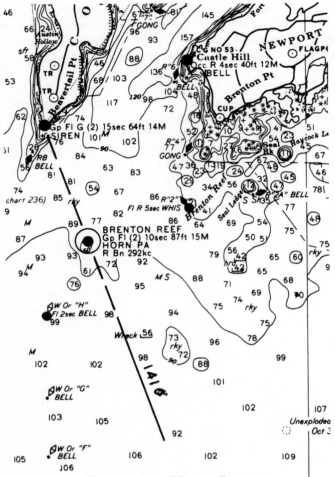

Figure 11-3.   LOP on a Range

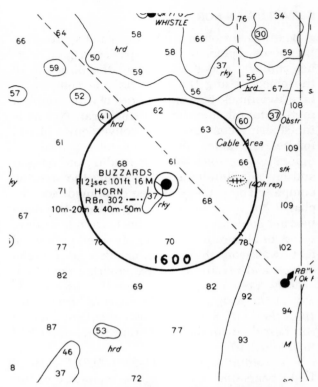

Figure 11-4.   A Distance Circle of Position

Labels

Note the labels used in figures 11-2, 11-3, and 11-4. A line of position should be labeled as soon as it is drawn; an unlabeled line can be a source of error.

A single *line of position* is labeled by putting four figures, denoting the hours and minutes at which it was obtained, on its *upper* side, as shown in figure 11-2. An example of a line obtained by observing a range is shown in figure 11-3.

THE FIX

We discussed the fix briefly in the chapter on dead reckoning (chapter 10); we will now consider it at greater length.

Always remember that *there is no relationship between the DR plot and lines of position.* The DR plot may be considered to be either a statement of intention or a graphic history of ordered courses and speeds. On the other hand, a line of position is a statement of fact, in that the vessel is located somewhere on that line at the time of observation, regardless of courses steered or speeds used. Also remember that there are an infinite number of possible positions on any single line of position. To fix the position of the vessel, it is necessary to plot two or more lines of position that intersect.

Lines of position can be combined to obtain a fix by using:

1. Cross bearings (two or more bearings).
2. Two ranges.
3. One range and a bearing.
4. Bearing and distance of the same object.
5. Bearing and distance of different objects.
6. A bearing (or distance) and soundings.
7. Passing close aboard an aid to navigation.

These are discussed in detail below.

Cross Bearings

A fix obtained by *cross bearings* is shown in figure 11-5. The fix is obtained by plotting the *reciprocals* of the observed bearings *from* the symbols, on the chart of the area, or the value of the observed bearing *toward* the symbol on the chart.

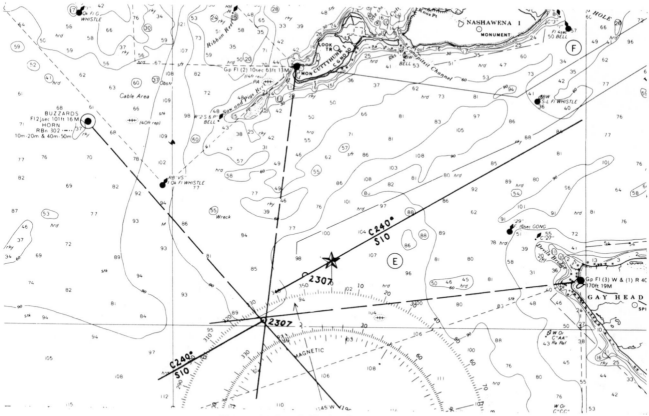

Figure 11-5.   A Fix by Cross Bearings

Note the manner in which the fix is labeled, by drawing a small circle around the point where the lines of position intersect and adding the time it was obtained. LOPs obtained from three simultaneous bearings are not labeled with a time, the time of the fix being sufficient. Also note that a new course line is drawn from the fix in accordance with the practice prescribed in chapter 10 for dead reckoning. This course line is immediately labeled with the course and speed. A third bearing should be obtained whenever possible as a check on the accuracy of the position. Three bearings will ordinarily form a small triangle; the fix is taken as lying at the center of the triangle. If the triangle, when plotted, is large, check all bearings for accuracy.

Two Ranges

When entering or leaving a harbor, it is frequently possible to fix position by means of two ranges. In figure 11-6, a vessel is entering port at ten knots and is steering a course that keeps lights X and W in line. At 1517, light Y and radio tower Z are observed to be in line. A fix is obtained as shown, and course is changed to 057° to pro-

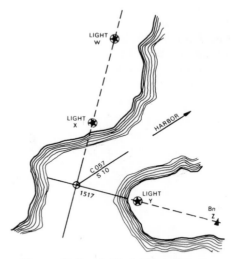

Figure 11-6.   A Fix by Two Ranges

ceed to the desired anchorage. Note that the range LOPs are not labeled with the time, as they are simultaneous.

One Range and a Bearing

A fix obtained by *one range and a bearing* is shown in figure 11-7. A vessel is on course 075°,

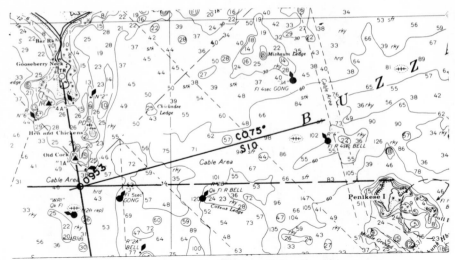

Figure 11-7.   One Range and a Bearing

speed 10 knots. At 0953 the tower on Gooseberry Neck and Old Cock daybeacon 1A are in line. At the same time, the left tangent of Penikese Island bears 090°. Note that neither LOP is labeled, as they are simultaneous. The fix is properly labeled at the intersection of the two lines of position, and the new course line is shown.

Bearing and Distance of Same Object

Figure 11-8 illustrates a fix obtained by a *bearing and distance of the same object*. At 1127, Brenton Reef Light bears 271°; its distance by stadimeter is 6,000 yards or approximately 2.95 nautical miles. A vertical sextant angle used in conjunction with table 9 *Bowditch* can also be used to determine distance off. The vessel is on

course 275°, speed 10 knots. The arc of a distance circle with a radius of 2.95 miles is drawn with the lighthouse as its center. The observed bearing is also plotted as an LOP, and the intersection of this line and the arc is labeled as the fix.

Radar can be of the greatest help in obtaining fixes of this type; even in zero visibility it permits accurate determination of both distance and bearing.

Bearing and Distance of Different Objects

A fix may be obtained by a *bearing of one object and distance of a second* as is shown in figure 11-9. At 1027, the house at Clay Head bears 221°, and Sandy Point Light is distant 2.0 miles by stadimeter. You are on course 187°, speed 8 knots.

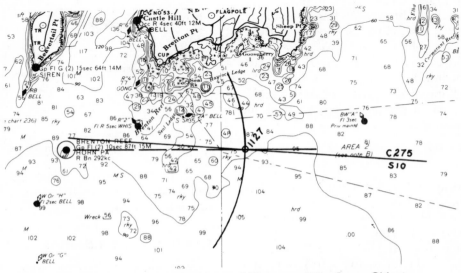

Figure 11-8.   A Fix by Bearing and Distance of the Same Object

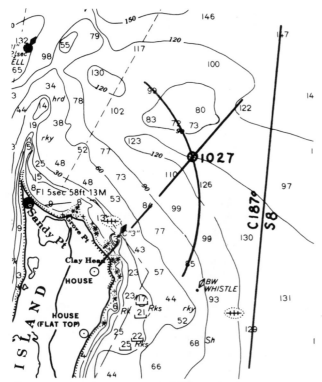

Figure 11-9. A Fix by Bearing of One Object and Distance of Another

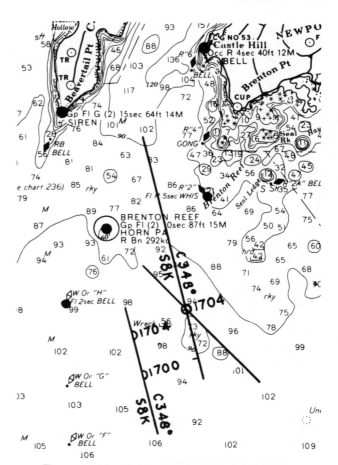

Figure 11-10. A Bearing and Line of Sounding

Draw the distance circle with a radius of two miles, centered on Sandy Point Light. Plot the observed bearing of the house. Ring the point where the circle and LOP intersect, and label it as the 1027 fix. It should be evident immediately that you are off course to starboard, and a turn to port is indicated.

Bearing (or Distance) and Soundings

An estimated position (EP) by *bearing (or distance) and soundings* can sometimes be obtained under favorable conditions. For example, assume that we are headed for Brenton Reef Light on course 348°, speed 8 knots, in fog. Our 1700 DR position is shown in figure 11-10. The depth finder is turned on and has been showing depths in the neighborhood of 100 feet.

At 1700 it indicates shoaling and reads 93 feet; at 1701 it reads 75 feet. At 1704, Brenton Reef Light is sighted through the fog, bearing 317°, and the depth finder reads 92 feet. Our navigator immediately plots the 1704 bearing and the 1704 DR position.

Obviously, we have crossed the slight rise in the sea bottom, bounded by the 90 foot curve to the northeast of our 1700 DR position, and the

1704 bearing was obtained as we recrossed the 90 foot curve.

The navigator now draws a line on a piece of tracing paper and, using the latitude scale on the chart, marks off a length of slightly more than one-half mile on it, representing our run for four minutes at eight knots from 1700, when the depth finder indicated the first shoaling, to 1704, when the bearing and the 92-foot sounding were obtained. He moves the tracing paper across the chart, keeping the marked line parallel to our course line until the mark at the upper end of the line coincides with the bearing line at a point just north of the 90-foot curve; this establishes the fix. This line, shown in figure 11-10, should in actual practice be drawn in red or any contrasting color. The mark near the southern end of the line, representing the 1700 sounding of 93 feet, helps to confirm the position, as it agrees with the indicated depth on the chart. The 1704 fix is plotted on the chart, and a new DR plot is started from that point.

If at 1704 we had obtained a *distance* from

Brenton Reef Light instead of a bearing, the navigator would have drawn the distance circle centered on the light and with the appropriate radius. The intersection of the line with this circle would then establish the 1704 fix.

Passing Close Aboard an Aid

Position can also be fixed approximately by *passing close aboard an aid to navigation,* which is shown on the chart. However, bear in mind that buoys sometimes are displaced by heavy weather or ice. Also, when using a small-scale chart, do not count on the buoy being *exactly* at its charted position, as the necessary scope of its mooring chain allows it to move somewhat in location.

Ranges estimated by eye are apt to be in error. Three hundred yards is about the upper limit that most people can estimate reasonably accurately; this may be considered acceptable for positioning when working on a chart prepared to a scale of 1:80,000 or more. Much shorter distances should be used when using harbor charts, which are on a much larger scale.

SELECTING OBJECTS TO OBTAIN A FIX

The primary consideration in selecting objects to obtain a fix is the angle between the resulting bearings. The best fix results when two bearing lines cross at 90 degrees, as an error in this case in either bearing results in the least error in the plotted fix. On the other hand, as the angle between the objects decreases, a given small error in either bearing causes an increase in the error of the plotted fix. This is illustrated in figure 11-11, in which the observer is presumed to be located at *O,* and *A* and *B* represent two objects on which bearings have been taken.

As an error in a bearing is always possible, it is good practice to take three bearings, whenever practicable; if the three resulting lines do not intersect in a point or a very small triangle, the navigator knows at once that one of the bearings is in error or that an error has developed in the compass system.

Figure 11-11 compares the errors to a fix arising from a five-degree error in one bearing when the observed objects differ 90 degrees in bearing and when they differ 20 degrees. *A, B,* and *C* each represent known objects. *O* is the observer's true position. *AOC* = 20°, and *AOB* = 90°. If a five-degree error is made in plotting the bearing of *B, OX* shows the resulting error; however, if a

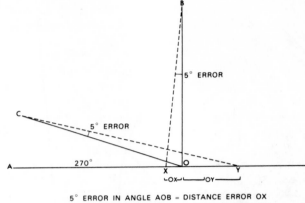

5° ERROR IN ANGLE AOB = DISTANCE ERROR OX
5° ERROR IN ANGLE AOC = DISTANCE ERROR OY

Figure 11-11.   Fix Errors

five-degree error is made in plotting the bearing of *C, OY* is the error.

It is obvious, therefore, that it is desirable to choose two objects separated by an angle as near 90 degrees as possible. If possible, check by a third bearing on an object located at about 45 degrees to the first two. If there is a serious error in one of the bearings, the three LOPs will form a large triangle instead of meeting at a single point.

Plotting Three Bearings

We have said that, whenever possible, three bearings should be observed to obtain a fix. It is important, when underway, that as little time as possible elapses between obtaining the first and the third bearing. The object that is changing least in bearing should always be observed first; that is, the object that is most nearly dead ahead or dead astern. Further, the object that is changing most rapidly in bearing, i.e., which is nearest the beam, should be observed last; the time of this bearing establishes the time of the fix.

Such bearings are plotted on the chart in the regular manner, using the reciprocals and plotting from the charted objects. A very small triangle usually results; we assume the fix to be at the center of the triangle.

When not underway and maximum accuracy is desired, three bearings may be conveniently plotted using a three-armed protractor, discussed in chapter 9.

SUMMARY

In this chapter, we have considered some of the elements of piloting and have seen how fixes can be determined by using bearings, distances, soundings, ranges, and circles of position. The navigator working alone cannot, of course, make two observations at exactly the same moment. What he should do under such conditions is observe the object that is changing least in bearing (i.e., the one most nearly dead ahead) first and then take the bearing on the second object; the time of the second bearing is the time of the fix. This will result in satisfactory fixes, except at very high speeds or when considerable time elapses between bearing observations.

Let us again stress the need for accuracy in piloting. Good piloting requires that accurate bearings and distances be obtained and that they be accurately plotted and labeled.

This does not mean that bearings and stopwatch times must be obtained for every buoy when you are traveling along a well-marked channel on a lovely day. It does mean that when aids to navigation or landmarks are few and far between or visibility is poor or might soon become poor, you must buckle down to your piloting in earnest. On the water, visibility can deteriorate very rapidly; under such conditions, a good DR plot is of the utmost assistance to the navigator. When taking departure, as when leaving the entrance of a buoyed channel, always note the time, course, and speed, even on a sunny day, as this data will permit constructing a DR plot should you subsequently need it.

chapter twelve

Piloting II

In this chapter, we will continue our discussion of piloting and will consider first the *running fix,* which is of great importance and is used in all branches of navigation. We will study how it is obtained and how it may be used to best advantage. We will also consider methods of safe piloting without a fix.

THE RUNNING FIX

Frequently it is impossible to obtain two simultaneous observations; at such times we must resort to a *running fix,* using two lines of position obtained at considerably different times. In order to plot a running fix, we must allow for the time lapse between the first and second observations. This is done by advancing the earlier LOP along your DR plot for the vessel's run to the time of the second LOP.

We assume that, for a comparatively limited time between two observations, our vessel makes good *over the ground* a definite distance in a definite direction. In other words, we move the first LOP *parallel to itself* forward along the course line for the distance the vessel moved over the ground since the LOP was obtained. The advanced LOP now represents all possible positions at the time of the second observation.

When an accurate running fix is established, a new DR plot is started, and the old one is discontinued, as would be the case with a fix. There is no set rule as to the length of time permissible for advancing an LOP to establish a running fix. This is a matter of judgment and depends chiefly on how accurately the course and speed being made good over the ground can be determined. Until the navigator has acquired considerable experience, a good general rule in piloting is to avoid advancing an LOP for more than 30 minutes. All else being equal, the shorter the time interval between LOPs, the more accurate will be the running fix.

Figure 12-1 shows an LOP advanced for a 20-minute run at 12 knots to the time a second LOP was obtained; in order that the method of advancing the first LOP may be entirely clear, the second LOP is not known in this figure.

A vessel is on course 012°, speed 12 knots. At 1500, light *E* is observed through the fog bearing 245°; no other identifiable object is in sight at the moment. At 1520 another object is observed, at which time light *E* is no longer visible.

In this case, the navigator assumes that for a 20-minute period, as there is no known current, his ship will make good both course 012° and speed 12 knots over the ground. He plots both the 1500 DR and the 1500 LOP; this LOP represents all possible positions of the ship at 1500. Note that the 1500 DR does not lie on the 1500 LOP, which indicates that the DR position does not coincide with the true position; the latter is not yet known.

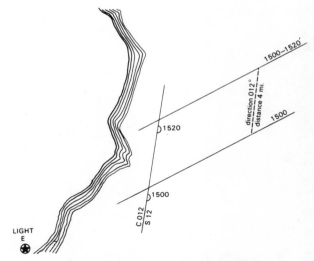

Figure 12-1.   Advancing a Line of Position

To advance the 1500 LOP to 1520, the time of the second observation, the navigator notes that at 12 knots the ship will steam four miles. From any point on the 1500 LOP, he measures off four miles in the direction, 012°, and draws a line through this point parallel to the 1500 line. He labels the new line with both the original time of observation, 1500, and the time to which it is advanced, 1520. Note that any point on the 1500 line, if advanced four miles in the direction 012°, will fall on the advanced line. The label, 1500-1520, means that the 1500 LOP has been advanced to 1520.

Now let us pass on to the second part of the running fix. Shortly after 1500 light *E* is obscured. At 1520, STACK *F* is sighted bearing 340°. Our navigator plots the new bearing line or LOP, as well as the 1520 DR position, as shown in figure 12-2. The intersection of the new LOP and the 1500 LOP advanced to 1520 constitutes the 1520 running fix. He next draws a new course line from the running fix and labels it as shown. Note that he plotted a DR position for each time he obtained an LOP; this is essential when plotting fixes or running fixes.

Probably the easiest way of advancing an LOP for a running fix is to set one leg of a pair of dividers to the DR position plotted for the time the first LOP was obtained—at 1500 in this case—and the other to the DR position for the time of the second LOP. Holding this setting, place one leg of the dividers on the point where the first LOP

crosses the course line drawn in the DR plot, prick the course line slightly with the other leg, and then mark this point with a pencil. A line is then drawn through this point, parallel to the first LOP; this new line is the first LOP, advanced. Be sure to label it correctly, with the time it was obtained and to which it was advanced on top, as shown in figure 12-2.

Sometimes an LOP must be advanced that is so nearly parallel to the course line that it does not intersect it in the area of the DR plot. In this case, draw a short line parallel to the course line, intersecting the LOP at any convenient point. Pick off the distance it is to be advanced from the DR plot, using the DR position for the time it was obtained and the DR position for the time to which it is to be advanced, as described above. Lay off this distance from the LOP along the short line, representing direction of travel, then draw the advanced LOP through this point. When two lines intersect at an acute angle, it is important to determine the point of intersection as precisely as possible.

Examples showing how running fixes may be obtained are given in the following sections.

A Running Fix with Bearings of the Same Object

A running fix can frequently be obtained by plotting two bearings, taken some time apart, of the same object (see figure 12-3).

Let us assume that we are on course 018°, speed 12 knots. At 1430, Buzzards Light bears 042°, and

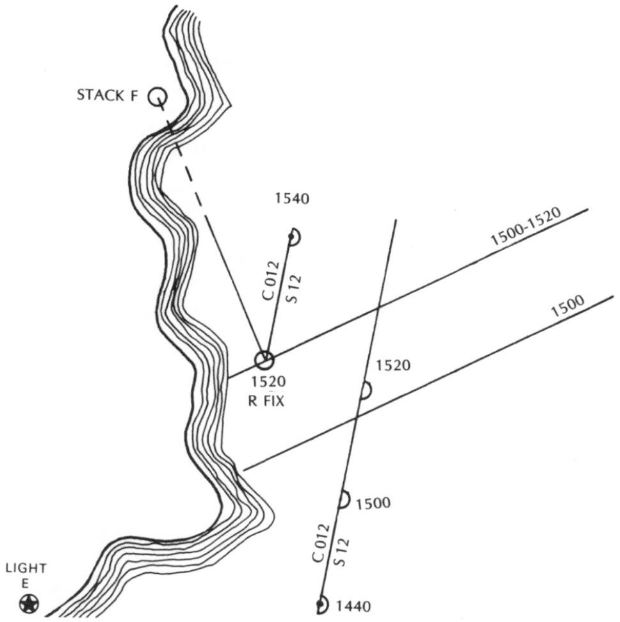

Figure 12-2. A Running Fix

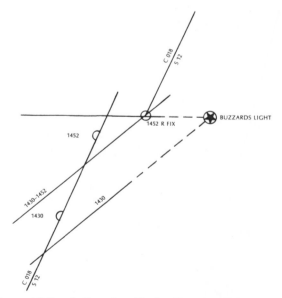

Figure 12-3. A Running Fix by Two Bearings on the Same Object

at 1452 it bears 083°. We mark and label the 1430 position on the DR plot, and then plot and label the 1430 LOP, as shown in figure 12-3. The second bearing is obtained at 1452, 22 minutes after the first. At 12 knots, this represents an advance of 4.4 miles; we use this distance to plot the 1452 DR and also for advancing the first LOP parallel to itself along the course line.

The point where the first LOP, advanced, intersects the second LOP is our running fix and is labeled accordingly. A new course line is drawn in from this point; this will be the basis of our new DR plot.

Distance Circle of Position

A distance circle of position may also be advanced to establish a running fix. This is accomplished by advancing the center of the circle, as illustrated in the following example. Let us assume that we are on course 076°, speed 15 knots; our 1440 DR position has been plotted, as shown in figure 12-4. At 1440, the distance to lightship *J* is found to be 4.7 miles; it is obscured by fog before a bearing can be obtained. The resulting distance circle of position is drawn in and labeled as shown. At 1508, we sight light *H* through a rift in the fog, bearing 040°. The 1508 DR position is immediately labeled on the DR plot, and the 1508 LOP is drawn from the light. The center of the circle of position (the lightship) is next advanced 7.0 miles parallel to our course line for our run from 1440 to 1508, and the advanced distance circle of position is drawn centered on this point. The intersection of the bearing LOP with the advanced distance circle of position marks the run-

ning fix. This we label as shown and start a new DR plot.

Remember that the bearing LOP can intersect the distance circle LOP at two points, only one of which is shown in figure 12-4. Ordinarily, the intersection that establishes the running fix can be determined quite readily. However, if there is any doubt, start a DR plot from both intersections, and assume that the vessel may be on the one that is potentially the more dangerous.

Course and Speed Changes

An LOP may be advanced to obtain a running fix even though course, speed, or both have been changed during the period between observations.

Let us first consider a problem involving only a single change of course, and no change of speed.

We are on course 063°, speed 18 knots at 2100. Our 2100 DR position is shown in figure 12-5. At 2105, light *P* is observed bearing 340° and disappears shortly thereafter. The 2105 DR position and the LOP are immediately plotted. At 2120 course is changed to 138°; the 2120 position is plotted, and the new course line is drawn. At 2132, light *Q* is observed, bearing 047°; the 2132 DR and the new LOP are immediately plotted.

The 2105 LOP is advanced by using the course and distance made good between the two DR positions corresponding in time to the two observations. This is shown by the dashed line in figure 12-5 connecting the two DR positions; it is shown here for purposes of illustration, although it is not ordinarily drawn on the chart. By advancing the 2105 LOP parallel to itself in the equivalent direction and for an equivalent distance, it becomes the 2105-2132 LOP. The intersection of this advanced LOP with the 2132 LOP establishes the running fix.

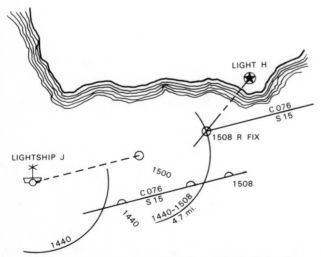

Figure 12-4. Advancing a Distance Circle of Position

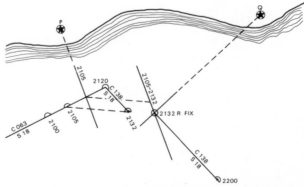

Figure 12-5. A Running Fix with a Single Course Change between Bearings

Problems involving multiple course changes, speed changes, or both are handled in exactly the same manner. The length and direction of the vector between the DR position for the time the first LOP was obtained and the DR position for the time of the second LOP establishes the advance for the first LOP.

MATHEMATICAL SOLUTIONS

In addition to the graphic methods of fixing position in piloting which we have discussed, two mathematical methods are sometimes employed. These are solution by table 7 in *Bowditch* and *special cases*. Both methods require taking two bearings of a fixed and known object and knowing the distance run between the bearings.

Complete instructions covering the use of table 7 are given in *Bowditch;* we will describe it only briefly (see figure 12-6). The table is entered with the angular difference between the course and the first bearing along the top of the table and the angular difference between the course and the second bearing at the left side. Two numbers will be found for each entry. Multiply the distance run between bearings by the first number in the column to find the distance of the object at the

second bearing, and by the *second* number to find the distance of the object when it is *abeam*.

Special cases are so called because they do not require the use of tables to obtain a solution when two bearings of an object are obtained and the run between bearings is known. Four of these special cases are described in the following sections.

Bow and Beam

The bow and beam bearing involves taking the first (or bow) bearing when the object is broad on the bow, bearing either 045° or 315° relative, and the beam bearing when it bears 090° or 270° relative. Given these two bearings, the distance from the object at the time of the second bearing will equal the distance run since the first bearing was obtained. This is illustrated in figure 12-7.

Doubling the Angle on the Bow

This case is illustrated in figure 12-8. If a relative bearing is obtained, followed by a second relative bearing of twice the angular value of the first, the run between bearings equals the distance to the object at the time of the second bearing.

TABLE 7
Distance of an Object by Two Bearings.

Difference between the course and second bearing.	Difference between the course and first bearing.													
	20°		22°		24°		26°		28°		30°		32°	
30°	1.97	0.98												
32	1.64	0.87	2.16	1.14										
34	1.41	0.79	1.80	1.01	2.34	1.31								
36	1.24	0.73	1.55	0.91	1.96	1.15	2.52	1.48						
38	1.11	0.68	1.36	0.84	1.68	1.04	2.11	1.30	2.70	1.66				
40	1.00	0.64	1.21	0.78	1.48	0.95	1.81	1.16	2.26	1.45	2.88	1.85		
42	0.91	0.61	1.10	0.73	1.32	0.88	1.59	1.06	1.94	1.30	2.40	1.61	3.05	2.04
44	0.84	0.58	1.00	0.69	1.19	0.83	1.42	0.98	1.70	1.18	2.07	1.44	2.55	1.77
46	0.78	0.56	0.92	0.66	1.09	0.78	1.28	0.92	1.52	1.09	1.81	1.30	2.19	1.58
48	0.73	0.54	0.85	0.64	1.00	0.74	1.17	0.87	1.37	1.02	1.62	1.20	1.92	1.43
50	0.68	0.52	0.80	0.61	0.93	0.71	1.08	0.83	1.25	0.96	1.46	1.12	1.71	1.31
52	0.65	0.51	0.75	0.59	0.87	0.68	1.00	0.79	1.15	0.91	1.33	1.05	1.55	1.22
54	0.61	0.49	0.71	0.57	0.81	0.66	0.93	0.76	1.07	0.87	1.23	0.99	1.41	1.14
56	0.58	0.48	0.67	0.56	0.77	0.64	0.88	0.73	1.00	0.83	1.14	0.95	1.30	1.08
58	0.56	0.47	0.64	0.54	0.73	0.62	0.83	0.70	0.94	0.80	1.07	0.90	1.21	1.03
60	0.53	0.46	0.61	0.53	0.69	0.60	0.78	0.68	0.89	0.77	1.00	0.87	1.13	0.98
62	0.51	0.45	0.58	0.51	0.66	0.58	0.75	0.66	0.84	0.74	0.94	0.83	1.06	0.94

Figure 12-6.   Extract from Table 7, *Bowditch, Pub. No. 9* (Washington: 1975)

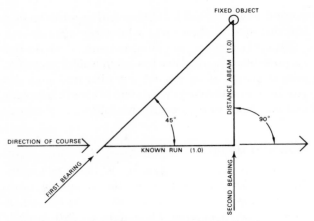

Figure 12-7.   The Bow and Beam Bearing

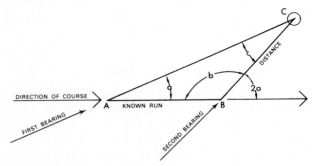

Figure 12-8.   Doubling the Angle on the Bow

The 22½°-45° Case

The 22½°-45° case, sometimes called the *7/10 rule,* is a specialized case of doubling the angle on the bow. However, in this instance, in addition to knowing the distance from the object at the time of the second bearing, we can predict the distance at which the object will be passed abeam. In this particular case, the distance abeam will equal 7/10 of the distance run between the two bearings.

The 30°-60° Case

The 30°-60° case, also called the *7/8 rule,* is another specialized case of doubling the angle on the bow. If the relative bearings obtained are 30 degrees and 60 degrees on the bow, the distance run between bearings equals the distance to the object at the second bearing. In addition, 7/8 of the distance run equals the distance at which the object will be passed abeam.

The 26½°-45° Case

If the first bearing is 26½° on the bow and the second is 45°, the object's distance when abeam

equals the run between bearings. This is true in other combinations of angles whose natural cotangents differ by unity. Some of these combinations are listed below in tabular form. The asterisked pairs are the most convenient to use, since they involve whole degrees only. In each case, the distance run between bearings equals the distance of passing the object abeam.

Table 12-1 Relative Bearings

1st Bearing	2d Bearing	1st Bearing	2d Bearing	1st Bearing	2d Bearing
°	°	°	°	°	°
20	29¾	28	48½	37	71¼
21	31¾	*29	51	38	74¼
*22	34	30	53¾	39	76¾
23	36¼	31	56¼	*40	79
24	38¾	*32	59	41	81¼
*25	41	33	61½	42	83½
26	43½	34	64¼	43	85¾
26½	45	35	66¾	*44	88
*27	46	36	69¼	*45	90

SAFE PILOTING WITHOUT A FIX

Keeping in safe water without a fix is sometimes possible, and under certain conditions may let you proceed to your destination in safety, even in heavy fog.

Essentially, most of these methods involve moving along a line of position. For example, in following a narrow channel, particularly one that is not well marked, a constant bearing on a distant *leading mark* (a prominent charted object) ahead or a range can be of the greatest value. A very slight deviation from the intended track will be immediately apparent when navigating by means of a range ahead; a range astern will serve the same purpose. Ranges may be navigational ranges; lacking such, natural ranges can often be found. Use a range whenever possible in restricted waters; however, *always determine how to identify the point at which it will be necessary to turn off the range.* Always study the chart in advance. Danger bearings and danger angles are very useful at times. These are discussed in the following section.

Danger Bearings

A *danger bearing* is used to keep a vessel clear of an offshore area of shoal water, close to which she must pass; the outer limit of such an area may not be marked by a buoy. If a charted object is

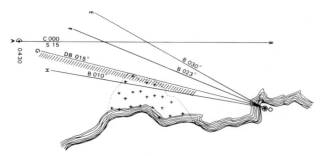

Figure 12-9. The Danger Bearing

visible well ahead, it may be useful for establishing a danger bearing; refer to figure 12-9.

A vessel is proceeding north along a rocky coast on course 000°, speed 15 knots. Her 0430 DR is shown. The foul area ahead on her starboard bow must be avoided. Lighthouse *O* is visible ahead to starboard. The navigator draws a line in red pencil from the light, passing clear of the foul area, and labels it *OG* as shown. He next measures the direction of the line from *G* toward *O*. This proves to be 015° and constitutes the danger bearing. As can be seen from the figure, as long as the danger bearing is *greater* than 015°, the vessel is in safe water. Needless to say, the bearing must be checked frequently.

Note that the farther ahead the leading mark is, the more satisfactory it is, as the value of a danger bearing decreases as the angle between the course and the danger bearing increases.

Position by Soundings

A line of position by soundings can also often be of great value. For example, a boat en route from Newport to Vineyard Haven encountered increasing fog in Vineyard Sound. At 1810, Tarpaulin Cove Light (Chart 1210TR) bore 012°, distant 1¾ miles by estimate. An inspection of the

Tidal Current Charts covering Vineyard Sound (see chapter 14) disclosed that a fair current was running stronger along the Martha's Vineyard shore and would continue to run longer there than in the main body of the Sound; in addition, much less commercial traffic could be expected on the eastern shore of the Sound. A course of 088° was therefore laid for Paul Point (see figure 12-10) and speed was set at 10 knots. Note that the 1810 position is marked EP, for *estimated position* (see chapter 10), as the distance from the light was only an estimate. At 1819, the depth finder indicated shoaling water and at 1821 showed a depth of 28 feet. This depth indicated that the boat was on course and was crossing the northern end of Lucas Shoal; directly thereafter, the indicated depth increased considerably. At 1828, shoaling water was again indicated, and at 1830, the indicated depth was 30 feet. The boat therefore turned towards the northeast and followed along this curve. When the indicated depth showed less than 30 feet, course was changed slightly to the left; conversely, when the depth increased beyond this limit, the boat came right. West Chop Light was rounded in due course, and the boat came safely to anchor in Vineyard Haven. The ease with which the passage along the Vineyard shore was made was noteworthy, as at times the visibility was reduced to less than 100 yards. The last part of this run is shown in figure 12-10; the course line along the five-fathom curve is not drawn.

The use of a depth curve as a course line was feasible in this instance, first, because the curve was reasonably straight and therefore easy to follow, and second, because no rocks or shoals lay close to it—the three-fathom curve lay some 200 yards farther to the southeast up to the point where the black can buoy, to the north of West Chop Light, was rounded.

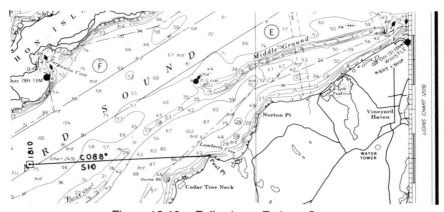

Figure 12-10. Following a Fathom Curve

Commercial shipping bound for the port of New York from the south has used a similar system for years. Off the New Jersey coast the ships are on the *continental shelf,* which is considered to extend out to the 100-fathom curve. The indicated depth of water remains quite constant for a considerable distance; suddenly it begins to deepen. This is the Hudson River gorge, which is an extension of the Hudson River and appears on the chart as a trough crossing the shelf and extending in about the same direction as the river. At this point, they turn toward the northwest and begin their approach toward the harbor.

Danger Angles

Two types of *danger angles* are sometimes used in piloting; both require the use of a sextant or similar instrument to permit precise measurement of angles.

The first type is the horizontal danger angle. This requires that two readily identifiable objects lying along the coast be shown on the chart; in addition, they must be sufficiently far apart to give a fair-sized horizontal angle.

Figure 12-11 shows a section of coastline; A and B are the two charted landmarks. S and S' are two outlying shoals with good water between them. To pass safely outside S', take the middle of the shoal as a center, and using the distance at which you wish to pass as a radius, strike in a circle. Next draw a second circle that passes through landmarks A and B and is also tangent to the seaward side of the first circle shown at E in the figure. To find the center for this second circle, draw a line from A to B and bisect it with

a perpendicular. The center of the second circle will lie on this line; its exact location can be found by trial. Now measure the angle AEB, which in this case is 60 degrees. *As long as the angle between A and B,* as measured with the sextant, *is 60 degrees or less, you are clear of the shoal, S'.*

The horizontal danger angle for shoal S is obtained in the same manner. Draw a circle, centered on the middle of shoal S and of sufficient radius so that it is well clear of all danger. Another circle is next drawn, passing through A and B, and tangent to the circle about S at G. From this point at G, measure the angle between A and B, which here is 50 degrees. Now, if the sextant angle measured between A and B is *not less than* 50 degrees, you will pass clear of the shoal, S.

In actual practice, the points E and G can usually be determined by eye, thus making it unnecessary to draw the circles about the shoal areas.

The vertical danger angle involves the same general principle, as can be seen in figure 12-12, in which AB represents a vertical object of known height. In this case, the tangent circles are centered on A, the charted position of the object. The limiting angles are determined by means of table 9 in *Bowditch* or by computation. This can be done very simply if a calculator with trigonometric scales is available. The height, AB, in feet is divided by the distance, AE, in feet; the result is the tangent of angle AEB.

The values of the danger angles and the arcs of the circles limiting the safe passage corridor should be marked in red pencil.

The Estimated Position

Sometimes the information available is insufficient to fix a vessel's position accurately. However, under such conditions it is often possible to improve the DR position by using all available information. A position so determined is termed the *estimated position (EP);* it is the vessel's most probable position, as based on all information available to the navigator.

Estimated positions may be determined from data obtained in many different ways. In a heavy sea, it is usually difficult to obtain bearings sufficiently accurate to determine a fix. Radio direction finder bearings (chapter 15) are not as accurate as visual bearings. Estimates of current and leeway due to wind and sea are rarely exact. Compass bearings are no more accurate than the deviation table. Many such factors affect the accuracy of a position; the exact value of each factor

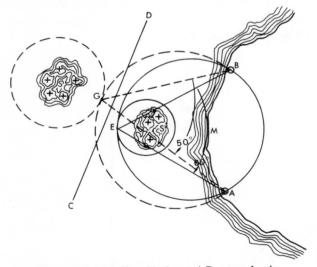

Figure 12-11.   The Horizontal Danger Angle

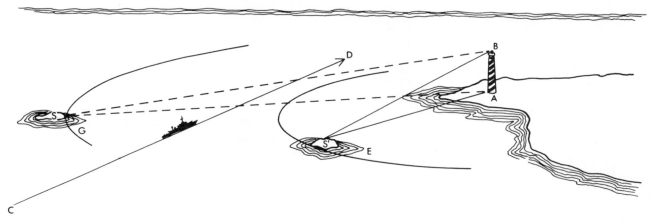

Figure 12-12. The Vertical Danger Angle

may not be known, but the navigator's experience and judgment permit him to assign an approximate value to each existing factor in order to obtain an estimated position.

An estimated position, therefore, is the best determinable position when no fix or running fix can be obtained. *All* available information must be taken into consideration, and each factor must be analyzed individually.

The factors most commonly involved in determining an EP are a single line of position, knowledge of the approximate direction of flow of a current, the approximate strength or speed of the current, the effect of any leeway, and helpful, but not conclusive, information obtained from soundings. The effects of currents and leeway will be discussed in chapter 13 *(Current Sailing)*; the use of a single line of position and of information gleaned from soundings is discussed in the following paragraphs.

When only a single LOP and no other positive information is available, the EP is determined by drawing a perpendicular from the LOP to the DR position for the time of the LOP. The intersection of this perpendicular and the LOP marks the EP.

For example, assume that we are on course 025°, speed 10 knots, as shown in the DR plot in figure 12-13. At 0627, our navigator observes the lighthouse A through a rift in the fog, bearing 260°.

He immediately plots and labels the bearing line and also the 0627 DR position. To determine the EP, he draws a line perpendicular to the LOP or bearing line from the 0627 DR position. He labels the intersection of the perpendicular and the LOP as the 0627 EP, as shown. The EP is normally marked with a square to distinguish it

from a DR position which is circled. This is the vessel's most probable position, as it not only lies on the LOP, but also represents the nearest point on the LOP to the 0627 DR position. If soundings or any knowledge of the current were available, a considerably better position could be determined.

A very good EP can sometimes be obtained by plotting a string of soundings if the seabed in the area is not flat and featureless. To use this method, draw a straight line on a piece of tracing paper or transparent plastic. Along this line mark off equal distances according to the vessel's speed and the chart scale. For example, if you are steaming at ten knots and using a fairly large-scale chart, each distance might be one-half mile, representing a three-minute run. When you obtain the first sounding, enter it against the first mark on the line with the time opposite it. Three minutes later note the next sounding and the time, and so on. When a number of soundings have been noted, lay the transparency on the chart in the area of your DR plot, and, with the base line kept oriented in the direction of your course line, move the transparency around until the charted and recorded soundings agree. The resulting position should be good, but for the sake of safety, make sure that there is no other area in the neighborhood where the same bottom contour might exist.

In connection with EPs, remember that you must use *all* available information in determining your most probable position. For example, never pass a buoy or a float on an anchored lobster pot without noting the direction in which any existing current may be flowing and estimating its speed. Such information may, a little later, be of the utmost value.

It is not general usage to start a new DR plot

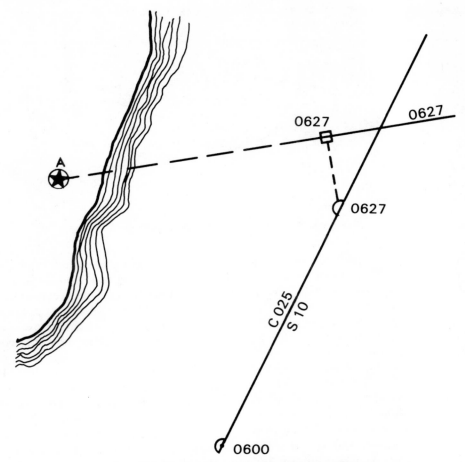

Figure 12-13.   The Estimated Position (EP)

from an EP, as the latter is not a definitely known position. However, run a line representing the *estimated* course and speed being made good from the EP to determine the possibility of standing into danger. In laying down the line, consider what you know definitely, what is probable, and what is possible. Using the DR plot and EP shown in figure 12-13 as an example, we know definitely that the vessel is making good better than 10 knots over the ground and that her track is probably to the left of the course line. However, the latter item is only a probability, based on the location of the EP. Having no additional information to guide us, it is possible that she is either farther inshore or offshore than the EP would indicate; both possibilities must be taken into consideration when planning any future action.

chapter thirteen

Current Sailing

So far, in discussing piloting, we have not considered the effect of current on a moving vessel. This chapter is concerned with *current sailing* and how the current may be determined and used for safe navigation. *Leeway,* the leeward motion of a vessel due to wind and sea action, also comes under the heading of current sailing, as the effect of leeway is the same as the effect of current, in that it affects the vessel's track, or course made good, as well as her speed over the bottom. Current sailing is defined in the following section.

In the chapter on dead reckoning, (chapter 10), we stated that in preparing a DR plot, only the true courses steered and the distance steamed as determined by ordered engine speeds are taken into consideration. In Coast Guard and naval practice, the total of all the forces that may cause a vessel to depart from its DR plot is termed *current.* The chief factors included in the term *current* are:

- Ocean Current
- Tidal or river current
- Wind
- Seas
- Inaccurate steering
- Undetermined compass error
- Errors in engine calibration
- Errors in log or speedometer calibration
- Excessively fouled bottom
- Unusual condition of trim

From the above, you will see that current may have two meanings. In the first sense it refers to the horizontal flow of water; in the second, it refers to the total of all the forces listed above. Current, in the navigational sense, may or may not include motion of the water in which the vessel is situated; in most cases, however, motion of the water, if it exists, usually is the factor having the greatest effect on the travel of the vessel.

DEFINITIONS

It is recommended that at this point the student review the definitions listed in chapter 10 on dead reckoning, as their meaning must be thoroughly understood. In addition, it is necessary to list some new definitions applying to current sailing.

Current sailing combines the determination of the actual current by the navigator and the use of this information, so that the vessel's intended track and her course made good will coincide as closely as possible.

The *estimated current* is the result of the evaluation of all the known or predicted forces that will make up the sum of current effects expected during a passage. If it is calculated before departure, it may be termed *pre-sailing current.*

The *actual current* is established by the exact measurement of the vessel's displacement from her intended track; it is the sum of all current effects encountered.

The *set* of a current is the direction *toward which it flows.* It is usually expressed in degrees true.

The *drift (D)* of a current is its velocity in knots. The drift of ocean currents is expressed in terms of nautical miles per day in some publications.

THE CURRENT TRIANGLE

A *current triangle* is a vector diagram constructed graphically, in which one side represents the vessel's course and speed, another side represents the set and drift of the current, and the third side represents the actual or intended track. If any two sides are known, the third can be determined by measurement.

Many times it is desirable to construct a current sailing vector triangle to assist in the graphic solution of the problem. However, the solution of the

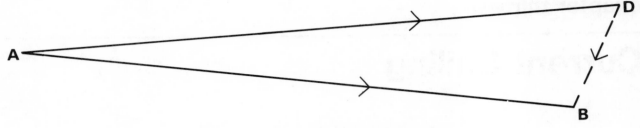

Figure 13-1. The Current Triangle and Its Parts

unknown parts of the triangle must be in terms of the given information of the known parts.

A complete current triangle equally applicable to the solutions of the current problem prior to departure, as well as to its solution after arrival, is illustrated in figure 13-1. A tabulation of the respective parts of each triangle is given in table 13-1.

Table 13-1

Part	Using Estimated Current	Using Actual Current
Point A	Present position (fix) of ship	Previous position (fix) of ship
Point D	DR position of ship at future time	DR position of ship at present time
Point B	Estimated position at future time	Present position (fix) at present time
Side AD	Course and speed vector	Course and speed vector
Side AB	Intended track and SOA	Actual track and SMG
Side DB	Anticipated or expected current	Actual current encountered

Note: Points B and D are always for the *same* time.

CURRENT SAILING

If a vessel were ordered to steam from point A to point D, bearing 090° and distant 10 miles, in an elapsed time of one hour, through a current setting 180° with a drift of two knots, the navigator would be faced with a typical problem in current sailing. Referring to figure 13-2, it is obvious that the direction of the intended track, ITR, is 090°, and the speed of advance, SOA, is 10 knots. It is equally obvious that if our navigator ordered a course of 090° and a speed of 10 knots, he would

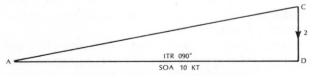

Figure 13-2. Allowing for Current

end up some two miles to the south of point D.

He therefore prepares a current triangle as shown in figure 13-2. The line, AD, represents his intended track; it is in the direction 090°, and its length is 10 convenient units, representing the intended speed to be made good. From point D he draws a line in the direction *opposite* to the set of the current; in this case it is drawn in the direction 000°, as the set is 180°. This line, DC, is two units in length, thus representing the two-knot drift of the current. Next he draws a line from A to C and measures its direction, which, to the nearest degree, proves to be 079°. This represents the direction in which the vessel must steam to reach point D in view of the existing current. The navigator next measures the length of the line AC, which proves to be 10.2 miles; this length represents the speed he must order to arrive at point D in one hour. When she departs point A, the ship will therefore be heading 11 degrees to the left of the intended track and will be "crabbing" over the bottom, heading 079° but moving in the direction 090°. The ordered speed, 10.2 knots, will result in a speed over the ground of 10 knots.

CURRENT AND THE EP

In our discussion of piloting, we stated that when no fix or running fix could be obtained, consideration of all available information would usually enable the navigator to estimate a position that was more correct than that shown by the DR. Such is the case when it is known that a current, in the sense of horizontal water motion, exists or will occur. The existence of a current may be determined by observing the water eddy caused by an anchored object; a predicted tidal current in bays and inlets may be obtained from the *Tidal Current Tables* (chapter 14). In addition, some charts show the average set and drift of currents obtained from many observations. When it is possible to estimate the current that a vessel will encounter, the EP is found by plotting the

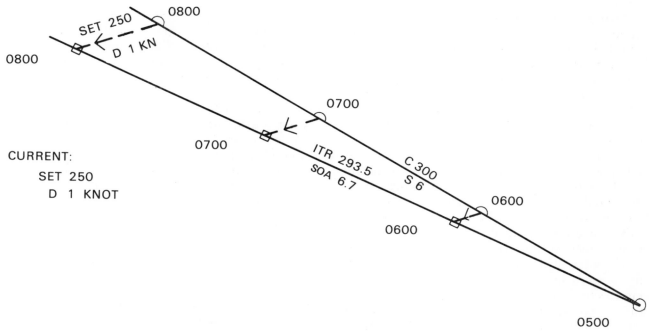

Figure 13-3. The EP Plot Using Current

predicted offset from the DR position caused by the current. To do this, plot the *set* from the DR position and measure off along this line the drift, multiplied by the number of hours it has been or will be acting.

For example, in figure 13-3, our vessel's 0500 fix is shown. She is on course 300°, speed 6 knots. A current has been observed to exist with an estimated set of 250° and a drift of 1.0 knot. The hourly DR positions are plotted to 0800; from each DR position, we plot a line in the direction 250° and measure off a length on each of these lines appropriate for the period of time the current is affecting our vessel. Thus, the 0600 line is one mile long, and the 0700 line is two miles in length, etc. The ends of each of these lines represent the EP for each hour, and the line drawn from the fix through each EP indicates the track we believe our vessel is making. The accuracy of the EP in this case, of course, depends on the accuracy of the estimate of the current. Do not assume that a current determined by the last fix will continue unless there is evidence that such is the case. It is unwise to assume that a current is regular and uniform near a coast, for local conditions usually cause irregularity. In bays, such as the Chesapeake and the Delaware, there is a very considerable difference both in the set and drift in different areas at any given time. Currents in such bodies of water usually have the greatest drift in the deepest part of the bay.

When there is doubt as to a curent, it is sometimes desirable to maintain both an EP plot, which allows for a possible current, and a DR plot, which does not. Both plots are then considered when selecting a safe course.

ALLOWING FOR CURRENT

Three problems frequently arise in connection with currents of estimated set and drift. These are:

1. To find the course a vessel should take to make good the intended track when steaming through a current at a given speed.
2. To find what course and speed must be used in a current to arrive at the destination on time.
3. To find the EP that will be reached at a given time when steaming on a given course at a given speed in a current.

If the current is setting along the course, either ahead or astern, the track will be the same as the course; the effect on speed can be found by adding or subtracting the drift. This condition frequently arises when entering or leaving port in a tidal stream. If a vessel is crossing a current, a solution can be obtained graphically by preparing a vector diagram, as the course and speed made good over the ground is the vector sum of the vessel's course and speed through the water and the set and drift of the water.

Such a vector solution can be conveniently on a compass rose or directly on the plot. The following examples will show how graphic solutions are obtained.

CASE 1. Let us assume that the estimated set of the current is 075°, and the drift is 3 knots. We wish to steam at 12 knots, and the direction of our intended track is 195°. We must determine what course to steer.

Referring to figure 13-4, A represents our vessel's position, and N indicates the direction of true north. Plot the line AD of indefinite length in the direction of our intended track, 195°. Plot the current vector, AC, in the direction of the set, 075°, for a length equal to the drift, 3 knots; N again indicates the direction of true north. With C as center, strike an arc with a radius equal to the vessel's speed through the water, 12 knots, intersecting AD at D. The direction CD represents the course we must steer; to the nearest whole degree, it proves to be 208°. The length, AD, is the speed we expect to make good over the

ground (the speed of advance); it proves to be 10.2 knots. Note that the vectors AD and AC, representing the intended track and current respectively, are plotted with respect to the earth (point A), while vector CD is plotted with respect to the water.

CASE 2. In this instance, we must determine what course and speed must be used, in view of an existing current, to reach our destination at a predetermined hour. Let us assume that at 1300 we are 12 miles due west of our destination, which we wish to reach at 1400. A current with an estimated set of 135° and a drift of 2.0 knots is predicted.

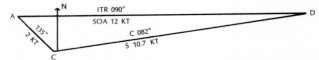

Figure 13-5.   Finding Course and Speed to Make Good an Intended Track

Refer to figure 13-5; our 1300 position is at point A; the line labeled N represents our meridian at that time. Our destination is at D in the direction 090° from A, distant 12 miles; obviously, therefore, we must make good 12 knots over the ground to reach D at 1400. We lay off AD in the direction 090° to represent the intended track and of a length equal to the necessary speed of advance of 12 knots. Next, we lay off the current vector, AC, in the direction of the set, 135°, from point A and of a length equal to the drift, 2.0 knots. We complete the current sailing vector diagram by drawing a line to join C and D. The direction of CD, 082° to the nearest degree, is the course we must steer, and its length, 10.7 knots to the nearest tenth, is the speed we must make good through the water to arrive at our destination on schedule. Again, note that the vectors AD and AC, which represent the intended track and the current respectively, are plotted with respect to the earth, while the vector CD is plotted with respect to the water.

DETERMINING ACTUAL CURRENT

If a DR plot is laid down from a fix (not a running fix) and at a later time a new fix is obtained that does not agree with the DR position for the same time, the difference between the DR position and the fix must represent the actual current encountered during passage. It is immediately apparent that current so determined will include all of the

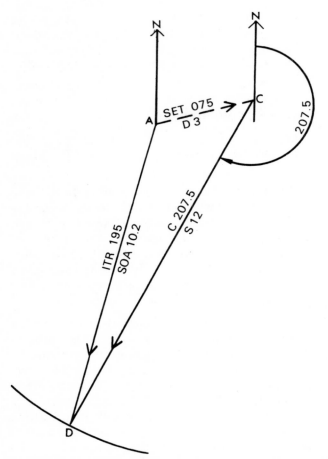

Figure 13-4.   Finding Course to Steer to Make Good an Intended Track

factors mentioned previously and, in addition, any errors in the fixes. It should also be apparent that if the estimated position on the intended track coincides with the fix on the actual track, the estimated current computed prior to departure would be exactly equal to the actual current encountered during passage. If the two positions are *not* identical, then the estimated current would be in error by an amount directly proportional to the rate and direction of separation of the two positions.

Three problems most frequently arise in determining the set and drift of an actual current:

1. To find the set and drift of an actual current for the run between two fixes, using the DR position for the time of the second fix.
2. To find the set and drift of an actual current for the run between two fixes when a second DR plot has been laid down from a running fix.
3. To find the set and drift of an actual current for the run between two fixes when an estimated position has been laid down.

CASE 1. We are on course 050°, speed 15 knots. Our 1815 DR position is shown in figure 13-6; it has been run forward from a fix obtained at 1445. At 1815 we obtained a new fix, as plotted; it is located 2.1 miles from the 1815 DR position. We want to determine the set and drift of the actual current.

We determine the set by measuring the direction in which the 1815 fix lies from the 1815 DR position; this proves to be 099°. The drift is found by measuring the distance between the 1815 DR and the 1815 fix, 2.1 miles, and then dividing it by the number of hours since the previous fix was

obtained at 1445; 2.1 miles divided by 3.5 hours shows the drift to be 0.6 knots.

CASE 2. In this instance, we must determine the set and drift of a current after a new DR plot has been started from a running fix. While we discuss later the problem of obtaining the best possible running fix in the presence of a current of unknown set and drift, the main point to remember is that a running fix never yields as reliable a position as a fix. In this case, we therefore do not use the current data obtained from the running fix, except for information while underway. Instead, we use a DR position developed from our first fix and compare this with the final fix to obtain current set and drift.

Referring to figure 13-7, assume that we are on course 080°, speed 10 knots, having taken departure from point A at 1000. At 1130 we obtain an LOP as shown; at 1230 we obtain a second LOP and advance the first line to obtain a running fix. The position of the first line clearly indicates that a very strong current is running; we therefore must *not* advance the first LOP for our run of 10 miles between 1130 and 1230. Instead, we measure the distance from point A to the point where the first LOP intersects our course line; this proves to be 12.5 miles. An hour and a half has elapsed between the time we departed point A and when the first LOP was obtained. We therefore divide the 12.5 miles by 1.5 hours to obtain the distance along the course line to advance the LOP for the one-hour run to 1230, when the second LOP is obtained; the answer is 8.3 miles. This, then, is the distance to advance the first LOP to form the running fix. Advancing an LOP in a known current is discussed later in this chapter.

At 1400 we obtain a good fix, which is shown

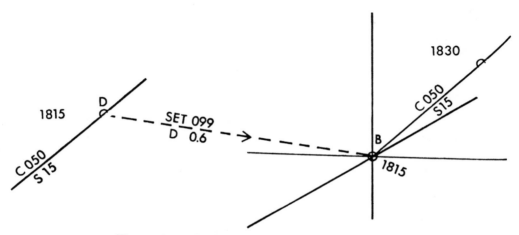

Figure 13-6.   Finding the Set and Drift of a Current

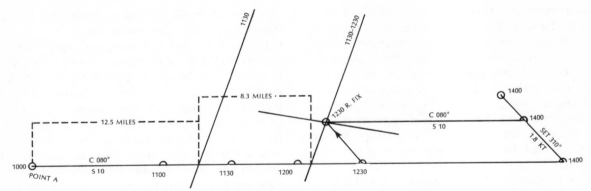

Figure 13-7.   Advancing an LOP When a Current Is Running

in the plot, and we wish to determine the total effect of the current since we took departure from point *A* at 1000. To do this, we ignore the DR plot that we started at the 1230 running fix and plot a 1400 DR position brought forward from point *A*. The direction from this DR position to the 1400 fix establishes the set, 310°; and the distance, 7.2 miles, divided by the elapsed time since departing point *A*, four hours, establishes the drift, 1.8 knots.

This gives us the total current effect we have encountered during the run. We did not use the running fix in making this determination; first, because no running fix yields an absolutely sure position, and second, because we wanted to determine the current effect since taking departure from *A*. The current might well have changed after we plotted the 1230 running fix, although in this case, it did not do so.

CASE 3. Here we must determine set and drift when we have plotted an EP on an erroneous estimate of set and drift. We selected a course and speed that we thought would bring us to an estimated position, allowing for a current that we believed would be running.

For example, let us assume that we obtained a fix at 0900, shown at *A* in figure 13-8. Our intended destination was point *D*, bearing 090° and distant 20 miles from *A*. We desired to arrive at *D* at 1000, and as we estimated the current would

be setting 135° with a drift of 6 knots, we selected a course of 075° and a speed of 16.3 knots, based on a current triangle. However, at 1000 we fixed our position at point *B*.

In this case, the 1000 DR position at *C* represents our location if there had been no current, and the 1000 fix at *B* is our actual position. The line *CB* is, therefore, the direction and distance the ship has been displaced by the actual current. The direction of the line from the DR position to the fix, 180°, is the set of the current. The drift is the length of this line, 8.0 miles, divided by the time between fixes, 1 hour; the drift is therefore 8.0 knots.

THE RUNNING FIX WITH KNOWN CURRENT

In case 2 of the previous section on determining actual current, we discussed briefly the manner of advancing an LOP for a running fix, when it was obvious that the vessel was encountering a current. The method of advancing an LOP when both the set and the drift of a current are known is discussed below.

Let us assume that we are on course 012°, speed 12 knots, when we observe light *E*, in figure 13-9, bearing 311° at 1500. We believe that a current exists, setting 030° with a drift of 3.0 knots. At 1520 we observe light *E* bearing 245°.

In the 20 minutes between the two LOPs, we have advanced 4.0 miles through the water in the direction 012°, so we advance the first LOP by a corresponding amount, as shown by the dashed line *AA'*. During this 20-minute period, the current has also moved us 1.0 mile in the direction 030°; we therefore advance the 1500 LOP for this additional amount to the solid line labeled 1500–1520. The intersection of the 1500 LOP advanced and the 1520 LOP marks our 1520 running fix. Note that, if we had not taken the current

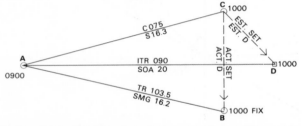

Figure 13-8.   Finding Actual Current, Having Allowed for Estimated Current

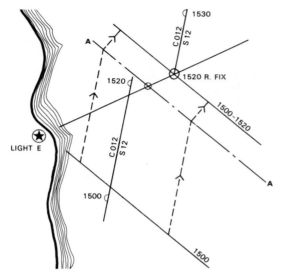

Figure 13-9. Plotting a Running Fix with Known Current

into consideration, our running fix would have been located at the dotted circle, over one mile from the established running fix.

CURRENTS AND THEIR EFFECT ON RUNNING FIXES

The inexperienced navigator is prone to make two errors in working with current. On the one hand, he either makes no allowance for it, or his allowance is seriously in error; on the other hand, he expects a given current to continue, when there is no valid reason for this expectation. There is, of course, no easy answer on how to avoid making such errors; the navigator can only be advised to gather all the experience he can, to consult all available data, including the *Tidal Current Tables* and *Current Charts* discussed in the next chapter, and above all, always to give each problem his full attention.

Wind causes some leeway for all ships; small craft are apt to be more affected than big vessels. The less a boat's draft and the higher her topside and house, the greater will be this effect. All sailboats make leeway when hard on the wind; this effect tends to decrease as the wind draws aft. In addition, seas on the beam tend to set a vessel leeward. No hard data can be laid down here; it is up to each navigator to determine what leeway he can expect his vessel to make under any given conditions of weather.

Wind tends to increase the drift of a predicted tidal current if both are moving in the same direction. The *Tidal Current Tables* give excellent information on average effects of wind on current along the coast. It may be noted that wind cur-

rents in completely open water tend to be deflected to the right of the wind in the northern hemisphere, often by as much as 30 degrees, due to the *Coriolis force*. This is an apparent force acting on a body in motion, caused by the earth's rotation. Data on the Gulf Stream are also included in the *Tidal Current Tables*.

Always remember that the drift of a tidal current changes constantly during a tidal cycle, even though its set may remain constant for several hours.

Poor helmsmanship is often a cause of apparent current. There is frequently a considerable difference in the track made good under identical conditions when two different people are at the helm.

All in all, conditions affecting the track are usually changing quite rapidly in coastal waters, and all the factors we have outlined should be taken into consideration when making an estimate of the current. Further, when making such an estimate, always assume that the most unfavorable conditions possible will prevail.

As to the accuracy of a running fix, remember that it hinges on the accuracy with which you estimate the course and speed you are making good over the ground. Since the current is rarely known exactly, the run between two bearings is often in error, and the running fix therefore gives a false position—the amount and direction of the error depends on the current that has not been allowed for. This is the basic reason for limiting the length of time allowable for advancing an LOP for a running fix.

Some indication of a current may be obtained by making several successive observations of the same object and plotting multiple-line running fixes. However, if the current is parallel to the course, its presence will not be revealed by this method, as the succession of running fixes will be either too far inshore or too far out, depending on whether the current is fair or foul. Successive running fixes will, nevertheless, show the vessel to be on the right course line, although not on the intended track. The effect of a fair current, parallel to the course, is shown in figure 13-10.

On the other hand, if there is a cross current, the running fixes will result in triangles, their size depending on the cross component of the current. A line through mean points of successive running fixes will show a track oblique to the course steered, to the right or to the left, depending on whether the current is setting to the right or to the left. This line will fall between the course steered and the actual track. The effect of a cur-

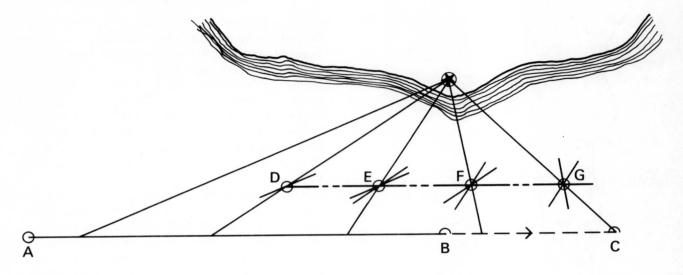

A-B   RUN BY DR

B-C   CURRENT

A-C   TRACK

D, E, F, G   POSITION SHOWN
BY RUNNING FIXES

Figure 13-10.   Error of Running Fix with Current Parallel to Course (based on a following current)

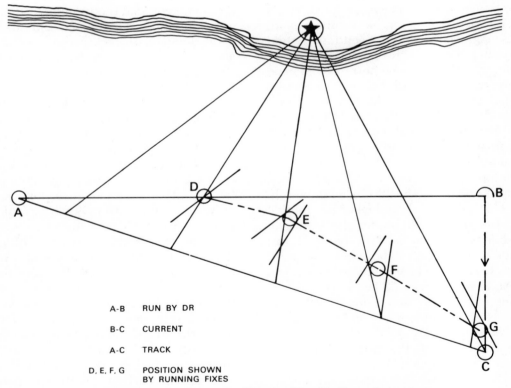

A-B   RUN BY DR

B-C   CURRENT

A-C   TRACK

D, E, F, G   POSITION SHOWN
BY RUNNING FIXES

Figure 13-11.   Error of a Running Fix with Cross Current

rent with a considerable component to the right of the vessel's course is shown in figure 13-11.

Obviously, a current acting against a vessel can present a hazard in restricted waters, as running fixes indicate a greater margin of safety relative to off-lying shoals than actually exists. Hence, if there is any possibility of the current being foul, always give off-lying hazards to navigation a wider berth than running fixes would seem to require.

SUMMARY

We have discussed current effect at considerable length in this chapter, as well as the hazards of overreliance on running fixes. Whenever possible, obtain fixes by simultaneous bearings of two or more objects; when only running fixes can be obtained, hold the time between bearings to the minimum consistent with obtaining a reasonable angular difference between the bearings. Last, *get soundings*. They can be of the utmost help and will resolve many of the problems caused by current.

chapter fourteen

Tides and Tidal Currents*

Tide is the vertical rise and fall of the ocean level caused chiefly by the gravitational pull of the moon and, to a lesser extent, of the sun. In most areas this rise and fall occurs twice during each lunar day, which on the average lasts 24 hours and 50 minutes. However, in some areas, due to the configuration of the land surrounding the body of water, there is only one high and one low tide during each lunar day. *High tide* or *high water* is the highest level reached by the ascending tide; the level of the water decreases from high tide until it reaches a minimum level called *low tide* or *low water*. At high and low water, there is a brief period when no change in the water level can be detected; this is called *stand*. The total rise or fall between high and low water is called the *range of the tide*. *Mean sea level* is the average level of the ocean, which differs slightly from the *half-tide level*, the plane midway between high and mean low water.

A knowledge of the times of high and low water and the amount of vertical rise and fall of the tide is of importance for vessels operating in areas where the charted depth is less than their draft. It is also useful to vessels running close along a coast, particularly in thick weather, as it enables them to anticipate the effects of tidal currents in setting them onshore or offshore.

REFERENCE PLANES FOR TIDAL DATA

In this section, we will cover a number of definitions used in connection with tidal phenomena and discuss the reference planes used for tidal data. The expression *height of tide* is not to be confused with *depth of water*. The latter refers to the vertical distance from the surface of the

* Portions of this chapter have been adapted from *Dutton's Navigation and Piloting*, 12th Ed. (Annapolis: Naval Institute Press, 1969).

water to the bottom; the former refers to the vertical distance from the surface of the water to an arbitrarily chosen *reference plane* or *datum plane*, such plane being based on a selected *low water* average. The *charted depth* is the vertical distance from this reference plane to the ocean bottom. A second reference plane based on a selected *high water* average is used as a basis for the measurement of *charted heights* and *vertical clearances* of objects above the water. If the selected low water average is mean low water, and the selected high water average is mean high water, then the difference between these two planes is called the *mean range of the tide*. The relationship of these terms is shown in figure 14-1.

It is important to remember that the water level is occasionally *below the reference plane*. That is, *the depth of water can be less than the charted depth*. This is indicated by a minus sign (−) placed before the height of tide as shown in the *Tide Tables*. The depth of water is equal to the alge-

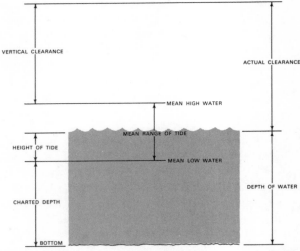

Figure 14-1.   Relationship of Terms Measuring Depths and Heights

braic sum of the charted depth and the height of tide, so that when there is a negative tide, the numerical value of the height of tide is subtracted from the charted depth to find the depth of water. Primarily because of wind, the water level sometimes differs from the predicted height.

The arbitrarily chosen reference plane differs with the locality and the country making the survey on which the chart is based. Before listing these, it will be in order to give a brief explanation and define some terms.

There are usually two high tides and two low tides each lunar day. Because of the relative position of the sun and moon with respect to the earth and each other, there is an infinite variety of tidal situations, so that the height varies from tide to tide and from day to day. The lower of the two low tides of any one day is called the *lower low water*.

Spring tides occur near the time of full moon and new moon when the tidal effects of sun and moon are in phase. When the sun and moon are thus acting together, high tides are higher than average and low tides are lower. When the moon is at quadrature, at first and last quarter, the tidal effects of the two bodies are opposing each other and the range of the tide is less than average. These are called *neap* tides.

The principal planes of reference used are derived from the approximation of:

Mean low water, the average of all low tides. This plane is used on charts of the Atlantic and Gulf coasts of the United States and on nearly all National Ocean Service charts based on its own surveys.

Mean lower low water, the average of the lower of the two daily tides. This plane is used on charts of the Pacific coast of the United States, the Hawaiian Islands, the Philippines, and Alaska.

Mean low water springs, the average of the low waters at spring tides. Most British Admiralty charts are based on this reference plane.

It is not necessary to know the reference planes of various localities, for the *Tide Tables* are always based on the same plane used for the largest scale charts of the locality, as stated in the tables. The reference plane for a given locality, when not one of the three listed above, is stated in reference to one of them.

Each chart generally carries a statement of the reference plane used for soundings. However, the plane of reference may be in doubt on charts compiled from old sources. When there is any doubt, assume that it is mean low water, for this assumption allows the greatest margin of safety in that it is the *highest* of the low water datum planes in use on nautical charts. A cautious navigator knows that the depth of the water at a low tide (mean low water springs, for example) can be *less* than the depth charted with reference to mean low water.

TIDE TABLES

Tide Tables enable the navigator to predict the state of the tide for any given place, date, and time. These tables are published annually by the National Ocean Service in four volumes as follows: (1) Europe and West Coast of Africa (including the Mediterranean Sea); (2) East Coast, North and South America (including Greenland); (3) West Coast, North and South America (including the Hawaiian Islands); (4) Central and Western Pacific Ocean and Indian Ocean. Together they contain daily predictions for 188 reference ports and difference data for about 5000 stations.

The make-up of the tables is illustrated in figure 14-2. Table 1 lists the time and height of the tide in both feet and meters at each high water and low water in chronological order for each day of the year at a number of places that are designated as *reference stations*. Because the lunar or tidal day is a little more than 24 hours in length (an average of about 24ʰ50ᵐ), the time between successive high or low tides is a little more than 12 hours. When a high (or low) tide occurs just before midnight, the next high (or low) tide occurs about noon of the following day, and the next one occurs just after midnight. Under these conditions, three consecutive high (or low) tides may occur on three different dates, although the total interval may be no more than the average period of a lunar day, 24ʰ50ᵐ. This means that on the middle of the three days, there is but one high (or low) water. An example of this occurrence can be seen in figure 14-2 on Monday, 3 March at Portland, Maine, when only one high tide occurs that day. During portions of each month the tide becomes diurnal at some stations; that is, there is only one high tide and one low tide each lunar or tidal day. This fact is indicated by blank entries in the tabulated data.

Secondary or *subordinate stations* are listed in geographical order in table 2. Given for each station are the latitude and longitude to the nearest

PORTLAND, MAINE

TIMES AND HEIGHTS OF HIGH AND LOW WATERS

JANUARY

DAY	TIME h.m.	HEIGHT ft.	HEIGHT m.		DAY	TIME h.m.	HEIGHT ft.	HEIGHT m.
1 TU	0349	-0.1	0.0		16 W	0310	0.4	0.1
	1003	10.1	3.1			0927	9.7	3.0
	1631	-1.2	-0.4			1555	-0.8	-0.2
	2240	8.8	2.7			2203	8.5	2.6
2 W	0435	0.0	0.0		17 TH	0358	-0.1	0.0
	1049	10.0	3.0			1011	10.2	3.1
	1715	-1.1	-0.3			1638	-1.3	-0.4
	2326	8.7	2.7			2248	9.0	2.7
3 TH	0520	0.1	0.0		18 F	0446	-0.4	-0.1
	1132	9.9	3.0			1100	10.5	3.2
	1757	-0.9	-0.3			1724	-1.7	-0.5
						2335	9.3	2.8
4 F	0006	8.6	2.6		19 SA	0534	-0.8	-0.2
	0602	0.2	0.1			1147	10.7	3.3
	1212	9.6	2.9			1810	-1.9	-0.6
	1835	-0.7	-0.2					
5 SA	0048	8.5	2.6		20 SU	0023	9.6	2.9
	0642	0.4	0.1			0623	-1.0	-0.3
	1253	9.3	2.8			1237	10.7	3.3
	1916	-0.5	-0.2			1859	-1.9	-0.6
6 SU	0126	8.3	2.5		21 M	0113	9.8	3.0
	0721	0.6	0.2			0715	-1.0	-0.3
	1333	9.0	2.7			1328	10.5	3.2
	1955	-0.2	-0.1			1949	-1.7	-0.5
7 M	0207	8.2	2.5		22 TU	0205	9.8	3.0
	0807	0.8	0.2			0812	-0.9	-0.3
	1415	8.6	2.6			1424	10.1	3.1
	2035	0.2	0.1			2043	-1.4	-0.4
8 TU	0251	8.0	2.4		23 W	0301	9.8	3.0
	0853	1.0	0.3			0912	-0.7	-0.2
	1501	8.2	2.5			1524	9.5	2.9
	2120	0.5	0.2			2138	-0.9	-0.3
9 W	0336	7.9	2.4		24 TH	0359	9.6	2.9
	0943	1.1	0.3			1017	-0.5	-0.2
	1551	7.8	2.4			1628	9.0	2.7
	2207	0.8	0.2			2240	-0.4	-0.1
10 TH	0425	7.9	2.4		25 F	0501	9.5	2.9
	1039	1.2	0.4			1123	-0.3	-0.1
	1643	7.5	2.3			1736	8.5	2.6
	2257	1.0	0.3			2345	0.0	0.0
11 F	0517	7.9	2.4		26 SA	0607	9.4	2.9
	1136	1.2	0.4			1232	-0.3	-0.1
	1742	7.3	2.2			1845	8.3	2.5
	2350	1.1	0.3					
12 SA	0610	8.1	2.5		27 SU	0050	0.2	0.1
	1234	1.0	0.3			0709	9.4	2.9
	1841	7.3	2.2			1337	-0.4	-0.1
						1951	8.2	2.5
13 SU	0042	1.1	0.3		28 M	0151	0.3	0.1
	0701	8.3	2.5			0809	9.5	2.9
	1327	0.6	0.2			1438	-0.5	-0.2
	1937	7.5	2.3			2049	8.3	2.5
14 M	0133	1.0	0.3		29 TU	0247	0.3	0.1
	0751	8.7	2.7			0904	9.5	2.9
	1419	0.2	0.1			1529	-0.6	-0.2
	2028	7.7	2.3			2141	8.3	2.5
15 TU	0223	0.7	0.2		30 W	0337	0.3	0.1
	0841	9.2	2.8			0952	9.6	2.9
	1507	-0.3	-0.1			1616	-0.7	-0.2
	2115	8.1	2.5			2227	8.4	2.6
					31 TH	0424	0.2	0.1
						1035	9.6	2.9
						1659	-0.7	-0.2
						2309	8.5	2.6

FEBRUARY

DAY	TIME h.m.	HEIGHT ft.	HEIGHT m.		DAY	TIME h.m.	HEIGHT ft.	HEIGHT m.
1 F	0505	0.2	0.1		16 SA	0426	-0.9	-0.3
	1115	9.5	2.9			1040	10.8	3.3
	1738	-0.6	-0.2			1702	-1.9	-0.6
	2345	8.5	2.6			2313	9.9	3.0
2 SA	0542	0.2	0.1		17 SU	0517	-1.3	-0.4
	1152	9.4	2.9			1130	11.0	3.4
	1813	-0.5	-0.2			1749	-2.1	-0.6
3 SU	0019	8.5	2.6		18 M	0003	10.3	3.1
	0619	0.2	0.1			0608	-1.6	-0.5
	1228	9.2	2.8			1222	10.9	3.3
	1846	-0.4	-0.1			1838	-2.1	-0.6
4 M	0056	8.5	2.6		19 TU	0051	10.5	3.2
	0656	0.3	0.1			0701	-1.6	-0.5
	1305	9.0	2.7			1313	10.7	3.3
	1921	-0.2	-0.1			1928	-1.8	-0.5
5 TU	0131	8.4	2.6		20 W	0144	10.4	3.2
	0734	0.4	0.1			0757	-1.5	-0.5
	1342	8.7	2.7			1408	10.1	3.1
	1958	0.1	0.0			2021	-1.4	-0.4
6 W	0208	8.4	2.6		21 TH	0237	10.2	3.1
	0816	0.6	0.2			0856	-1.1	-0.3
	1424	8.3	2.5			1506	9.5	2.9
	2035	0.4	0.1			2116	-0.8	-0.2
7 TH	0250	8.3	2.5		22 F	0336	9.9	3.0
	0901	0.7	0.2			0957	-0.7	-0.2
	1506	8.0	2.4			1610	8.9	2.7
	2120	0.7	0.2			2218	-0.1	0.0
8 F	0335	8.1	2.5		23 SA	0439	9.5	2.9
	0949	0.9	0.3			1106	-0.4	-0.1
	1557	7.6	2.3			1718	8.3	2.5
	2206	1.0	0.3			2324	0.4	0.1
9 SA	0421	8.1	2.5		24 SU	0544	9.2	2.8
	1043	1.0	0.3			1213	-0.1	0.0
	1653	7.4	2.3			1828	8.0	2.4
	2257	1.2	0.4					
10 SU	0516	8.1	2.5		25 M	0031	0.6	0.2
	1141	0.9	0.3			0650	9.0	2.7
	1753	7.2	2.2			1319	-0.1	0.0
	2353	1.2	0.4			1935	8.0	2.4
11 M	0613	8.3	2.5		26 TU	0135	0.7	0.2
	1244	0.6	0.2			0753	9.0	2.7
	1853	7.4	2.3			1420	-0.1	0.0
						2033	8.0	2.4
12 TU	0050	1.1	0.3		27 W	0231	0.6	0.2
	0711	8.7	2.7			0846	9.1	2.8
	1340	0.2	0.1			1513	-0.2	-0.1
	1949	7.7	2.3			2122	8.2	2.5
13 W	0148	0.9	0.3		28 TH	0321	0.5	0.2
	0807	9.2	2.8			0935	9.2	2.8
	1433	-0.3	-0.1			1557	-0.3	-0.1
	2044	8.2	2.5			2207	8.4	2.6
14 TH	0241	0.2	0.1		29 F	0407	0.3	0.1
	0859	9.8	3.0			1017	9.2	2.8
	1526	-0.9	-0.3			1636	-0.3	-0.1
	2135	8.8	2.7			2245	8.5	2.6
15 F	0334	-0.4	-0.1					
	0950	10.3	3.1					
	1614	-1.5	-0.5					
	2224	9.4	2.9					

MARCH

DAY	TIME h.m.	HEIGHT ft.	HEIGHT m.		DAY	TIME h.m.	HEIGHT ft.	HEIGHT m.
1 SA	0445	0.2	0.1		16 SU	0407	-1.3	-0.4
	1054	9.2	2.8			1022	10.8	3.3
	1712	-0.3	-0.1			1638	-1.9	-0.6
	2320	8.6	2.6			2251	10.5	3.2
2 SU	0522	0.1	0.0		17 M	0501	-1.8	-0.5
	1131	9.2	2.8			1114	11.0	3.4
	1745	-0.3	-0.1			1727	-2.0	-0.6
	2353	8.7	2.7			2340	10.9	3.3
3 M	0554	0.1	0.0		18 TU	0552	-2.0	-0.6
	1203	9.1	2.8			1205	10.9	3.3
	1817	-0.2	-0.1			1816	-1.9	-0.6
4 TU	0025	8.8	2.7		19 W	0030	11.0	3.4
	0630	0.1	0.0			0645	-2.0	-0.6
	1238	8.9	2.7			1257	10.6	3.2
	1849	0.0	0.0			1907	-1.6	-0.5
5 W	0057	8.8	2.7		20 TH	0121	10.8	3.3
	0705	0.1	0.0			0739	-1.8	-0.5
	1313	8.7	2.7			1351	10.0	3.0
	1921	0.2	0.1			2000	-1.0	-0.3
6 TH	0132	8.7	2.7		21 F	0213	10.4	3.2
	0744	0.2	0.1			0836	-1.3	-0.4
	1351	8.4	2.6			1450	9.4	2.9
	2000	0.4	0.1			2055	-0.4	-0.1
7 F	0210	8.6	2.6		22 SA	0312	9.9	3.0
	0824	0.4	0.1			0936	-0.8	-0.2
	1433	8.1	2.5			1551	8.7	2.7
	2037	0.7	0.2			2154	0.3	0.1
8 SA	0251	8.5	2.6		23 SU	0413	9.4	2.9
	0909	0.5	0.2			1042	-0.2	-0.1
	1519	7.8	2.4			1658	8.2	2.5
	2122	1.0	0.3			2300	0.8	0.2
9 SU	0338	8.4	2.6		24 M	0519	9.0	2.7
	1001	0.7	0.2			1149	0.1	0.0
	1613	7.5	2.3			1806	7.9	2.4
	2213	1.2	0.4					
10 M	0432	8.4	2.6		25 TU	0009	1.0	0.3
	1100	0.7	0.2			0626	8.7	2.7
	1711	7.4	2.3			1255	0.3	0.1
	2311	1.2	0.4			1911	7.9	2.4
11 TU	0532	8.5	2.6		26 W	0114	1.0	0.3
	1202	0.5	0.2			0729	8.7	2.7
	1814	7.6	2.3			1352	0.3	0.1
						2006	8.0	2.4
12 W	0015	1.0	0.3		27 TH	0211	0.9	0.3
	0634	8.8	2.7			0825	8.7	2.7
	1303	0.1	0.0			1445	0.2	0.1
	1916	8.0	2.4			2057	8.2	2.5
13 TH	0116	0.6	0.2		28 F	0300	0.7	0.2
	0735	9.3	2.8			0911	8.8	2.7
	1402	-0.4	-0.1			1529	0.1	0.0
	2014	8.6	2.6			2139	8.5	2.6
14 F	0217	0.0	0.0		29 SA	0343	0.4	0.1
	0833	9.9	3.0			0952	8.9	2.7
	1457	-1.0	-0.3			1606	0.1	0.0
	2108	9.3	2.8			2216	8.7	2.7
15 SA	0314	-0.7	-0.2		30 SU	0422	0.2	0.1
	0929	10.4	3.2			1032	9.0	2.7
	1548	-1.5	-0.5			1643	0.0	0.0
	2200	9.9	3.0			2251	8.9	2.7
					31 M	0457	0.1	0.0
						1106	9.0	2.7
						1714	0.1	0.0
						2322	9.0	2.7

TIME MERIDIAN 75° W.   0000 IS MIDNIGHT.   1200 IS NOON.
HEIGHTS ARE REFERRED TO MEAN LOW WATER WHICH IS THE CHART DATUM OF SOUNDINGS.

Figure 14-2. *Tide Tables,* Table 1, Portland, Maine

TABLE 2.—TIDAL DIFFERENCES AND OTHER CONSTANTS

No.	PLACE	POSITION		DIFFERENCES				RANGES		MEAN TIDE LEVEL
		Lat.	Long.	Time		Height		Mean	Spring	
				High water	Low water	High water	Low water			
		°N.′	°W.′	h. m.	h. m.	feet	feet	feet	feet	feet
	MAINE				on, PORTLAND, p.32					
	Time meridian, 75°W.									
	Mount Desert Island									
709	Salsbury Cove	44 26	68 17	−0 15	−0 12	+1.6	0.0	10.6	12.2	5.3
711	Bar Harbor	44 23	68 12	−0 22	−0 16	+1.5	0.0	10.5	12.1	5.2
713	Southwest Harbor	44 16	68 19	−0 22	−0 12	+1.2	0.0	10.2	11.7	5.1
715	Mount Desert	44 22	68 20	−0 16	−0 08	+1.6	0.0	10.6	12.2	5.3
717	Bass Harbor	44 14	68 21	−0 18	−0 11	+0.9	0.0	9.9	11.3	5.0
719	Pretty Marsh Harbor	44 20	68 25	−0 13	−0 13	+1.2	0.0	10.2	11.7	5.1
	Blue Hill Bay									
721	Union River	44 30	68 26	−0 09	−0 08	+1.4	0.0	10.4	11.9	5.2
723	Blue Hill Harbor	44 24	68 34	−0 13	−0 08	+1.1	0.0	10.1	11.6	5.0
725	Allen Cove	44 18	68 33	−0 12	−0 12	+1.3	0.0	10.3	11.8	5.1
727	Mackerel Cove	44 10	68 26	−0 20	−0 13	+1.0	0.0	10.0	11.5	5.0
729	Burnt Coat Harbor, Swans Island	44 09	68 27	−0 23	−0 13	+0.5	0.0	9.5	10.8	4.7
	MAINE, Penobscot Bay									
	Eggemoggin Reach									
731	Naskeag Harbor	44 14	68 33	−0 16	−0 14	+1.2	0.0	10.2	11.6	5.1
733	Center Harbor	44 16	68 35	−0 13	−0 07	+1.1	0.0	10.1	11.5	5.0
735	Sedgwick	44 18	68 38	−0 11	−0 06	+1.2	0.0	10.2	11.7	5.1
736	Isle Au Haut	44 04	68 38	−0 23	−0 19	+0.3	0.0	9.3	10.7	4.7
737	Head Harbor, Isle Au Haut	44 01	68 37	−0 20	−0 20	+0.1	0.0	9.1	10.4	4.6
739	Kimball Island	44 04	68 39	−0 20	−0 22	+0.6	0.0	9.6	10.9	4.8
741	Oceanville, Deer Isle	44 12	68 38	−0 18	−0 17	+1.1	0.0	10.1	11.5	5.0
743	Stonington, Deer Isle	44 09	68 40	−0 18	−0 17	+0.7	0.0	9.7	11.0	4.8
745	Northwest Harbor, Deer Isle	44 14	68 41	−0 12	−0 12	+1.1	0.0	10.1	11.5	5.0
747	Matinicus Harbor	43 52	68 53	−0 17	−0 12	0.0	0.0	9.0	10.4	4.5
749	Vinalhaven, Vinalhaven Island	44 03	68 50	−0 13	−0 06	+0.3	0.0	9.3	10.7	4.6
751	Iron Point, North Haven Island	44 08	68 52	−0 13	−0 13	+0.5	0.0	9.5	10.8	4.8
753	Pulpit Harbor, North Haven Island	44 09	68 53	−0 13	−0 15	+0.8	0.0	9.8	11.1	4.9
755	Castine	44 23	68 48	−0 04	−0 01	+0.7	0.0	9.7	11.1	4.8
757	Pumpkin Island, South Bay	44 25	68 44	+0 11	+0 29	+1.3	0.0	10.3	11.7	5.1
	Penobscot River									
759	Fort Point	44 28	68 49	−0 06	−0 05	+1.3	0.0	10.3	11.8	5.1
761	Bucksport	44 34	68 48	−0 02	−0 01	+2.0	0.0	11.0	12.5	5.5
763	South Orrington	44 42	68 49	+0 01	+0 04	+3.3	0.0	12.3	14.0	6.1
765	Hampden	44 45	68 50	+0 02	+0 06	+3.8	0.0	12.8	14.6	6.4
767	Bangor	44 48	68 46	+0 04	+0 13	+4.1	0.0	13.1	14.9	6.5
769	Belfast	44 26	69 00	−0 08	−0 01	+1.0	0.0	10.0	11.5	5.0
771	Camden	44 12	69 03	−0 12	−0 06	+0.6	0.0	9.6	10.9	4.8
773	Rockland	44 06	69 06	−0 16	−0 10	+0.7	0.0	9.7	11.2	4.8
775	Owls Head	44 06	69 03	−0 16	−0 13	+0.4	0.0	9.4	10.7	4.7
777	Dyer Point, Weskeag River	44 02	69 07	−0 10	−0 10	+0.6	0.0	9.6	10.9	4.8
	MAINE, Outer Coast									
779	Tenants Harbor	43 58	69 12	−0 11	−0 11	+0.3	0.0	9.3	10.6	4.6
781	Monhegan Island	43 46	69 19	−0 13	−0 09	−0.2	0.0	8.8	10.1	4.4
783	Burnt Island, Georges Islands	43 52	69 18	−0 13	−0 12	−0.1	0.0	8.9	10.2	4.4
	St. George River									
785	Port Clyde	43 56	69 16	−0 11	−0 07	−0.1	0.0	8.9	10.2	4.4
787	Otis Cove	43 59	69 14	−0 15	−0 14	+0.1	0.0	9.1	10.5	4.5
789	Thomaston	44 04	69 11	−0 04	−0 03	+0.4	0.0	9.4	10.8	4.7
791	New Harbor, Muscongus Bay	43 52	69 29	−0 10	−0 05	−0.2	0.0	8.8	10.1	4.4
793	Muscongus Harbor, Muscongus Sound	43 58	69 27	−0 09	−0 03	0.0	0.0	9.0	10.4	4.5
795	Friendship Harbor	43 58	69 20	−0 18	−0 11	0.0	0.0	9.0	10.4	4.5
	Medomak River									
797	Jones Neck	44 01	69 23	−0 10	−0 05	+0.1	0.0	9.1	10.5	4.5
799	Waldoboro	44 06	69 23	−0 16	−0 04	+0.5	0.0	9.5	10.9	4.8
801	Pemaquid Harbor, Johns Bay	43 53	69 32	−0 05	−0 01	−0.2	0.0	8.8	10.1	4.4
	Damariscotta River									
803	East Boothbay	43 52	69 35	−0 02	+0 04	−0.1	0.0	8.9	10.2	4.4
805	Newcastle	44 02	69 32	+0 16	+0 28	+0.3	0.0	9.3	10.7	4.6
807	Damariscove Harbor, Damariscove I	43 46	69 37	−0 09	−0 10	−0.2	0.0	8.8	10.1	4.4
809	Boothbay Harbor	43 51	69 38	−0 06	−0 05	−0.2	0.0	8.8	10.1	4.4
811	Southport, Townsend Gut	43 51	69 40	+0 01	+0 01	−0.1	0.0	8.9	10.2	4.4

Figure 14-3. *Tide Tables*, Table 2

minute, and certain information to be applied to the predictions at a stated reference station to obtain the tidal information for the subordinate station.

A separate time difference is tabulated for high and low water as shown in figure 14-3. Each time difference is added to or subtracted from the time of the respective high or low water at the reference station in accordance with its sign. Be alert to changes of date when the time difference is applied. For example, if a high water occurs at a reference station at 2300 on 23 March and the tide at the subordinate station occurs two hours later, then high water will occur at 0100 on 24 March at the subordinate station. Conversely, if a high water at a reference station occurs at 0100 on 29 March, and the tide at the subordinate station occurs two hours earlier, the high water at the subordinate station will occur at 2300 on 28 March.

The height of the tide is found in several ways, depending on local conditions. If the difference for height of high water is given, with 0.0 feet tabulated as the low-water difference, apply the high-water difference in accordance with its sign to the height of high water at the reference station. The height of low water will be, of course, the same as at the reference station. If a difference for height of low as well as high water is given, each must be applied in accordance with its sign to the height of the corresponding tide at the reference station, adding the difference if its sign is plus (+) and subtracting if its sign is minus (−). If a ratio of ranges is given, the height of the tides at the subordinate station can be obtained by multiplying the heights of both high and low tides at the reference station by the respective ratios. If a ratio of ranges and an arithmetical difference are given in a form such as "*0.7 − 5.4 feet," multiply the heights of high and low water at the reference station by the ratio, 0.7, and then apply the correction, 5.4 feet, in accordance with its sign, (−).

Any unusual conditions pertaining to the subordinate stations are listed in keyed footnotes.

The mean tide level and the ranges of tide given in the last three columns are not generally used. An explanation of them is given in the *Tide Tables*.

The height of the tide at a specific time other than those tabulated in table 1 or computed using table 2 can be found by means of table 3, illustrated in figure 14-4, which is used without interpolation. This table is easy to use and the instructions given below the table are explicit.

TABLE 3.—HEIGHT OF TIDE AT ANY TIME

Duration of rise or fall, see footnote	Time from the nearest high water or low water														
h. m.	h. m.	h. m.	h. m.	h. m.	h. m.	h. m.	h. m.	h. m.	h. m.	h. m.	h. m.	h. m.	h. m.	h. m.	h. m.
4 00	0 08	0 16	0 24	0 32	0 40	0 48	0 56	1 04	1 12	1 20	1 28	1 36	1 44	1 52	2 00
4 20	0 09	0 17	0 26	0 35	0 43	0 52	1 01	1 09	1 18	1 27	1 35	1 44	1 53	2 01	2 10
4 40	0 09	0 19	0 28	0 37	0 47	0 56	1 05	1 15	1 24	1 33	1 43	1 52	2 01	2 11	2 20
5 00	0 10	0 20	0 30	0 40	0 50	1 00	1 10	1 20	1 30	1 40	1 50	2 00	2 10	2 20	2 30
5 20	0 11	0 21	0 32	0 43	0 53	1 04	1 15	1 25	1 36	1 47	1 57	2 08	2 19	2 29	2 40
5 40	0 11	0 23	0 34	0 45	0 57	1 08	1 19	1 31	1 42	1 53	2 05	2 16	2 27	2 39	2 50
6 00	0 12	0 24	0 36	0 48	1 00	1 12	1 24	1 36	1 48	2 00	2 12	2 24	2 36	2 48	3 00
6 20	0 13	0 25	0 38	0 51	1 03	1 16	1 29	1 41	1 54	2 07	2 19	2 32	2 45	2 57	3 10
6 40	0 13	0 27	0 40	0 53	1 07	1 20	1 33	1 47	2 00	2 13	2 27	2 40	2 53	3 07	3 20
7 00	0 14	0 28	0 42	0 56	1 10	1 24	1 38	1 52	2 06	2 20	2 34	2 48	3 02	3 16	3 30
7 20	0 15	0 29	0 44	0 59	1 13	1 28	1 43	1 57	2 12	2 27	2 41	2 56	3 11	3 25	3 40
7 40	0 15	0 31	0 46	1 01	1 17	1 32	1 47	2 03	2 18	2 33	2 49	3 04	3 19	3 35	3 50
8 00	0 16	0 32	0 48	1 04	1 20	1 36	1 52	2 08	2 24	2 40	2 56	3 12	3 28	3 44	4 00
8 20	0 17	0 33	0 50	1 07	1 23	1 40	1 57	2 13	2 30	2 47	3 03	3 20	3 37	3 53	4 10
8 40	0 17	0 35	0 52	1 09	1 27	1 44	2 01	2 19	2 36	2 53	3 11	3 28	3 45	4 03	4 20
9 00	0 18	0 36	0 54	1 12	1 30	1 48	2 06	2 24	2 42	3 00	3 18	3 36	3 54	4 12	4 30
9 20	0 19	0 37	0 56	1 15	1 33	1 52	2 11	2 29	2 48	3 07	3 25	3 44	4 03	4 21	4 40
9 40	0 19	0 39	0 58	1 17	1 37	1 56	2 15	2 35	2 54	3 13	3 33	3 52	4 11	4 31	4 50
10 00	0 20	0 40	1 00	1 20	1 40	2 00	2 20	2 40	3 00	3 20	3 40	4 00	4 20	4 40	5 00
10 20	0 21	0 41	1 02	1 23	1 43	2 04	2 25	2 45	3 06	3 27	3 47	4 08	4 29	4 49	5 10
10 40	0 21	0 43	1 04	1 25	1 47	2 08	2 29	2 51	3 12	3 33	3 55	4 16	4 37	4 59	5 20
Range of tide, see footnote	Correction to height														
Ft.	Ft.	Ft.	Ft.	Ft.	Ft.	Ft.	Ft.	Ft.	Ft.	Ft.	Ft.	Ft.	Ft.	Ft.	Ft.
0.5	0.0	0.0	0.0	0.0	0.0	0.0	0.1	0.1	0.1	0.1	0.1	0.2	0.2	0.2	0.2
1.0	0.0	0.0	0.0	0.0	0.1	0.1	0.1	0.2	0.2	0.2	0.3	0.3	0.4	0.4	0.5
1.5	0.0	0.0	0.0	0.1	0.1	0.1	0.2	0.2	0.3	0.4	0.4	0.5	0.6	0.7	0.8
2.0	0.0	0.0	0.0	0.1	0.1	0.2	0.3	0.3	0.4	0.5	0.6	0.7	0.8	0.9	1.0
2.5	0.0	0.0	0.1	0.1	0.2	0.2	0.3	0.4	0.5	0.6	0.7	0.9	1.0	1.1	1.2
3.0	0.0	0.0	0.1	0.1	0.2	0.3	0.4	0.5	0.6	0.8	0.9	1.0	1.2	1.3	1.5
3.5	0.0	0.0	0.1	0.2	0.2	0.3	0.4	0.6	0.7	0.9	1.0	1.2	1.4	1.6	1.8
4.0	0.0	0.0	0.1	0.2	0.3	0.4	0.5	0.7	0.8	1.0	1.2	1.4	1.6	1.8	2.0
4.5	0.0	0.0	0.1	0.2	0.3	0.4	0.6	0.7	0.9	1.1	1.3	1.6	1.8	2.0	2.2
5.0	0.0	0.1	0.1	0.2	0.3	0.5	0.6	0.8	1.0	1.2	1.5	1.7	2.0	2.2	2.5
5.5	0.0	0.1	0.1	0.2	0.4	0.5	0.7	0.9	1.1	1.4	1.6	1.9	2.2	2.5	2.8
6.0	0.0	0.1	0.1	0.3	0.4	0.6	0.8	1.0	1.2	1.5	1.8	2.1	2.4	2.7	3.0
6.5	0.0	0.1	0.2	0.3	0.4	0.6	0.8	1.1	1.3	1.6	1.9	2.2	2.6	2.9	3.2
7.0	0.0	0.1	0.2	0.3	0.5	0.7	0.9	1.2	1.4	1.8	2.1	2.4	2.8	3.1	3.5
7.5	0.0	0.1	0.2	0.3	0.5	0.7	1.0	1.2	1.5	1.9	2.2	2.6	3.0	3.4	3.8
8.0	0.0	0.1	0.2	0.3	0.5	0.8	1.0	1.3	1.6	2.0	2.4	2.8	3.2	3.6	4.0
8.5	0.0	0.1	0.2	0.4	0.6	0.8	1.1	1.4	1.8	2.1	2.5	2.9	3.4	3.8	4.2
9.0	0.0	0.1	0.2	0.4	0.6	0.9	1.2	1.5	1.9	2.2	2.7	3.1	3.6	4.0	4.5
9.5	0.0	0.1	0.2	0.4	0.6	0.9	1.2	1.6	2.0	2.4	2.8	3.3	3.8	4.3	4.8
10.0	0.0	0.1	0.2	0.4	0.7	1.0	1.3	1.7	2.1	2.5	3.0	3.5	4.0	4.5	5.0
10.5	0.0	0.1	0.3	0.5	0.7	1.0	1.3	1.7	2.2	2.6	3.1	3.6	4.2	4.7	5.2
11.0	0.0	0.1	0.3	0.5	0.7	1.1	1.4	1.8	2.3	2.8	3.3	3.8	4.4	4.9	5.5
11.5	0.0	0.1	0.3	0.5	0.8	1.1	1.5	1.9	2.4	2.9	3.4	4.0	4.6	5.1	5.8
12.0	0.0	0.1	0.3	0.5	0.8	1.1	1.5	2.0	2.5	3.0	3.6	4.1	4.8	5.4	6.0
12.5	0.0	0.1	0.3	0.5	0.8	1.2	1.6	2.1	2.6	3.1	3.7	4.3	5.0	5.6	6.2
13.0	0.0	0.1	0.3	0.6	0.9	1.2	1.7	2.2	2.7	3.2	3.9	4.5	5.1	5.8	6.5
13.5	0.0	0.1	0.3	0.6	0.9	1.3	1.7	2.2	2.8	3.4	4.0	4.7	5.3	6.0	6.8
14.0	0.0	0.2	0.3	0.6	0.9	1.3	1.8	2.3	2.9	3.5	4.2	4.8	5.5	6.3	7.0
14.5	0.0	0.2	0.4	0.6	1.0	1.4	1.9	2.4	3.0	3.6	4.3	5.0	5.7	6.5	7.2
15.0	0.0	0.2	0.4	0.6	1.0	1.4	1.9	2.5	3.1	3.8	4.4	5.2	5.9	6.7	7.5
15.5	0.0	0.2	0.4	0.7	1.0	1.5	2.0	2.6	3.2	3.9	4.6	5.4	6.1	6.9	7.8
16.0	0.0	0.2	0.4	0.7	1.1	1.5	2.1	2.6	3.3	4.0	4.7	5.5	6.3	7.2	8.0
16.5	0.0	0.2	0.4	0.7	1.1	1.6	2.1	2.7	3.4	4.1	4.9	5.7	6.5	7.4	8.2
17.0	0.0	0.2	0.4	0.7	1.1	1.6	2.2	2.8	3.5	4.2	5.0	5.9	6.7	7.6	8.5
17.5	0.0	0.2	0.4	0.8	1.2	1.7	2.2	2.9	3.6	4.4	5.2	6.0	6.9	7.8	8.8
18.0	0.0	0.2	0.4	0.8	1.2	1.7	2.3	3.0	3.7	4.5	5.3	6.2	7.1	8.1	9.0
18.5	0.1	0.2	0.5	0.8	1.2	1.8	2.4	3.1	3.8	4.6	5.5	6.4	7.3	8.3	9.2
19.0	0.1	0.2	0.5	0.8	1.3	1.8	2.4	3.1	3.9	4.8	5.6	6.6	7.5	8.5	9.5
19.5	0.1	0.2	0.5	0.8	1.3	1.9	2.5	3.2	4.0	4.9	5.8	6.7	7.7	8.7	9.8
20.0	0.1	0.2	0.5	0.9	1.3	1.9	2.6	3.3	4.1	5.0	5.9	6.9	7.9	9.0	10.0

Obtain from the predictions the high water and low water, one of which is before and the other after the time for which the height is required. The difference between the times of occurrence of these tides is the duration of rise or fall, and the difference between their heights is the range of tide for the above table. Find the difference between the nearest high or low water and the time for which the height is required.

Enter the table with the duration of rise or fall, printed in heavy-faced type, which most nearly agrees with the actual value, and on that horizontal line find the time from the nearest high or low water which agrees most nearly with the corresponding actual difference. The correction sought is in the column directly below, on the line with the range of tide.

When the nearest tide is high water, subtract the correction.

When the nearest tide is low water, add the correction.

National Ocean Survey

Figure 14-4. *Tide Tables,* Table 3

Note that all entries in the main body of the *Tide Tables* are for *standard time.* Do not forget to add one hour if you are operating on Daylight Saving Time.

The use of the *Tide Tables* is illustrated in the following example. The form given may seem lengthy; however, its use is recommended, as it has been found to reduce the risk of errors. Experience has shown that for tide problems a well-organized form permits easy and correct solutions.

The most common errors encountered in completion of a tide table for a subordinate station occur due to:

1. Applying the high water difference to the height of low water at the reference station as well as to the height of high water.
2. Not being alert to a change in date at the subor-

dinate station after applying the high-water or low-water time difference to the reference station.

3. Failing to apply the difference factor from table 3 with the proper sign to a rising or falling tide at the station in question. When the nearest tide is high water, subtract the correction factor given in table 3 from the nearest high tide; when the nearest tide is low water, add the correction to the nearest low tide.

4. Failing to add one hour to the tabulated time when Daylight Saving Time is being used.

Always refer to the explanatory notes given at the bottom of table 3 when using that table.

Example

Using the excerpts from the *Tide Tables* (figures 14-2, 14-3, and 14-4), we need to determine:

1. The time and heights of all tides at Southwest Harbor, Maine, on 9 March.
2. The height of the tide at 1100 on 9 March.
3. The depth of water at 1100 on 9 March at a certain point in Southwest Harbor having a charted depth of four feet.

On certain days, as for example on 18 March, the tabulated low water in table 1 is preceded with a minus sign, as "0552 −2.0 ft." This means that at that time, 2.0 feet must be subtracted from the charted depths.

COMPLETE TIDE TABLE

Substation <u>Southwest Harbor</u>   Date: <u>**9 March**</u>

Reference station <u>Portland</u>

HW time diff. <u>(−) 0h 22m</u>   Diff. in height of HW <u>+ 1.2 ft.</u>

LW time diff. <u>(−) 0h 12m</u>   Diff. in height of LW <u>0.0 ft.</u>

Ref. Sta. <u>**Portland**</u>   Sub Sta. <u>Southwest Harbor</u>

LW					
HW	0338	8.4 ft.		0316	9.6 ft.
LW	1001	0.7 ft.		0949	0.7 ft.
HW	1613	7.5 ft.		1551	8.7 ft.
LW	2213	1.2 ft.		2201	1.2
HW					

HEIGHT OF TIDE AT ANY TIME

Locality: <u>**Southwest Harbor**</u> Time: <u>1100</u> Date: <u>**9 March**</u>

Duration of Rise or Fall: <u>(0949 − 1551) 6h 02 m</u>

Time From Nearest Tide: <u>(Lw 0949 − 1100) 1h 11 m</u>

Range of Tide: <u>(8.7 − 0.7)   8 ft.</u>

Height of Nearest Tide: <u>(Lw)   0.7 ft.</u>

Corr. from Table 3: <u>+0.8 ft.</u>

Ht of Tide at: <u>1100</u> <u>1.5 ft.</u>

Height of tide at 1100   + 1.5 ft.
Charted depth   4.0 ft
Depth of water 1100   5.5 ft.

Tidal Predictions

Always remember that the data given in the *Tide Tables* are predictions based on the assumption that normal weather conditions will prevail. In general, these predictions are surprisingly accurate; however, they can be greatly modified in many areas by wind and also by barometric pressure. For example, at Annapolis, Maryland, the water level will be greatly reduced by strong northwesterly winds blowing over a considerable period of time. Conversely, the water level will be increased by southerlies.

Barometric pressure has a considerable effect on the water level both at sea and along our coasts. Water depths are given for a normal barometer reading of 29.92 inches; the level is raised by about one foot if the reading falls to 28.92 inches.

TIDAL CURRENTS

Tidal currents are caused by the same phenomena that cause the tides. The water moving toward the area of high tide is said to be *flooding;* it is *ebbing* as it moves away. In the open sea, the periods of flood and ebb coincide with the rise and fall of the tides. However, when affected by a land mass, this timing is forced out of phase. In bays, harbors, etc., it is usually impossible to determine the times a tidal current will be flowing from the times of high and low water.

The prevailing wind can have a considerable effect on tidal currents. It can increase or decrease the drift considerably and also can cause a given flow somewhat longer than the period tabulated in the *Tidal Current Tables*. However, overall, these tables can be considered highly reliable.

Tidal Current Tables

The *Tidal Current Tables* are published annually by the Department of Commerce (National Ocean Survey) in two volumes; one for the Atlantic Coast of North America and the other for the Pacific Coast of North America and Asia.

For a number of principal points called reference stations, table 1 of these tables lists the predicted times of slack water in chronological order in the left-hand column, and the predicted times and velocities of maximum flood *(F)* and ebb *(E)* currents, also in chronological order, in the center and right-hand columns respectively for each day of the year. Flood and ebb current directions appear at the top of each page. See figure 14-5.

Table 2 contains a list of secondary or *subordinate stations,* arranged in geographic order. Given for each station is its position in terms of latitude and longitude to the nearest minute and the name of its reference station. At many locations the current may not diminish to a true slack water or zero speed stage. For that reason, the phrases, "Minimum before flood" and "Minimum before ebb" are used in table 2 rather than the term Slack Water as used in table 1. The table lists the average speed and direction of the maximum floods and maximum ebbs. The directions are given in degrees, true, and are the directions toward which the currents flow.

The principal use of table 2 is to provide mean time differences for compiling approximate times for the minimum and maximum current phases at the subordinate stations. Four columns give these time differences for Min. before Flood, Flood, Min. before Ebb, and Ebb. Speed ratios for Flood and Ebb are also given to be applied as a percentage to the velocity at the reference station. The arrangement of table 2 is illustrated in figure 14-6. Note particularly the printing of the name of the reference station in the center of the page above the group of subordinate stations to which it applies.

The respective time differences are added to or subtracted from the time of slack water and maximum current (maximum flood or ebb) at the reference station according to their signs to obtain the times of occurrence of the respective events in the current cycle at the subordinate station. The velocity of the maximum currents at the subordinate station is found by multiplying the velocity of either the flood or ebb current at the reference station by the respective speed ratio listed for the subordinate station.

The set of maximum ebb tabulated in table 2 generally differs from the flood direction by about 180 degrees, as an examination of figure 14-6 will indicate. The average flood velocity is the mean of all the maximum flood currents, while the average ebb velocity is the mean of all the maximum ebb currents.

Table 3 is used to find the velocity of the current at a specific time. Full instructions for its use are given below the table. See figure 14-7.

Table 4 is used to find the duration of slack. Although slack water, or the time of zero velocity, lasts but an instant, there is a period each side of slack during which the current is so weak that for practical purposes it can be considered as negligible. From table 4, the period (half on each side

PORTSMOUTH HARBOR ENTRANCE (OFF WOOD I.), N.H., 1980

F-FLOOD, DIR. 355° TRUE   E-EBB, DIR. 195° TRUE

MARCH

DAY	SLACK WATER TIME H.M.	MAXIMUM CURRENT TIME H.M.	VEL. KNOTS	DAY	SLACK WATER TIME H.M.	MAXIMUM CURRENT TIME H.M.	VEL. KNOTS
1 SA	0020	0309	1.6E	16 SU		0236	2.3E
	0643	0916	1.0F		0620	0829	1.7F
	1231	1524	1.9E		1209	1502	2.5E
	1913	2108	1.0F		1848	2058	1.8F
2 SU	0100	0339	1.7E	17 M	0040	0327	2.4E
	0725	0918	1.1F		0710	0922	1.8F
	1310	1556	1.9E		1300	1551	2.6E
	1951	2143	1.1F		1936	2150	1.9F
3 M	0138	0414	1.7E	18 TU	0130	0418	2.5E
	0805	0959	1.1F		0801	1013	1.9F
	1347	1632	1.9E		1350	1642	2.6E
	2029	2222	1.2F		2025	2239	1.9F
4 TU	0214	0452	1.8E	19 W	0219	0508	2.5E
	0846	1040	1.2F		0853	1102	1.8F
	1421	1711	1.9E		1441	1731	2.5E
	2107	2304	1.2F		2115	2328	1.8F
5 W	0248	0532	1.8E	20 TH	0310	0559	2.5E
	0927	1121	1.2F		0946	1151	1.7F
	1452	1752	1.8E		1533	1820	2.3E
	2145	2345	1.3F		2207		
6 TH	0320	0616	1.8E	21 F		0017	1.7F
	1011	1206	1.1F		0402	0650	2.3E
	1518	1835	1.8E		1042	1244	1.5F
	2225				1629	1913	2.1E
					2302		
7 F		0028	1.2F	22 SA		0108	1.5F
	0350	0701	1.7E		0457	0745	2.1E
	1057	1251	1.1F		1141	1336	1.2F
	1542	1920	1.7E		1728	2007	1.9E
	2308						
8 SA		0117	1.2F	23 SU	0000	0159	1.3F
	0422	0748	1.7E		0555	0840	1.9E
	1148	1339	1.0F		1242	1431	1.0F
	1616	2009	1.6E		1830	2106	1.6E
	2357						
9 SU		0204	1.2F	24 M	0101	0253	1.0F
	0504	0837	1.7E		0655	0941	1.8E
	1242	1432	0.9F		1345	1746	0.8F
	1709	2101	1.5E		1932	2209	1.5E
10 M	0050	0257	1.1F	25 TU	0203	0350	0.9F
	0604	0932	1.7E		0755	1053	1.7E
	1339	1527	0.9F		1446	1850	0.8F
	1832	2154	1.5E		2033	2336	1.4E
11 TU	0148	0349	1.1F	26 W	0303	0709	0.8F
	0717	1028	1.7E		0853	1240	1.7E
	1436	1622	1.0F		1543	1945	0.9F
	1957	2253	1.6E		2130		
12 W	0246	0446	1.2F	27 TH		0115	1.5E
	0826	1125	1.8E		0359	0802	0.9F
	1530	1719	1.1F		0947	1335	1.7E
	2105	2351	1.7E		1634	2034	1.0F
					2222		
13 TH	0342	0545	1.3F	28 F		0203	1.5E
	0928	1222	2.0E		0450	0850	0.9F
	1622	1817	1.2F		1036	1414	1.7E
	2204				1720	2111	1.0F
					2308		
14 F		0050	1.9E	29 SA		0236	1.6E
	0437	0642	1.4F		0537	0850	0.8F
	1025	1317	2.2E		1122	1425	1.7E
	1712	1914	1.4F		1801	2111	0.9F
	2259				2351		
15 SA		0143	2.1E	30 SU		0242	1.7E
	0529	0735	1.6F		0620	0851	0.9F
	1118	1410	2.4E		1204	1451	1.8E
	1800	2007	1.6F		1841	2111	1.0F
	2351						
				31 M	0030	0311	1.7E
					0701	0851	1.0F
					1244	1524	1.8E
					1918	2111	1.2F

APRIL

DAY	SLACK WATER TIME H.M.	MAXIMUM CURRENT TIME H.M.	VEL. KNOTS	DAY	SLACK WATER TIME H.M.	MAXIMUM CURRENT TIME H.M.	VEL. KNOTS
1 TU	0107	0346	1.8E	16 W	0108	0358	2.6E
	0741	0932	1.1F		0744	0953	1.7F
	1321	1603	1.8E		1333	1619	2.4E
	1956	2152	1.2F		2001	2214	1.9F
2 W	0142	0425	1.9E	17 TH	0157	0447	2.6E
	0821	1013	1.2F		0835	1042	1.7F
	1355	1642	1.8E		1424	1708	2.3E
	2033	2233	1.3F		2051	2303	1.8F
3 TH	0213	0504	1.9E	18 F	0246	0536	2.5E
	0902	1056	1.2F		0928	1133	1.6F
	1426	1721	1.8E		1517	1759	2.2E
	2111	2316	1.3F		2143	2351	1.6F
4 F	0242	0547	1.9E	19 SA	0337	0627	2.3E
	0944	1140	1.2F		1022	1220	1.4F
	1454	1805	1.7E		1611	1847	1.9E
	2150	2359	1.3F		2238		
5 SA	0307	0632	1.9E	20 SU		0041	1.4F
	1029	1225	1.1F		0429	0719	2.1E
	1521	1852	1.7E		1119	1311	1.2F
	2233				1708	1942	1.7E
					2335		
6 SU		0048	1.3F	21 M		0129	1.2F
	0337	0719	1.8E		0525	0811	1.9E
	1117	1314	1.1F		1217	1405	1.0F
	1559	1941	1.6E		1807	2040	1.5E
	2323						
7 M		0136	1.2F	22 TU	0035	0224	1.0F
	0419	0808	1.8E		0622	0907	1.7E
	1210	1405	1.0F		1315	1459	0.8F
	1657	2032	1.6E		1907	2138	1.4E
8 TU	0019	0227	1.2F	23 W	0136	0317	0.8F
	0517	0902	1.8E		0721	1009	1.6E
	1306	1458	1.0F		1413	1557	0.8F
	1818	2129	1.6E		2005	2249	1.4E
9 W	0119	0324	1.1F	24 TH	0235	0413	0.7F
	0635	0959	1.8E		0818	1113	1.6E
	1402	1556	1.1F		1507	1916	0.8F
	1935	2227	1.6E		2059		
10 TH	0220	0421	1.2F	25 F		0039	1.4E
	0752	1056	1.9E		0331	0510	0.7F
	1458	1653	1.2F		0912	1214	1.6E
	2042	2326	1.8E		1557	1959	0.9F
					2149		
11 F	0319	0520	1.3F	26 SA		0122	1.5E
	0859	1155	2.0E		0423	0605	0.7F
	1552	1752	1.3F		1003	1257	1.6E
	2142				1642	1959	0.9F
					2235		
12 SA		0025	2.0E	27 SU		0135	1.6E
	0416	0617	1.4F		0510	0652	0.8F
	1000	1253	2.2E		1049	1335	1.7E
	1643	1849	1.5F		1725	1959	1.0F
	2236				2318		
13 SU		0122	2.2E	28 M		0206	1.7E
	0509	0715	1.5F		0554	0738	0.9F
	1056	1347	2.3E		1133	1413	1.7E
	1733	1943	1.7F		1805	1959	1.1F
	2328				2358		
14 M		0216	2.4E	29 TU		0239	1.8E
	0601	0808	1.7F		0636	0823	1.0F
	1149	1439	2.4E		1214	1451	1.7E
	1822	2036	1.8F		1844	2040	1.2F
15 TU	0019	0308	2.5E	30 W	0035	0317	1.9E
	0653	0901	1.7F		0717	0904	1.1F
	1241	1530	2.5E		1253	1531	1.8E
	1911	2127	1.9F		1922	2123	1.3F

TIME MERIDIAN 75° W.   0000 IS MIDNIGHT.   1200 IS NOON.

Figure 14-5. *Tidal Current Tables*, Table 1

TABLE 2. – CURRENT DIFFERENCES AND OTHER CONSTANTS

No.	PLACE	METER DEPTH (feet)	POSITION Lat. N.	POSITION Long. W.	TIME DIFF. Min. before Flood (h.m.)	TIME DIFF. Flood (h.m.)	TIME DIFF. Min. before Ebb (h.m.)	TIME DIFF. Ebb (h.m.)	SPEED RATIOS Flood	SPEED RATIOS Ebb	Minimum before Flood knots	deg	Maximum Flood knots	deg	Minimum before Ebb knots	deg	Maximum Ebb knots	deg
200	**KENNEBEC RIVER** *Time meridian, 75°W.* Bath, 0.2 mile south of bridge(3)		43 54.5	69 48.5	+0 29	+1 28	+0 43	+0 23	0.8	0.8	0.0	--	1.0	003	0.0	--	1.5	177
	on PORTSMOUTH HARBOR ENTRANCE, p.10																	
	CASCO BAY																	
205	Broad Sound, west of Eagle Island		43 42.7	70 03.8	-1 16	-1 05	-1 27	-0 59	0.8	0.7	0.0	--	0.9	010	0.0	--	1.3	168
210	Hussey Sound, SW. of Overset Island		43 40.27	70 10.52	-1 28	-1 18	-0 58	-1 30	0.9	0.6	0.0	--	1.1	316	0.3	189	1.2	153
	...do...	15	43 40.27	70 10.52	-1 39	-1 19	-1 06	-1 32	0.9	0.6	0.0	--	1.1	318	0.3	211	1.1	155
	...do...	25	43 40.27	70 10.52	-1 58	-1 16	-1 05	-1 32	0.9	0.6	0.1	228	1.1	314	0.1	200	1.1	154
212	Hussey Sound, SE. of Pumpkin Nob	40	43 40.45	70 10.78	-2 21	-1 29	-1 32	-1 14	1.0	0.5	0.1	068	1.2	346	0.1	066	0.9	168
215	Hussey Sound, east of Crow Island	40	43 41.33	70 10.79	-2 18	-0 42	-0 55	-1 24	0.7	0.4	0.1	114	0.9	016	0.0	--	0.8	197
220	Portland Hbr. ent., SW. of Cushing I.	40	43 37.9	70 12.7	-1 43	-1 11	-1 20	-0 58	0.8	0.6	0.0	--	1.0	322	0.0	--	1.1	154
225	Diamond I. Ledge, midchannel SW. of		43 39.6	70 13.5	-1 26	-1 12	-1 11	-1 06	0.8	0.5	0.0	--	0.9	300	0.0	--	0.9	150
230	Portland Breakwater Lt., 0.3 mi. NW. of(1)(4)		43 39.5	70 14.5	--	-0 47	--	-1 07	0.3	0.3	0.0	--	0.4	--	0.0	--	0.5	048
235	Grand Trunk Wharves, off ends(1)		43 39.5	70 14.7	--	-1 45	--	-1 50	0.5	0.2	0.0	--	0.6	250	0.0	--	0.4	040
240	Portland Bridge, center of draw		43 38.7	70 15.5	-1 06	-0 17	-0 38	-0 15	0.8	0.6	0.0	--	0.9	225	0.0	--	1.0	050
	MAINE COAST—Continued																	
250	Cape Elizabeth		43 34	70 11	-0 35	-1 35	-1 35	-1 35	0.2	0.2	0.0	--	0.3	340	0.0	--	0.3	160
255	Cape Porpoise		43 22	70 24	-0 55	-0 55	-0 55	-0 55	0.2	0.2	0.0	--	0.3	035	0.0	--	0.3	215
260	Cape Neddick		43 10	70 35	-0 20	-0 20	-0 20	-0 20	0.3	0.3	0.0	--	0.4	025	0.0	--	0.4	205
265	York Harbor ent., 3 miles south of		43 08	70 33	-0 15	-0 15	-0 15	-0 15	0.3	0.3	0.0	--	0.4	025	0.0	--	0.4	205
	PORTSMOUTH HARBOR																	
270	Kitts Rocks, 0.2 mile west of		43 03	70 42	0 00	0 00	0 00	0 00	0.7	0.9	0.0	--	0.8	325	0.0	--	1.6	175
275	Little Harbor entrance		43 03	70 43	-1 00	-1 00	-1 00	-1 00	0.6	0.6	0.0	--	0.7	310	0.0	--	1.1	130
280	PORTLAND HARBOR ENT. (off Wood I.)		43 03.8	70 42.3	Daily predictions				1.2	1.1	0.0	--	1.2	355	0.0	--	1.8	195
285	Fort Point		43 04	70 42	+0 05	+0 05	+0 05	+0 05	1.1	0.7	0.0	--	1.5	350	0.0	--	2.0	130
290	Salamander Point		43 05	70 43	+0 10	+0 10	+0 10	+0 10	0.8	1.1	0.0	--	1.3	260	0.0	--	1.3	085
295	Between Hick Rocks and Clarks Island		43 05	70 43	-0 35	-0 50	-0 35	-0 50	0.8	0.8	0.0	--	0.9	335	0.0	--	0.8	195
300	Kittery Point Bridge		43 05	70 43	-1 10	-1 10	-1 10	-1 10	0.7	0.4	0.0	--	0.8	020	0.0	--	1.1	200
305	Jamaica Island, NE of		43 05	70 44	-0 25	-0 25	-0 25	-0 25	0.8	0.6	0.0	--	1.0	315	0.0	--	1.0	135
310	Seavey Island, north of		43 05	70 44	+0 15	+0 15	+0 15	+0 15	1.2	0.7	0.0	--	1.4	260	0.0	--	1.8	080
315	Between Clarks I. and Seavey I(5)		43 05	70 44	+0 15	+0 15	+0 15	+0 15	1.5	1.0	0.0	--	1.8	200	0.0	--		
320	Clarks Island, south of		43 04	70 44	-1 00	-1 00	-1 00	-1 00	1.7	1.7	0.0	--	2.1	260	0.0	--	3.1	080
325	Seavey Island, south of		43 04	70 44	+0 15	+0 15	+0 15	+0 15	2.5	2.1	0.0	--	3.0	260	0.0	--	3.8	090
330	Between Marvin I. and Goat I.		43 04	70 44	-1 00	-1 00	-1 00	-1 00	1.0	0.4	0.0	--	1.2	160	0.0	--	0.8	340
335	Henderson Point, west of		43 05	70 44	+0 30	+0 30	+0 30	+0 30	2.2	1.3	0.0	--	2.6	340	0.0	--	2.3	170
340	Off Gangway Rock		43 05	70 45	+0 30	+0 30	+0 30	+0 30	1.7	1.7	0.0	--	2.1	280	0.0	--	3.0	110
345	Badgers Island, east of		43 05	70 45	+0 25	+0 25	+0 35	+0 25	0.9	0.2	0.0	--	1.1	240	0.0	--	0.4	050
350	Badgers Island, SW of		43 05	70 45	+0 30	+0 30	+0 30	+0 30	2.7	2.0	0.0	--	3.3	330	0.0	--	3.7	125
	PISCATAQUA RIVER and TRIBUTARIES																	
355	NW of Nobles Island (RR. bridge)		43 05	70 46	+0 35	+0 35	+0 35	+0 35	1.3	0.5	0.0	--	1.6	050	0.0	--	0.9	200
360	Nobles Island, north of		43 06	70 46	+0 30	+0 30	+0 30	+0 30	3.0	2.4	0.0	--	3.6	305	0.0	--	4.4	140
365	Frankfort Island, south of		43 06	70 48	+0 30	+0 30	+0 30	+0 30	2.2	1.6	0.0	--	2.6	310	0.0	--	2.9	130
370	Little Bay entrance, Dover Point		43 07	70 50	+0 35	+0 35	+0 35	+0 35	3.2	2.3	0.0	--	3.8	270	0.0	--	4.2	095
375	Furber Strait		43 05	70 52	+0 40	+0 40	+0 40	+0 40	1.7	1.2	0.0	--	2.0	185	0.0	--	2.1	010

Endnotes can be found at the end of Table 2.

Figure 14-6. *Tidal Current Tables, Table 2*

COMPLETE CURRENT TABLE

Locality: Broad Sound

Date: 15 April

Reference Station: Portsmouth Harbor Entrance

Time Diff:
- Min. before Flood: −1hr 16 m
- Flood: −1h 05 m
- Min. before Ebb: −1h 27 m
- Ebb: −0h 59m

Speed Ratio:
- Flood: 0.8
- Ebb: 0.7

Flood Direction: 010°

Ebb Direction: 168°

Ref. Sta: Portsmouth Har. Ent.		Locality: Broad Sound	
0019	0	2252(14th)	0
0308	2.5E	0209	1.8E
0653	0	0537	0
0901	1.7F	0756	1.4F
1241	0	1114	0
1530	2.5E	1431	1.8E
1911	0	1755	0
2127	1.9F	2022	1.5F
0108(16th)	0	2341	0

VELOCITY OF CURRENT AT ANY TIME - Broad Sound 1300

Int. between slack and desired time	1h 46m
Int. between slack and max. current	3h 17 m
Max. Current	1.8 Kt. (Ebb) ~~(Flood)~~
Factor, Table 3	0.7
Velocity	1.3
Direction	168°

DURATION OF SLACK

Times of Max. Current	0756	1431
Max. Current	1.4 F	1.8 E
Desired Max.	0.2	0.2
Period – Table 4	34 m	26 m
Sum of Periods		60 m
Average Period		30 m
Duration of Period	1114 ± 15	1059 – 1129

TABLE 3.—VELOCITY OF CURRENT AT ANY TIME

TABLE A														
Interval between slack and maximum current														
h. m. 1 20	h. m. 1 40	h. m. 2 00	h. m. 2 20	h. m. 2 40	h. m. 3 00	h. m. 3 20	h. m. 3 40	h. m. 4 00	h. m. 4 20	h. m. 4 40	h. m. 5 00	h. m. 5 20	h. m. 5 40

Interval between slack and desired time:

h. m.	f.	f.	f.	f.	f.	f.	f.	f.	f.	f.	f.	f.	f.	f.
0 20	0.4	0.3	0.3	0.2	0.2	0.2	0.2	0.1	0.1	0.1	0.1	0.1	0.1	0.1
0 40	0.7	0.6	0.5	0.4	0.4	0.3	0.3	0.3	0.3	0.2	0.2	0.2	0.2	0.2
1 00	0.9	0.8	0.7	0.6	0.6	0.5	0.5	0.4	0.4	0.4	0.3	0.3	0.3	0.3
1 20	1.0	1.0	0.9	0.8	0.7	0.6	0.6	0.5	0.5	0.5	0.4	0.4	0.4	0.4
1 40	---	1.0	1.0	0.9	0.8	0.8	0.7	0.7	0.6	0.6	0.5	0.5	0.5	0.4
2 00	---	---	1.0	1.0	0.9	0.9	0.8	0.8	0.7	0.7	0.6	0.6	0.6	0.5
2 20	---	---	---	1.0	1.0	0.9	0.9	0.8	0.8	0.7	0.7	0.7	0.6	0.6
2 40	---	---	---	---	1.0	1.0	1.0	0.9	0.9	0.8	0.8	0.7	0.7	0.7
3 00	---	---	---	---	---	1.0	1.0	1.0	0.9	0.9	0.8	0.8	0.8	0.7
3 20	---	---	---	---	---	---	1.0	1.0	1.0	0.9	0.9	0.9	0.8	0.8
3 40	---	---	---	---	---	---	---	1.0	1.0	1.0	0.9	0.9	0.9	0.9
4 00	---	---	---	---	---	---	---	---	1.0	1.0	1.0	1.0	0.9	0.9
4 20	---	---	---	---	---	---	---	---	---	1.0	1.0	1.0	1.0	0.9
4 40	---	---	---	---	---	---	---	---	---	---	1.0	1.0	1.0	1.0
5 00	---	---	---	---	---	---	---	---	---	---	---	1.0	1.0	1.0
5 20	---	---	---	---	---	---	---	---	---	---	---	---	1.0	1.0
5 40	---	---	---	---	---	---	---	---	---	---	---	---	---	1.0

1. From predictions find the time of slack water and the time and velocity of maximum current (flood or ebb), one of which is immediately before and the other after the time for which the velocity is desired.
2. Find the interval of time between the above slack and maximum current, and enter the top of Table A or B with the interval which most nearly agrees with this value.
3. Find the interval of time between the above slack and the time desired, and enter the side of Table A or B with the interval which most nearly agrees with this value.
4. Find, in the table, the factor corresponding to the above two intervals, and multiply the maximum velocity by this factor. The result will be the approximate velocity at the time desired.

Figure 14-7. *Tidal Current Tables,* Table 3A

of slack) during which the current does not exceed a given velocity (0.1 to 0.5 knot) is tabulated for various maximum currents. See figure 14-8.

Table 5 (Atlantic tables only) gives information regarding *rotary tidal currents,* or currents which change their direction continually and never come to a slack, so that in a tidal cycle of about 12.5 hours they set in all directions successively. Such currents occur offshore and in some wide indentations of the coast. The values given are average velocities due to tidal action only. When a steady wind is blowing, the effect of the current due to wind should be added vectorially to the

TABLE A					
Maximum current	Period with a velocity not more than—				
	0.1 knot	0.2 knot	0.3 knot	0.4 knot	0.5 knot
Knots	*Minutes*	*Minutes*	*Minutes*	*Minutes*	*Minutes*
1.0	23	46	70	94	120
1.5	15	31	46	62	78
2.0	11	23	35	46	58
3.0	8	15	23	31	38
4.0	6	11	17	23	29
5.0	5	9	14	18	23
6.0	4	8	11	15	19
7.0	3	7	10	13	16
8.0	3	6	9	11	14
9.0	3	5	8	10	13
10.0	2	5	7	9	11

Figure 14-8. *Tidal Current Tables,* Table 4A

current due to tidal action. An example using table 5 is not given, since this table is seldom used. Instructions for the use of this table as well as for tables 1 through 4 are given in the publications themselves.

The example on page 111–12 illustrates the use of the current tables. While the form may appear to be somewhat lengthy, its use is recommended to avoid errors. The necessary tabular data for solution are included in the illustrations in this section.

Example (see page 111–12)

We expect to be operating in Broad Sound in the Casco Bay, Maine, area on 15 April. We require:

1. A complete current table for Broad Sound for 15 April.
2. The set and drift of the current in Broad Sound at 1300.
3. The length of the period during the midday slack at Broad Sound when the drift will be 0.2 knots or less.

Comments on Tidal Current Problems

As the period of the tidal cycle is about 12 and a half hours, two cycles are not completed in one day. Hence, as in the *Tide Tables*, on some days one entry is left blank.

Because of the difference of time between the reference and subordinate stations, it is sometimes necessary to pick values from the preceding or the following day at the reference station.

In computing the period at the time of slack water when the current will not exceed a selected maximum, you will find that when one current, the flood or the ebb, is the stronger, the period of minimum set for that current will be shorter than that for the other. Thus, in the example in the previous section, the ebb has a maximum drift of 1.8 knots, and the period during which it does not exceed 0.2 knots is 26 minutes, while the flood, having a maximum drift of 1.4 knots, permits a period of 34 minutes.

Always remember that the values given in the *Tidal Current Tables* are predictions based on normal meteorological conditions; while they are remarkably accurate, by and large, they can be radically affected by weather.

Do not forget to add an hour to the tabulated times if you are operating on Daylight Saving Time.

Current Diagrams

Current diagrams for the principal tidal waterways of our coasts are included in the *Tidal Current Tables*. As used in the *Tables*, a current diagram is a graphic table that shows the velocities of the flood and ebb currents and the times of slack and strength over a considerable stretch of the channel of a tidal waterway. At selected points along the channel, the drifts of the current are shown with reference to the times of slack water at a reference station. This makes it a simple matter to determine the velocity of the current at any point in the channel or the average current along the channel for any desired time. The optimum time for leaving a place to take maximum advantage of a favorable current can also be determined, as well as the time we will be able to remain in that current, provided a fixed speed through the water is maintained. Detailed instructions for their use are included with each of these diagrams.

Tidal Current Charts

Tidal Current Charts for selected areas are published by the National Ocean Service to supplement the *Tidal Current Tables*. Twelve small charts, one for each hour of the tidal cycle based on a reference station, are bound together for each area. On each chart, the set of the current at various places is shown by arrows, and the drift by numbers.

The areas included are Boston Harbor, Long Island Sound and Block Island Sound, Narragansett Bay to Nantucket Sound, New York Harbor, Delaware Bay and River, Upper Chesapeake Bay, Charleston Harbor, San Francisco Bay, and Puget Sound.

These charts can be of great assistance, particularly aboard sailboats cruising in such waters as Long Island Sound, Buzzards Bay, and Vineyard and Nantucket Sounds. Their small size makes them easy to stow, and their price is low.

SUNRISE AND SUNSET

In addition to the material we have discussed, table 4 in the *Tide Tables* gives the *local mean time* of sunrise and sunset to the nearest minute for every fifth day of the current year for even latitudes from the equator to 76°N and 60°S. Local mean time differs from the time shown by our clocks and watches, which are set to a zone or standard time. Each time zone is approximately

15 degrees of longitude in width, thus enabling people in the same zone to share a common time. Local mean time, on the other hand, is the time established by the mean sun at a given meridian, thus local mean time is four minutes earlier at a spot one degree of longitude west of us, and an hour later at a spot fifteen degrees of longitude east of us. Table 5 in the *Tide Tables* enables us to convert local mean time to our clock time, if we know our longitude.

The use of these two tables is best illustrated by an example; figure 14-9 is an excerpt from table

4 in the *Tide Tables*, while table 5 is reproduced in figure 14-10.

Let us assume that we are in L 39°36′N, λ 72°24′W on 11 August and wish to determine the time of sunrise and sunset.

Starting with sunrise, we note the times of this phenomenon from the tables (see table 14-1), and by mental interpolation note that to the nearest minute, the sun will rise at 0511 local mean time in L 38°N and at 0508 in L 40°N on 11 August. Now our latitude is 39°36′N, or 1.6° north of latitude 38°N, so we must find $1.6 \div 2$ and multiply

TABLE 4.-SUNRISE AND SUNSET

Date		30° N.		32° N.		34° N.		36° N.		38° N.		40° N.	
		Rise	Set	Rise	Set	Rise	Set	Rise	Set	Rise	Set	Rise	Set
		h. m.	h. m.	h. m.	h. m.	h. m.	h. m.	h. m.	h. m.	h. m.	h. m.	h. m.	h. m.
Jan.	1	6 56	17 11	7 01	17 07	7 06	17 01	7 11	16 56	7 16	16 50	7 22	16 44
	6	6 57	17 14	7 02	17 09	7 07	17 04	7 12	16 59	7 17	16 54	7 22	16 49
	11	6 57	17 19	7 02	17 14	7 07	17 09	7 12	17 04	7 17	16 59	7 22	16 54
	16	6 57	17 23	7 01	17 18	7 06	17 13	7 11	17 09	7 15	17 04	7 20	16 59
	21	6 56	17 27	7 00	17 23	7 04	17 18	7 09	17 14	7 09	17 09	7 18	17 05
	26	6 54	17 31	6 58	17 27	7 02	17 23	7 06	17 19	7 10	17 15	7 14	17 11
	31	6 51	17 36	6 55	17 32	6 58	17 28	7 02	17 25	7 06	17 21	7 10	17 17
Feb.	5	6 49	17 40	6 52	17 37	6 55	17 33	6 59	17 30	7 03	17 26	7 06	17 23
	10	6 45	17 44	6 48	17 41	6 51	17 38	6 54	17 35	6 57	17 32	7 00	17 29
	15	6 41	17 48	6 43	17 45	6 46	17 43	6 49	17 40	6 51	17 38	6 54	17 35
	20	6 36	17 52	6 38	17 50	6 41	17 48	6 43	17 45	6 46	17 43	6 48	17 41
	25	6 31	17 56	6 33	17 54	6 35	17 52	6 37	17 50	6 39	17 48	6 41	17 46
Mar.	1	6 26	17 59	6 28	17 58	6 29	17 56	6 31	17 55	6 32	17 53	6 34	17 52
	6	6 21	18 03	6 22	18 02	6 23	18 01	6 24	17 59	6 25	17 58	6 26	17 57
	11	6 15	18 06	6 15	18 05	6 16	18 05	6 17	18 04	6 17	18 04	6 18	18 03
	16	6 09	18 09	6 09	18 09	6 09	18 09	6 10	18 08	6 10	18 08	6 10	18 08
	21	6 03	18 12	6 03	18 12	6 03	18 12	6 02	18 13	6 02	18 13	6 02	18 13
	26	5 57	18 15	5 56	18 16	5 56	18 16	5 55	18 17	5 55	18 17	5 54	18 18
	31	5 51	18 18	5 50	18 19	5 49	18 20	5 48	18 21	5 47	18 22	5 46	18 23
Apr.	5	5 45	18 21	5 44	18 22	5 42	18 24	5 41	18 25	5 39	18 27	5 38	18 28
	10	5 39	18 24	5 37	18 26	5 35	18 28	5 34	18 29	5 32	18 31	5 30	18 33
	15	5 33	18 27	5 31	18 29	5 29	18 31	5 26	18 34	5 24	18 36	5 22	18 38
	20	5 28	18 30	5 25	18 33	5 23	18 36	5 20	18 38	5 18	18 41	5 15	18 44
	25	5 23	18 33	5 20	18 36	5 17	18 39	5 14	18 43	5 11	18 46	5 08	18 49
	30	5 18	18 37	5 15	18 40	5 11	18 44	5 08	18 47	5 04	18 51	5 01	18 54
May	5	5 14	18 40	5 10	18 44	5 06	18 48	5 03	18 51	4 59	18 55	4 55	18 59
	10	5 10	18 43	5 06	18 47	5 02	18 51	4 58	18 56	4 54	19 00	4 50	19 04
	15	5 07	18 46	5 03	18 50	4 58	18 55	4 54	18 59	4 49	19 04	4 45	19 08
	20	5 04	18 49	4 59	18 54	4 54	18 59	4 50	19 03	4 45	19 08	4 40	19 13
	25	5 02	18 53	4 57	18 58	4 52	19 03	4 47	19 07	4 42	19 12	4 37	19 17
	30	5 00	18 55	4 55	19 00	4 50	19 05	4 44	19 11	4 39	19 16	4 34	19 21
June	4	4 59	18 58	4 54	19 03	4 48	19 09	4 43	19 14	4 37	19 20	4 32	19 25
	9	4 58	19 00	4 53	19 06	4 47	19 11	4 42	19 17	4 36	19 22	4 31	19 28
	14	4 58	19 02	4 52	19 08	4 47	19 13	4 41	19 19	4 36	19 24	4 30	19 30
	19	4 59	19 04	4 54	19 10	4 48	19 15	4 42	19 21	4 37	19 26	4 31	19 32
	24	5 00	19 05	4 54	19 11	4 49	19 16	4 43	19 22	4 38	19 27	4 32	19 33
	29	5 02	19 05	4 56	19 11	4 51	19 16	4 45	19 22	4 40	19 27	4 34	19 33
July	4	5 04	19 05	4 58	19 10	4 53	19 16	4 47	19 21	4 42	19 27	4 36	19 32
	9	5 06	19 04	5 01	19 09	4 55	19 15	4 50	19 20	4 44	19 26	4 39	19 31
	14	5 08	19 03	5 03	19 08	4 58	19 13	4 53	19 18	4 48	19 23	4 43	19 28
	19	5 11	19 01	5 06	19 06	5 01	19 11	4 57	19 15	4 52	19 20	4 47	19 25
	24	5 14	18 58	5 09	19 03	5 05	19 07	5 00	19 12	4 56	19 16	4 51	19 21
	29	5 17	18 55	5 13	18 59	5 03	19 04	5 04	19 08	4 59	19 13	4 55	19 17
Aug.	3	5 20	18 52	5 16	18 56	5 12	19 00	5 08	19 04	5 04	19 08	5 00	19 12
	8	5 23	18 48	5 19	18 52	5 16	18 55	5 12	18 59	5 09	19 02	5 05	19 06
	13	5 26	18 43	5 23	18 46	5 20	18 49	5 16	18 53	5 13	18 56	5 10	18 59
	18	5 29	18 38	5 26	18 41	5 23	18 44	5 20	18 47	5 17	18 50	5 14	18 53
	23	5 32	18 33	5 29	18 35	5 27	18 38	5 24	18 40	5 22	18 43	5 19	18 45
	28	5 35	18 27	5 33	18 29	5 31	18 31	5 28	18 34	5 26	18 36	5 24	18 38
Sept.	2	5 37	18 21	5 35	18 23	5 34	18 25	5 32	18 26	5 31	18 28	5 29	18 30
	7	5 40	18 15	5 39	18 16	5 37	18 18	5 36	18 19	5 34	18 21	5 33	18 22
	12	5 43	18 09	5 42	18 10	5 41	18 11	5 40	18 12	5 39	18 13	5 38	18 14
	17	5 45	18 03	5 45	18 04	5 44	18 04	5 44	18 05	5 43	18 05	5 43	18 06
	22	5 48	17 57	5 48	17 57	5 48	17 57	5 47	17 57	5 47	17 57	5 47	17 57
	27	5 51	17 50	5 51	17 50	5 51	17 50	5 52	17 49	5 52	17 49	5 52	17 49
Oct.	2	5 54	17 44	5 55	17 43	5 55	17 43	5 56	17 42	5 56	17 42	5 57	17 41
	7	5 57	17 38	5 58	17 37	5 59	17 36	6 00	17 35	6 01	17 34	6 02	17 33
	12	6 00	17 33	6 01	17 31	6 03	17 30	6 04	17 28	6 06	17 27	6 07	17 25
	17	6 03	17 27	6 05	17 25	6 07	17 23	6 08	17 22	6 10	17 20	6 12	17 18
	22	6 07	17 22	6 09	17 20	6 11	17 18	6 14	17 15	6 16	17 13	6 18	17 11
	27	6 10	17 17	6 13	17 14	6 15	17 12	6 18	17 09	6 20	17 07	6 23	17 04
Nov.	1	6 14	17 13	6 17	17 10	6 20	17 07	6 23	17 04	6 26	17 01	6 29	16 58
	6	6 18	17 09	6 21	17 06	6 25	17 02	6 28	16 59	6 32	16 55	6 35	16 52
	11	6 22	17 06	6 26	17 02	6 29	16 58	6 33	16 55	6 36	16 51	6 40	16 47
	16	6 26	17 03	6 30	16 59	6 34	16 55	6 38	16 51	6 42	16 47	6 46	16 43
	21	6 30	17 02	6 34	16 58	6 39	16 53	6 43	16 49	6 48	16 44	6 52	16 40
	26	6 34	17 00	6 39	16 55	6 43	16 51	6 48	16 46	6 52	16 42	6 57	16 37
Dec.	1	6 38	17 00	6 43	16 55	6 48	16 50	6 53	16 45	6 58	16 40	7 03	16 35
	6	6 42	17 00	6 47	16 55	6 52	16 50	6 57	16 45	7 02	16 40	7 08	16 35
	11	6 46	17 01	6 51	16 56	6 56	16 51	7 02	16 45	7 07	16 40	7 12	16 35
	16	6 49	17 02	6 54	16 58	6 59	16 52	7 05	16 46	7 10	16 41	7 15	16 36
	21	6 52	17 05	6 57	17 00	7 02	16 54	7 08	16 49	7 13	16 43	7 18	16 38
	26	6 54	17 07	6 59	17 02	7 04	16 57	7 10	16 51	7 15	16 46	7 20	16 41
	31	6 56	17 10	7 01	17 05	7 06	17 00	7 12	16 54	7 17	16 49	7 22	16 44

Local mean time.   To obtain standard time of rise or set, see Table 5.

Figure 14-9.   *Tide Tables*, Table 4

TABLE 5.—REDUCTION OF LOCAL MEAN TIME TO STANDARD TIME

Difference of longitude between local and standard meridian	Correction to local mean time to obtain standard time	Difference of longitude between local and standard meridian	Correction to local mean time to obtain standard time	Difference of longitude between local and standard meridian	Correction to local mean time to obtain standard time
° ′ ° ′	Minutes	° ′ ° ′	Minutes	°	Hours
0 00 to 0 07	0	7 23 to 7 37	30	15	1
0 08 to 0 22	1	7 38 to 7 52	31	30	2
0 23 to 0 37	2	7 53 to 8 07	32	45	3
0 38 to 0 52	3	8 08 to 8 22	33	60	4
0 53 to 1 07	4	8 23 to 8 37	34	75	5
1 08 to 1 22	5	8 38 to 8 52	35	90	6
1 23 to 1 37	6	8 53 to 9 07	36	105	7
1 38 to 1 52	7	9 08 to 9 22	37	120	8
1 53 to 2 07	8	9 23 to 9 37	38	135	9
2 08 to 2 22	9	9 38 to 9 52	39	150	10
2 23 to 2 37	10	9 53 to 10 07	40	165	11
2 38 to 2 52	11	10 08 to 10 22	41	180	12
2 53 to 3 07	12	10 23 to 10 37	42		
3 08 to 3 22	13	10 38 to 10 52	43		
3 23 to 3 37	14	10 53 to 11 07	44		
3 38 to 3 52	15	11 08 to 11 22	45		
3 53 to 4 07	16	11 23 to 11 37	46		
4 08 to 4 22	17	11 38 to 11 52	47		
4 23 to 4 37	18	11 53 to 12 07	48		
4 38 to 4 52	19	12 08 to 12 22	49		
4 53 to 5 07	20	12 23 to 12 37	50		
5 08 to 5 22	21	12 38 to 12 52	51		
5 23 to 5 37	22	12 53 to 13 07	52		
5 38 to 5 52	23	13 08 to 13 22	53		
5 53 to 6 07	24	13 23 to 13 37	54		
6 08 to 6 22	25	13 38 to 13 52	55		
6 23 to 6 37	26	13 53 to 14 07	56		
6 38 to 6 52	27	14 08 to 14 22	57		
6 53 to 7 07	28	14 23 to 14 37	58		
7 08 to 7 22	29	14 38 to 14 52	59		

If local meridian is east of standard meridian, subtract the correction from local time.

If local meridian is west of standard meridian, add the correction to local time.

For differences of longitude less than 15°, use the first part of the table. For greater differences use both parts thus: 47°23′ is equivalent to 45°+2°23′, the correction for 45° is 3 hours, the correction for 2°23′ is 10 minutes, therefore the total correction for the difference in longitude 47°23′ is 3 hours and 10 minutes.

Figure 14-10.   *Tide Tables*, Table 5

Table 14-1 (see figure 14-9)

	L 38°N	L 40°N
8 August	5h 09m	5h 05m
13 August	5h 13m	5h 10m

the result times three minutes; this comes to two minutes to the nearest minute. Sunrise for us will therefore occur at 0509 (0511 minus two minutes) local mean time.

The next step is to convert 0509 local mean time to our clock time. The 75° meridian establishes our time zone; hence our clocks are set to Eastern Standard Time, or Zone + 5 time as it is called in the Coast Guard and Navy. As our longitude is 72°24'W, we are 2°36' *east* of our standard meridian. From table 5, we note that this comes to 10 minutes, and in accordance with the instructions given, we *subtract* this from the local mean time of sunrise; 0509 minus 10 minutes equals 0459, which will therefore be the clock time of sunrise.

Note that this example is based on Eastern Standard Time; if our clocks are set to Eastern Daylight Time, sunrise would be at 0559.

The time of sunset is similarly determined; in this example, it would come at 1901 local mean time or 1851 Eastern Standard Time, which would be 1951 Eastern Daylight Time.

SUMMARY

We have dwelt at considerable length in this chapter both on determining the depth of water due to the tide at a given location and time, and on determining the set and drift of a tidal current. The first problem is not one frequently encountered by the small-craft operator in his daily work; however, under certain conditions such as a grounding in tidal waters, it can be of very considerable importance.

The determination of current set and drift, on the other hand, is a matter of regular interest, particularly for the navigators of sailing and comparatively low-speed power craft. It is desirable, therefore, that every navigator have a thorough grasp of these subjects, as even an express cruiser must make considerable allowance when crossing a strong tidal current, and it is occasionally necessary to assist a boat which has run aground in tidal waters. The sample pages shown herein are illustrative only. The *Tide Tables* and *Tidal Current Tables* for the current year must be used in practice, as times shown are not repetitive in successive years.

chapter fifteen

Radio Navigation

In 1895, Guglielmo Marconi transmitted a radio message over a distance of about one mile; by 1901, he was able to communicate between stations more than 2,000 miles apart. The first application of radio in navigation was the transmission of time signals in 1903, which enabled the navigator to obtain a chronometer check, thus increasing the accuracy of celestial navigation.

By the latter part of World War I, the directional properties of the loop antenna were successfully utilized in the *radio direction finder (RDF);* the first radio beacon went into commission in 1921.

Since then, the strides in this field have been rapid; they were greatly accelerated by the operational requirements of World War II. Radar has been developed as a precise tool for the navigator; Loran-C provides good position-fixing capability over the most widely traveled portions of the Atlantic and Pacific oceans, and Omega provides world-wide navigational coverage.

The advent of these sophisticated systems has led to a tendency to call this type of navigation *electronic* rather than *radio;* as, in this chapter, we are concerned primarily with radio direction finding, we will use the older term.

HERTZ (Hz) CYCLE(S) PER SECOND

For many decades, alternating current frequency was expressed in *cycles per second.* This seemed the natural term to indicate the complete reversal of the polarity of the voltage and the direction of flow of the current in alternating current circuits. However, the use of the term *cycles* has decreased in recent years and it is being replaced by the term *Hertz,* which is synonymous with *cycles per second.* The term Hertz has been adopted as a replacement by many countries as well as the United States. It honors the German scientist Heinrich Hertz, who was a pioneer in the field of electromagnetic radiation. A Hertz is a unit of frequency equivalent to one cycle per second. The terms *Hertz (Hz)* and *cycle(s) per second* are synonymous and may be used interchangeably. Kilohertz (kHz) is used instead of kilocycle for 1000 Hz and megahertz (MHz) for 1000 kHz.

MARINE RADIO BEACONS

Marine radio beacons, operated by the U.S. Coast Guard, are strategically located at many lighthouses and aboard lightships along our coasts, including the Great Lakes; they fall into two classes. Some are intended for homing; that is, when the radio beacon bears in the proper direction by compass for entering an inlet, the vessel turns in that direction and runs in, keeping the marker dead ahead by adjusting course to compensate for any current.

The *major marine radio beacons* are of considerably greater power and have nominal service ranges of from 10 miles to as high as 170 miles. Like the channel beacons, they may be used for homing, but their primary purpose is to enable the mariner to determine a fix by means of bearings on two or more beacons.

The designation *NDB* for nondirectional beacons is often used to describe these radio beacons as the transmitted signal does not itself give any directional information. Commercial broadcast stations are also generally nondirectional, and can be used for navigation in the same manner as the marine radio beacons, provided the exact location of the transmitting towers is known.

Because of the very limited width of the radio

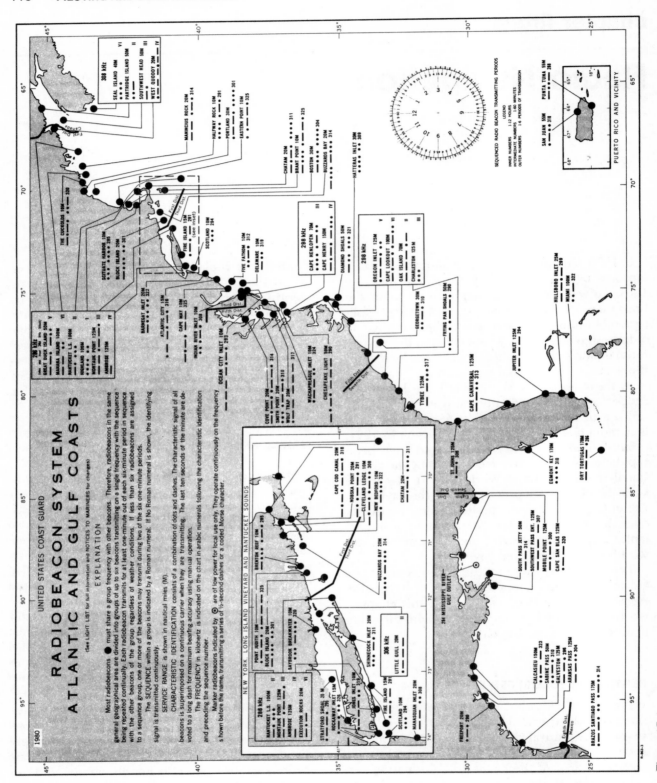

Figure 15-1.

frequency band assigned for the use of marine radio beacons (285 to 325 kHz), the same frequency is often shared by a group of beacons located in the same general area. There are up to six beacons in each group; each transmits for exactly one minute on the group frequency and in its proper sequence within the group.

A few beacons transmit for one minute, followed by two minutes of silence, and some others operate continuously.

Beacons, whether operating continuously or in sequence, operate at all times, regardless of weather conditions. Their locations are shown on charts and are listed in the *Light List*; in addition, each *Light List* includes a chartlet showing the location, frequency, nominal range, and identification signal of beacons, as well as their order of transmission, if sequenced. Figure 15-1 is taken from a *Light List* and shows the beacons serving the Atlantic and Gulf Coasts, including an inset for the area from New York to Cape Cod.

Each radio beacon can be identified by its individual signal, consisting of a simple combination of dots and dashes. It is usually helpful if the dots are thought of as "dits," and the dashes as "dahs"; this is pretty much as they sound when heard on a radio direction finder. No knowledge of the Morse code is required for station identification.

Marine Radio Beacon Operation

We have stated previously that, in many cases, the major radio beacons in a given area share a frequency with other beacons and transmit in a definite sequence within the group for exactly one minute. Each beacon in such a group transmits its identifying signal for 48 seconds, succeeded by two seconds of silence; this is followed by a 10-second dash. The next station in the group then transmits its identifying signal for 48 seconds and the 10-second dash after a two-second silence, and so forth until the cycle is completed, and the first beacon again goes on the air.

All necessary data for using a marine radio beacon may be obtained from the chartlets found in each copy of the *Light List*. Referring to figure 15-1, which is reproduced from the *Light List* (Volume I), the frequency on which the beacon operates is given beside its name. The major beacons are shown as black dots. The name of each station is given, followed by its service range. Below this ap-

pears its identifying signal, followed by the frequency on which it operates, shown in arabic numerals. For the sequenced stations this is followed by a roman numeral, denoting its sequence within the group. For example, when referring to figure 15-1 the beacon in the Nantucket Light Ship is listed as follows (Nantucket L.S. 2100 M __. . . . II) and this is in a block of stations labeled 286 kHz. This means the beacon has a service range of 100 miles, the identifying signal consists of a dash and dot followed by three dots (which is Morse Code for the letters NS) and the transmission is on 286 kHz. The radio beacon is second in sequence within its group. Several major beacons operate continuously; for them the roman numerals are omitted.

The identifying signal of all radio beacons is superimposed on a continuous carrier wave while they are transmitting. Remember that many beacons transmit only once every six minutes so that it is absolutely necessary to listen to the dot dash pattern of the signal to be certain that you are not taking a bearing on a different station than desired, although on the same radio frequency.

The transmission sequence of each beacon in the 286 kHz group in the New York-Cape Cod area is shown in table 15-1. The timing of the start of each transmission is very precise and can be helpful as a check on your timepiece. The minutes of each hour during which a sequenced beacon can be received are shown in table 15-2.

RADIO DIRECTION FINDER

A typical *radio direction finder (RDF)* is shown in figure 15-2; this instrument is representative of the RDFs used aboard small craft. The great majority of RDFs are portable units, containing flashlight dry cells for power. They are a specialized type of radio receiver, having a rotatable antenna, often called a *loop*, although on many models it is now a flat bar. The bearing of a radio beacon, or its reciprocal, is determined by means of the rotating antenna. Unfortunately, the loop antenna, by itself, cannot determine from which side the signal is coming. Methods of making this determination are discussed later in the chapter.

Portable RDFs of the sort we are considering are readily available. The majority will receive on three radio bands. These bands are the *marine beacon band*, between 285 and 325 kHz but usually also extending down to 190 kHz and up to about 400 kHz so that aero radio beacons may also be received; the *marine band*, from 1850 kHz

Table 15-1

Position within the Transmission Sequence of the Group	Name	Frequency	Approximate Range in Miles	Characteristic Code
I	Highland	286 kHz	100	· · · · · ·
II	Nantucket L.S.	286 kHz	100	— · · · ·
III	Montauk Point	286 kHz	125	— — · · — — ·
IV	Ambrose Light	286 kHz	125	—
V	Great Duck Island	286 kHz	50	— — · — · ·
VI	Manana Island	286 kHz	100	— — · ·

Table 15-2

Group	Exact minutes of each hour signal will be broadcast. Each signal will broadcast for 48 seconds followed by 2 seconds of silence and a 10-second dash.									
I	0	6	12	18	24	30	36	42	48	54
II	1	7	13	19	25	31	37	43	49	55
III	2	8	14	20	26	32	38	44	50	56
IV	3	9	15	21	27	33	39	45	51	57
V	4	10	16	22	28	34	40	46	52	58
VI	5	11	17	23	29	35	41	47	53	59

Figure 15-2. A Radio Direction Finder (Courtesy Newport Marine Engineering, Inc.)

to 2850 kHz; and the regular *broadcast band*, between 535 and 1620 kHz.

RDF receivers, of course, vary from model to model, but most receivers include certain controls and equipment in common. These include a band-selector switch, which enables the operator to select the band he wishes to receive, an on-off switch combined with a gain or volume control, and a tuning control to permit finding the desired station on the selected band. Many sets also have a *beat frequency oscillator (BFO)* switch, which greatly facilitates reception of *continuous wave (CW)* transmissions. Almost all RDFs have a *nullmeter,* which permits visual determination of the *minimum* signal strength; radio bearings are determined by means of the *null* or minimum signal, as is described later. In addition, the higher priced sets have a whip antenna, which may be extended. This is used to give the receiver *sense;* that is, to permit determining, when a bearing is obtained, whether the bearing is towards or away from the beacon.

The antenna, which is rotatable, is mounted on top of the receiver. Below it, on the top of the set, is a bearing circle, which permits reading the relative bearing when the null, or minimum signal, is obtained by rotating the antenna.

Hand-held portable RDF sets are also available. The configuration includes a small hand-bearing compass mounted on top of the RDF. There is, of course, some loss of accuracy as an assumption of no deviation of the compass and of the RDF must be used. On a glass or wood boat, if one stands away from the shrouds, mast, or known metal objects, the error can be reduced. The RDF problem is simplified by obtaining the direct magnetic bearing. The unit should not be used on a steel boat.

Detailed instructions are furnished by the manufacturer covering the operation of each set; we will, therefore, only discuss briefly the operation of a typical RDF receiver, assuming that we wish to obtain a bearing on a marine beacon. First, however, we will discuss the installation and calibration of the RDF.

RDF Installation

There are two schools of thought in regard to placing an RDF aboard a boat—those who want the set permanently secured in place and those who prefer to keep it stowed out of the way, bringing it out only when it is to be used. In either case, the same considerations govern its placement for satisfactory use.

First, it must be placed so that the zero line on the bearing scale is exactly parallel to the fore-and-aft axis of the boat, and it must be in a place where the controls can be used conveniently. In addition, it should be situated near enough to the compass, so that a compass heading can readily be obtained from the helmsman at the moment the RDF bearing is obtained. In this connection, remember that the loudspeaker in most RDFs contains a powerful permanent magnet, so the set must not be installed too near the compass.

Another factor affecting the location of the RDF is *deviation*. As with the compass, metal, such as wire lifelines, rigging, etc., can affect the accuracy of the bearings obtained by re-radiating the beacon signal. Under extreme conditions, such metal may prevent reception of any signals; usually, however, it only causes an error of a few degrees in the accuracy of the bearing. Aboard the great majority of boats, this error is minimal for bearings received from dead ahead or dead astern and maximal for bearings broad on the bow and broad on the quarter. It may be necessary to experiment with the set at several locations before optimum reception is achieved.

Because of the effect of this deviation on RDF bearings, it is important that a deviation card be prepared, as discussed in the following section, unless the RDF is to be used solely for homing, that is for obtaining bearings dead ahead. If you prepare a deviation card, remember that it is valid only when the RDF is in the same location as when the card was prepared.

Preparing an RDF Deviation Card

To prepare an RDF deviation card, which is also called a *calibration card*, the antenna of the transmitting beacon must be nearby within plain sight. Five miles is usually considered to be the absolute limit at which calibration should be attempted; preferably, the distance should be much shorter.

The Coast Guard maintains a few stations that may be used for calibration by advance application to the commander of the appropriate Coast Guard District. These stations are listed in each volume of the *Light List*, together with exact data on the location of the transmitting antenna, etc. Alternately, the short-range homing beacons can be used very conveniently as can the nonsequentially operating radio beacons, as both types operate continuously. The sequential beacons, on the other hand, are not very satisfactory as they are usually on the air only for one minute out of every six. Signals from commercial broadcasting stations, operating in the 535 to 1620 kHz band, may be used if nothing else is available, provided their antennas are visible and can be exactly identified and found on the chart, although this procedure is not as satisfactory as using a marine radio beacon. Radio waves are frequently *refracted*, or bent, when they cross from land to the water.

We will assume that we have found a satisfactory location for the RDF and are within sight of the beacon which we propose to use for calibration purposes. What we need to determine is the error or deviation of the RDF on regularly spaced relative bearings, preferably for every 5 degrees. Start taking bearings when the beacon antenna is dead ahead; have the helmsman sing out "Mark" when it is dead over the bow. Obtain the bearing of the null, and record it; it should read 000° or very close to it. Let us assume that we are going to swing in a counterclockwise direction. The next bearing should be obtained when the antenna bears 005° relative; this may best be determined by a pelorus. The helmsman again sings out "Mark" when he is on the appropriate heading, and then we obtain a new null and record the relative bearing. This process is repeated through 360°, and each relative bearing is noted. Should any gross error appear on any heading, obtain a second bearing on that particular heading. In the event that the received signal is very weak on any series of headings, the implication is that the RDF is in a shielded spot in the boat, and a new location for it should be found. Remember, when taking bearings, that there are two nulls, 180 degrees apart.

Even with the receiver carefully adjusted, the null may cover several degrees of arc. Establish

Table 15-3 Partially Completed Deviation Card for the RDF

Relative Bearing of Antenna	Bearing of Center of Null
000°	000°
005°	004°.5
010°	009°.5
015°	014°
020°	019°
025°	023°.5
030°	028°
035°	033°
040°	038°

the midpoint of the null; this will be the bearing to be recorded. Record the bearings as shown in table 15-3.

When the deviation card is completed, it is often helpful to plot the findings on graph paper. A graph of typical RDF deviation is shown in figure 15-3.

Obtaining Bearings with an RDF

Let us assume that we are en route to Buzzards Bay from Delaware Bay; we came up offshore and made a landfall on Block Island, passing about one mile to the south of Block Island Southeast Light (see Chart TR 1210). Soon after changing course to 052° true off Block Island for the green

flashing black whistle buoy in the center of the entrance to Buzzards Bay, fog sets in, and we decide that it is desirable to obtain an RDF bearing on the radio beacon at Buzzards Light as soon as it comes within range, in order to check our heading. We turn to the *Light List,* the chart of which is produced in figure 15-1, to obtain the necessary data on the Buzzards Light radio beacon. (All lights are listed alphabetically in the index of the *Light List* with a number showing its consecutive listing in the main body of the tables.) It transmits on a frequency of 314 kHz, has a range of approximately 20 miles, and its identifying signal is —... —... (Morse Code for the letters BB). This is a different code and radio frequency than is shown on training chart 1210 TR, which has not been updated.

We now set the RDF in the location for which it is calibrated, being careful to determine that the zero degree line of the RDF bearing scale is aligned parallel to the fore-and-aft line of the boat. We then turn the band selector switch on the RDF to the marine beacon band, tune the receiver to 314 kHz, and turn the set on. We will hear the signal —... —... repeated. (Note that if we had been using a sequenced station on some other frequency we would have received a signal on the frequency but it might not be transmitting

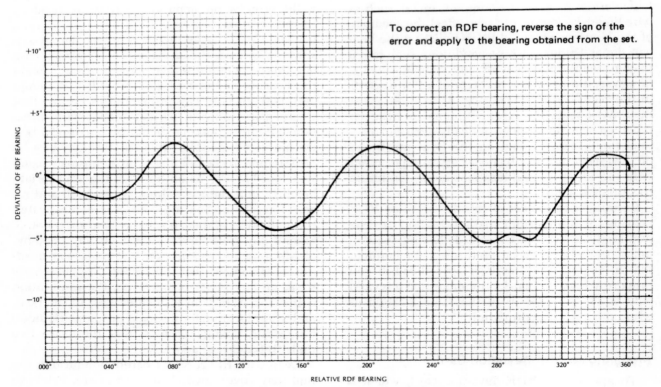

To correct an RDF bearing, reverse the sign of the error and apply to the bearing obtained from the set.

Figure 15-3.   Plot of Typical RDF Deviation

the correct code signal, and we would have to wait for the correct minute out of the sequence of six minutes and obtain the bearing within that limited time period.) We next retune or fine tune the station to obtain maximum signal strength and adjust the volume control to a satisfactory level. The nullmeter is turned on, and with the antenna turned to obtain maximum signal strength, the nullmeter knob is turned to bring the needle to the optimum reading, indicated by a hair line on the dial. The antenna is now rotated to obtain the null, or minimum signal, both visually on the nullmeter and by ear from the loudspeaker. "Mark" is then called to the helmsman, who sings out the boat's heading by compass, which is noted, as is the relative corrected bearing from the RDF bearing circle. These are combined, and the variation and deviation, if any, are applied to obtain the true bearing of Buzzards Light, as described in the following section. The RDF bearing is relative to the fore-and-aft line of the boat. The true course being steered must be applied to the relative bearing to obtain the true bearing of the station.

It is far better practice to establish the null visually, by means of the nullmeter, than to try to do it by ear. Some receivers have a gain control as well as the volume control. Read the instructions furnished by the manufacturer, so that you may obtain optimum readings from the nullmeter. It may be that your set cannot be tuned to give a sharp null point; for example, let us assume that the null is in the vicinity of 030° but cannot be determined precisely. In such a case, note the nullmeter reading slightly to the left of 030°—say the nullmeter reads "1" when the loop antenna is set at 027°. Now rotate the loop to the right of the null until the meter again reads "1." Assume that this occurs when the loop is set at 031°; in this case the null would be read as 029° ($\frac{031° + 027°}{2}$). This process should be repeated several times and the results averaged to get as good a bearing as possible.

Note that in the preceding paragraph, only one bearing was listed as being obtained from Buzzards Light. In actual practice, several bearings would be observed and averaged for maximum accuracy. The reason the bearing is obtained on the null is because this point is relatively easy to determine as compared to the maximum signal. The loop can be swung over a considerable arc while the maximum signal is observed without any apparent diminution of signal strength; on the other hand, only a very small arc is shown for the null.

If we had required an RDF fix instead of the single bearing on Buzzards Light, we could have obtained a bearing on the beacon at Point Judith, remembering that it has only a 10-mile range and might be very weak or not heard at all. As we were almost on a line between Buzzards Light and the radio beacon on Block Island, the latter would not have served to give a good line of position for a fix, although it would provide a good check on the accuracy of the bearing of Buzzards Light.

It sometimes happens that there is doubt as to the direction from which a signal is being received, as an RDF antenna cannot distinguish from which side the signals are coming, and there is therefore an ambiguity of 180 degrees. This doubt can readily be resolved if the set is equipped with a *sense* antenna. Without such an antenna, the problem can be solved by coming to a course that will bring the signal close to the beam and then noting how the bearing changes. For example, in figure 15-4, we obtain a bearing from beacon A, which when converted bears either 045° or 225° true; we do not know which bearing is correct. We come to a heading of 315° true, which brings the relative bearing on our beam, and run on this heading until the relative bearing changes appreciably. In figure 15-4, after running on course 315° for a time, we now obtain a bearing of 090° (or 270°), when converted to true. In actual fact, we would not have needed so great a change in bearing to determine on which side of the beacon we were located; it is used to clarify the illustration.

It is now obvious that we must be to the *west* of the beacon, as it is impossible to reconcile the second bearing when converted to true with any position to the eastward; if we had been to the eastward, the bearing would have had to have changed in a southerly direction.

As a rule of thumb, we can state the beacon lies on that side of the boat on which the relative bearing draws aft.

Correcting RDF Bearings

When an RDF fix is required, several bearings (at least five) should be obtained on each beacon, as it is often difficult to determine the exact null. This may require 18 or 24 minutes, as it is difficult to obtain more than two bearings on each beacon during the minute it is on the air. A great deal of practice is required with the RDF to become really proficient in its use.

The best helmsman should take the wheel when

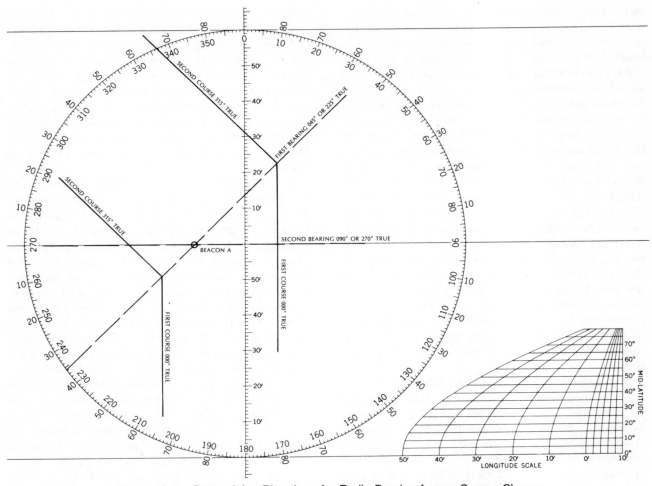

Figure 15-4.   Determining Direction of a Radio Bearing from a Course Change

the RDF is being used. Tell him to concentrate on the compass and hold to the course as closely as possible. When the navigator obtains a null, he will sing out "Mark," and the helmsman then gives the boat's *exact heading* at that instant. The heading and the relative bearing of the null is then entered in a form similar to the one shown in table 15-4. The variation for the locality, the deviation of the compass, and the calibration error of the RDF on that relative bearing are also entered in the form. These three elements are combined and applied to the average of the compass bearings (heading and RDF bearing) when the string of bearings on that beacon is completed.

Table 15-4 Form for Reading RDF Bearings

						Course	032° true 045° per compass
Beacon Point Judith			kHz 325				
Boat's head + RDF bearing = Compass bearing.			Variation	Deviation		Calibration error	
1 043° + 309°	=	352°	15°W	2°E		+1°	
2 045° + 311°	=	356°					
3 044° + 310°	=	354°					
4 046° + 308°	=	354°					
5 044° + 309°	=	353°					
	5	1769					
Average		354°					
RDF calibration error		+1°					
		355° − Var 15°W + Dev 2°E = 342°					

An additional correction or conversion is required for RDF bearings obtained at considerable distances from the transmitting beacon. This is because radio waves travel in great circles; they must, therefore, be converted to rhumb lines for plotting on a Mercator chart. The conversion angle may be obtained conveniently from table 1 in *Bowditch*. However, if you are mathematically inclined and have a slide rule, it may readily be calculated by means of the following formula:

$$\text{Conversion angle} = \sin \text{mid-latitude} \times \tan \tfrac{1}{2} \text{DLO}.$$

The sign of the conversion angle is given in the following table:

Your Latitude	*Direction of Transmitter From You*	*Conversion Angle*
North	Eastward	Plus
North	Westward	Minus
South	Eastward	Minus
South	Westward	Plus

Accuracy of RDF Bearings

The accuracy of the radio direction finder bearings you obtain will depend primarily on your proficiency in using the set, although it will also be affected by other factors, including the quality and design of the receiver. It is, of course, considerably more difficult to get good bearings in rough water: Since the bearings are relative, compass error will also affect the final true bearing which is plotted on the chart.

Due to the peculiarities of the propagation of radio waves, bearings obtained during daylight hours are usually more reliable than those obtained at night. Bearings obtained during the periods of sunrise and sunset tend to be unreliable. In addition, bearings obtained over water tend to be more reliable than those which travel from inland before reaching out to sea; radio waves tend to refract or bend somewhat when passing from over the land to the water.

As a general rule, it may be assumed that an experienced RDF operator in a small vessel can obtain an accuracy of about two degrees at a distance of five miles from the beacon. At a distance of 50 miles, it is not realistic to expect an accuracy of better than five degrees. Any unknown compass error will further deteriorate the final accuracy of the bearing as plotted.

To sum up, prepare an accurate RDF deviation table, get all the practice possible with your set, and get as many bearings as possible on each beacon, averaging the results.

AUTOMATIC DIRECTION FINDERS (ADF)

Automatic direction finders were originally developed for use aboard aircraft, but marine models are on the market and are coming into increasing use afloat.

The earlier ADF's differed from the RDF in that a small loop antenna was spun by a small electric motor, sensing the incoming signal on each revolution. On some modern sets, the same effect is achieved electronically; the signal pick-up is by means of a crossed-loop antenna, placed as high aloft as possible.

To operate, the proper band for the desired station is selected, and the station is tuned in; the automatic portion of the instrument is then turned on, and on the newer models, a needle then turns on a dial, calibrated in degrees, to the bearing of the station without ambiguity as to the reciprocal. Such sets cover the frequency band of 190 to 2550 kHz. The power drain is quite low.

The accuracy that can be obtained with a modern ADF is usually better than that of the RDFs used aboard small craft; however, the ADF is considerably more expensive.

Figure 15-5. A Typical Modern ADF

RADIO TIME SIGNALS

Continuous radio time signals are broadcast from the National Bureau of Standards stations, WWV, at Fort Collins, Colorado, and WWVH at

Kauai, Hawaii, on frequencies of 2.5, 5, 10, 15, and 20 MHz. A voice announcement at the end of each minute gives the call letters of the station and its location and states: "At the tone _____ hours _____ minutes coordinated Universal Time." In the broadcasts from WWV, this announcement is made by a male voice between $7\frac{1}{2}$ and 0 seconds before the minute, while a female voice makes the announcement from WWVH between 15 and $7\frac{1}{2}$ seconds before the minute. Each second, with the exception of the 29th and 59th, is marked by an audible tick.

For ordinary navigational purposes, Coordinated Universal Time may be considered to be the same as Greenwich Mean Time.

During daylight hours, the 15 MHz transmission generally comes in clearly; during night time, on the other hand, best reception is generally obtained by tuning in the 5 MHz broadcast.

The Canadian station, CHU, located at Ottawa, Ontario, also broadcasts a continuous time signal on 3330, 7335, and 14670 kHz. The broadcast is generally similar to that of WWV with a voice announcement at the end of every minute, except that the upcoming time is announced as Eastern Standard Time. These signals are at times easier to receive along the East Coast than those broadcast from WWV.

RADIO WEATHER INFORMATION

Excellent weather information by voice radio transmission is available to boatmen on both coasts as well as on the Great Lakes; it is foolish not to avail oneself of these services when planning a trip on open water.

These broadcasts emanate from a number of sources. The most widely used is that of the National Oceanic and Atmospheric Administration's National Weather Service, which operates a chain of stations on both coasts. Their continuous voice broadcasts are in the FM band, on frequencies of 162.40, 162.475 or 162.55 MHz. The range of transmission of these stations varies between 20 and 40 miles, depending in part upon the height of the transmitting station's antenna above sea level and also upon the configuration of the terrain between the transmitting and receiving antennas. Nearly all VHF radios used by yachtsmen are equipped with at least one of the continuous weather broadcast channels.

The location of all radio stations transmitting weather information, together with their frequencies and scheduled times of transmission—described in the following paragraphs—may be found on the small and inexpensive *Marine Weather Services Charts,* published by the National Weather Service under the National Oceanic and Atmospheric Administration of the U.S. Department of Commerce.

Marine forecasts and warnings, direct from National Weather Service offices, are also broadcast in the AM and FM bands by various commercial radio stations.

Radio telephone communications stations also broadcast weather information at scheduled times.

The weather broadcasts emanating from some airports, while primarily intended for the use of aviators, can also be very helpful to the boatman. These broadcasts are in the 325 to 410 kHz band; this band is included on most radio direction finders.

Radio stations WWV at Fort Collins, Colorado, and WWVH at Kauai, Hawaii, broadcast hourly reports covering the Atlantic and Pacific Coasts, as well as the Central Pacific area.

The U.S. Coast Guard also issues weather advisories for both the Atlantic and Pacific Coasts; the broadcasts for the Atlantic emanate from Portsmouth, VA, while those for the Pacific are transmitted from San Francisco. These latter broadcasts are single side band transmissions, directed primarily towards vessels carrying single side band radio telephones; however, some shortwave radio receivers can be tuned to receive these signals clearly.

As stated above, full information on the frequencies and times of the above weather broadcasts for a given area will be found on the appropriate *Marine Weather Services Chart,* which also shows the location of the visual storm warning displays. These charts may be obtained from:

National Ocean Service
Distribution Division (C44)
Riverdale, MD 20840
Telephone: (301) 436-6990

chapter sixteen

The Scientific Calculator in Piloting

The scientific calculator differs from the common electronic calculator in that it is designed to handle trigonometric functions—sines, cosines, tangents, and cotangents—in addition to the arithmetical functions of addition, subtraction, multiplication, and division. It is a comparatively new and tremendously powerful tool for the navigator; the simpler models, capable of a rapid and accurate solution of all problems encountered in piloting, can be purchased at quite inexpensive prices. More sophisticated models, which are programmable, are capable of repeated solution of the same type of problem; all that is required is to key in the new data and then press the "Start" button. The calculator proceeds to produce the answer or answers without further ado. These latter models, which are extremely well adapted to the solution of problems encountered in celestial navigation, also frequently have a decision-making capability in that, if an intermediate answer is greater than a given quantity, they will follow one routine; if it is smaller, they will follow a different routine to produce the answer.

Most programmable calculators also can convert polar to rectangular coordinates, and vice versa. One advantage of this feature, when combined with several addressable memory compartments in which data can be stored for future retrieval, is discussed under the section on plane sailing.

As the manuals supplied by the manufacturers ordinarily do not devote much space to the use of the calculator aboard ship, examples illustrating the calculator solution of typical problems encountered in piloting are included herewith. *The Calculator Afloat*, published by the U.S. Naval Institute, will be of interest to those who are interested in further consideration of the many uses to which the calculator can be put aboard any vessel.

It is wise to protect calculators aboard ship by keeping them in sealable plastic bags; this will keep out moisture. The calculator should always be stored in such a manner that it is protected from shock. For boats having 12-volt electric systems, and calculators having rechargeable batteries, an inverter, which converts 12v to 115v AC current, will help to keep the batteries charged and permit the operation of other small electric motor-operated devices designed for use with 115v AC current. Where the inverter is not available, spare, fully charged batteries should be kept on board.

A cautionary note: never rely solely on your calculator for the solution of navigational problems. Always have the requisite tables for the solution of problems on board and know how to use them. Murphy's Law works well at sea, "What can go wrong will go wrong."

Speed-time-distance problems may be solved with the calculator using the formulas given on page 72. Fuel consumption problems may also be solved easily and rapidly. However, the scientific calculator really proves its worth when vector problems, such as determining the direction and strength of the true wind when underway, or those encountered in current or traverse sailing, must be solved. The solution of such problems is discussed below.

DETERMINING THE DIRECTION AND STRENGTH OF THE TRUE WIND WHEN UNDER WAY

Figure 16-1A represents a vessel underway, with the apparent wind forward of the beam; the vessel is moving in the direction A towards B; side c represents both the direction of the vessel's travel and her speed. Side b represents the relative direction and strength of the apparent wind

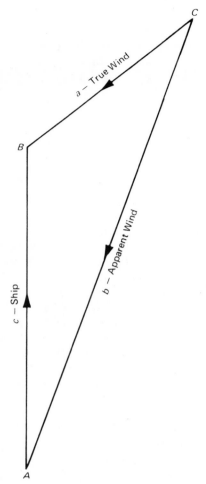

Figure 16-1A.

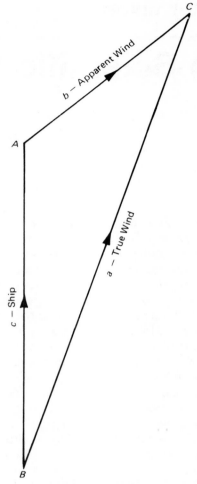

Figure 16-1B.

and side *a* represents the direction and strength of the true wind.

Figure 16-1B shows the vessel with a fair wind; in this instance, she is traveling in the direction *B* towards *A;* side *c* represents both the direction of her travel and her speed. Side *a* again represents the strength and relative direction of the true wind, and side *b* is the apparent wind vector.

The determination of the strength and direction of the true wind involves the use of the same formulas both when the wind is abaft or forward of the beam. The direction of the true wind, relative to the vessel's head, is found by the formula:

$$\tan B = \frac{b \times \sin A}{c\,(-)\,b \times \cos A} \qquad (1)$$

To find the speed of the true wind, we use the formula:

$$a = \frac{b \times \sin A}{\sin B} \qquad (2)$$

In the following examples, we will work to two decimal places, more than enough for the requirements of ordinary navigation. The calculator, while instructed to show values to only two decimal places, will, however, work to eight or more decimal places. It is possible, therefore, that if in working the examples only two decimal places are entered, answers differing slightly from those in the examples will be obtained.

Example 1: We are on course 270° True, making 12 knots, and the apparent wind is from 030° relative or 300° True, speed 25.0 knots. We require the direction and speed of the true wind. We write formula (1):

$$\tan B = \frac{b\,25 \times \sin A\,30°}{c\,12\,(-)\,b\,25 \times \cos A\,30°}$$

$$= \frac{12.50}{(-)\,9.65} = (-)\,1.30$$

Tan⁻¹ (−) 1.30 converts to (−) 52.33°, which means

that the angle B in the triangle is 127.67° (180° (−) 52.33°). However, we need not make this conversion; the angle 52.33°, which we will call 52°, is the angle of the true wind, relative to our course, 270°. As it is on the starboard bow, we add it to 270° and find the true wind is from 322° True, or approximately NW.

To find the true wind speed, we write formula (2):

$$a = \frac{b\,25 \times \sin A\,30°}{\sin B\,127.67°} = \frac{12.50}{0.79} = 15.79$$

We would, therefore, say that the strength of the true wind, to the nearest knot, is 16K.

Example (2): Our course is 125° True, speed 15.0 knots, and the apparent wind is from 230° relative, on our port quarter, at 8 knots. We need to determine the direction and strength of the true wind.

In this instance, the angle A, in the triangle ABC, equals 130° as the relative angle, 230°, subtracted from 360°, gives us 130°. Formula (1) becomes:

$$\tan B = \frac{b\,8 \times \sin A\,130°}{c\,15\,(-)\,b\,8 \times \cos A\,130°} = \frac{6.13}{20.14} = 0.30$$

The angle B, therefore, is 16.92°, which we will call 17°, making the true wind direction from 197° (180° + 17°) relative to our vessel's heading; to this we add our course 125°T to get the direction from which the true wind is blowing, 322°.

To find the strength of the true wind, we write formula (2):

$$a = \frac{b\,8 \times \sin A\,130°}{\sin B\,16.92°} = \frac{6.13}{0.29} = 21.06$$

The wind strength, therefore, is 21 knots, blowing from 322°, or, just north of northwest.

CURRENT SAILING

The scientific calculator lends itself well to the solution of current sailing problems. The first type of problem we will consider is one frequently encountered afloat: we know the set (direction) and drift (speed) of the current; we know the speed at which we can move through the water, and wish to determine the course to steer to reach our destination and how long it will take us to get there.

Figure 16-2A represents a fair current situation, that is, the current is helping the vessel in her movement towards her destination. In figure 16-2B, the current is foul.

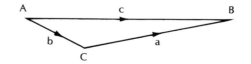

FAIR CURRENT
Figure 16-2A.

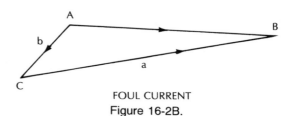

FOUL CURRENT
Figure 16-2B.

In both triangles, the vector c represents the desired track the vessel must follow in order to reach her destination, the vector b represents the set and drift of the current, and the vector a represents the course the vessel must steer in order to reach her destination and the speed at which she will move over the bottom. The angle A represents the difference between the set of the current and the desired track, and the angle B represents the correction angle, that is, the angle we must apply to the direction of the track along which we wish to move, in order to allow for the motion of the current.

Our first step is to determine the value of the correction angle B. To find the value of B, we use the formula:

$$\sin B = \frac{b \times \sin A}{a} \tag{1}$$

Having found the value of the angle B, we proceed to determine our speed of advance, that is, the speed we will make good over the bottom; this is represented by the length of the vector c. To find the value of c, we use the formula:

$$c = \frac{a \times \sin\,[180°\,(-)\,(A + B)]}{\sin A} \tag{2}$$

A couple of examples will illustrate the use of these formulas.

Example (1): We wish to make good a track of 109°; our speed is 11.0 knots. The current is setting 068°; its drift is 1.5 knots. We need to know what course we should steer to offset the current, and what our speed of advance will be.

To find the conversion angle B, we write formula (1):

sin B

$$= \frac{b \; 1.5 \times \sin A \; 41° \; (\text{Track } 109° \; (-) \; \text{set } 068°)}{c \; 11.0}$$

$$= \frac{0.98}{11.0} = 0.09 = B \; 5.13°$$

The correction angle, for steering purposes, we will call 5°. As the current is on our starboard quarter, we will steer 5° to the right of the desired track, making our course 114°.

Next, we will determine our speed of advance, for which we use formula (2):

$$c = \frac{11.0 \times \sin [180° \; (-) \; (A \; 41.0° + B \; 5.13°)]}{\sin A \; 41.0°}$$

$$= \frac{11.0 \times \sin 133.87°}{0.66} = \frac{7.93}{0.66} = 12.09$$

We would, therefore, call our speed of advance 12.1 knots.

Example (2): Our speed is 12.0 knots and we wish to make good a track of 340°; the current set is 195° and its drift is 2.0 knots. What should be our course, and what will our speed of advance be?

Formula (1) becomes:

sin B

$$= \frac{b \; 2.0 \times \sin A \; 145.0° \; (\text{Track } 340° \; (-) \; \text{set } 195°)}{c \; 12.0}$$

$$= \frac{2.0 \times 0.57}{12.0} = 0.10 = B \; 5.49°$$

For steering purposes, we would call the correction angle 5.5°. As the set is on our starboard bow, we would steer 5.5° to the right of the desired track, making our course 345.5°.

To find the speed of advance, we write formula (2):

$$c = \frac{a \; 12.0 \times \sin [180° \; (-) \; (A \; 145.0° + B \; 5.49°)]}{\sin A \; 145.0°}$$

$$= \frac{12.0 \times \sin 29.51°}{0.57} = \frac{5.91}{0.57} = 10.31$$

Our speed of advance will, therefore, be 10.3 knots.

DISTANCE TO THE HORIZON

Knowing your height of eye above the water, the distance to the horizon in nautical miles may be found with the calculator by means of the formula:

$$D = 1.144 \; \sqrt{\text{HE in feet}}$$

For finding the distance in statute miles, the formula is:

$$D = 1.317 \; \sqrt{\text{HE in feet}}$$

Thus, when you sight the bow wave of a steamer just appearing on the horizon, you can determine the range.

Example (1): The height of eye is 11 feet. What is the distance to the horizon in nautical miles?

$$D = 1.144 \; \sqrt{11} = 3.79$$

The distance to the horizon is, therefore, 3.79 miles.

Example (2): The height of a lighthouse above the water is listed in the *Light List* as 114 feet. The observer's height of eye is 8 feet. At what distance, in nautical miles, can he expect to sight the light on a clear night?

The height of the light is 114 feet. The distance from the light to the horizon is found by formula (1):

$$D = 1.144 \; \sqrt{114} = 12.21$$

The distance from the light to the horizon is, therefore, 12.21 nautical miles.

The observer's height of eye is 8 feet. To find the distance to the horizon for his height of eye by formula (1) we write:

$$D = 1.144 \; \sqrt{8} = 3.24$$

Next we add the two distances, 12.21 and 3.24 miles, to find that he should sight the light at a distance of 15.45 miles.

DISTANCE BY BEARINGS

The following examples assume that no current is flowing.

Distance Off When Abeam by One Bearing and Run to Beam

The distance off a stationary object when abeam can be calculated by first taking a bearing on the bow and noting the distance run from the time of that bearing to the time the object is abeam. The distance is found by the formula:

$$D = \frac{R \times \sin A}{\cos A}$$

D being the distance off when abeam, R is the distance run, and A is the relative angle on the bow.

Example (1): A lighthouse is sighted bearing 323° relative and after running 5.0 miles, it is abeam. What is our distance from the lighthouse at this moment?

When the light bore 323° relative, it was 37° on the port bow (360° (−) 323°); we will use this value in writing formula (1):

$$D = \frac{R\ 5.0 \times \sin A\ 37°}{\cos A\ 37°} = \frac{5.0 \times 0.60}{0.80} = 3.77$$

The light, therefore, was distant 3.77 miles at the moment it was abeam.

Note: Here we converted the relative bearing, 323°, to a bearing on the bow, as sines of angles greater than 180° carry a minus prefix, and, had we used 323°, our distance would have appeared as (−) 3.77 miles.

Cosines of angles between 90° and 270° also carry a minus prefix.

Distance Off at Second Bearing by Two Bearings

The distance off a fixed object can also be determined at the time of a second bearing, if two bearings on the bow are obtained, and the distance run between them is noted. The greater the angular spread between the two bearings, the more accurate will be the distance obtained.

Solution is by the formula:

$$D = \frac{R \times \sin A}{\sin (A \sim B)}$$

in which D is the distance at the moment the second bearing is obtained, A is the first bearing on the bow, B is the second bearing on the bow, and R is the distance run between the two bearings.

Example (1): A lighthouse bore 025° relative; after running 6.0 miles, the light bears 075° relative. We require the distance off the light at the time of the second bearing.

We write the formula:

$$D = \frac{R\ 6.0 \times \sin A\ 25°}{\sin 50° (A\ 25° \sim B\ 75°)} = \frac{2.54}{0.77} = 3.31$$

Our distance off the light, at the time of the second bearing, was, therefore, 3.31 miles.

Distance Off When Abeam by Two Bearings on the Bow and the Run Between

We can determine the distance we will be off a fixed object when it is abeam, by taking two bearings on the bow, and noting the distance run between the bearings.

Our first step is to determine the distance off the object at the time of the first bearing. This we do at the time the second bearing is obtained, by determining the angle at the object formed by the two bearing lines; this angle forms the apex of a triangle, whose base is formed by the run between bearings. To illustrate how the value of the angle at the apex is determined, suppose the first bearing on the bow were 30° and the second were 50°, the angle at the object would be 20°, as we can see from figure 16-3; 180° (−) (130° + 30°) = 20°.

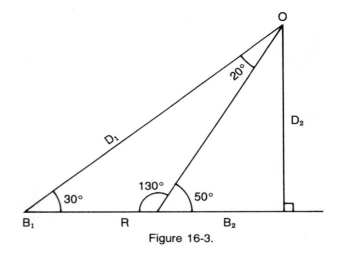

Figure 16-3.

We then find the distance off the object at the time of the first bearing by the formula:

$$D_1 = \frac{R \times \sin B_2}{\sin O} \qquad (1)$$

where D_1 is the distance off at the first bearing, R is the distance run between the bearings, B_2 is the second bearing on the bow, subtracted from 180°, and O is the angle between the two bearings at the object.

Having found D_1, we can determine our distance off the object when it is abeam, D_2, by the formula:

$$D_2 = \frac{D_1 \times \sin A}{\sin 90°}$$

which we can write as:

$$D_2 = D_1 \times \sin A \qquad (2)$$

as sin 90° is equal to 1.

In this formula, D_1 is the distance off the object at the time of the first bearing, and A is the first angle on the bow.

Example (1): We pick up a light bearing 30° on the bow; after sailing 5.8 miles it bears 57° on the bow. What will be our distance off the light when it is abeam?

Our first step is to determine the value of the angle O, formed by the two bearing lines. The first bearing on the bow is 30°, and the second is 57°; subtracting 57° from 180°, we get 123°, the value of B_2. To 123° we add the first bearing on the bow, 30°; the sum is 153°. This value, in turn, is subtracted from 180°, which makes the angle at the object, O, 27°.

We can now write formula (1):

$$D_1 = \frac{R\ 5.8 \times \sin B_2\ 123°}{O \sin 27°} = \frac{4.86}{0.45} = 10.71$$

At the time the first bearing was obtained, we were, therefore, 10.71 miles off the light.

Formula (2) becomes, therefore:

$$D_2 = D_1\ 10.71 \times \sin A\ 30° = 5.36$$

When abeam, the light will therefore be distant 5.36 miles.

PLANE AND TRAVERSE SAILING

A "sailing" is defined by *Bowditch* as a method of solving the various problems involving course, distance, difference of latitude and longitude and departure. Departure is defined as the distance between two meridians at any given parallel of latitude, expressed in linear units, usually nautical miles.

In piloting, we are usually concerned with only two of the sailings, plane sailing and traverse sailing. In both these sailings the earth is assumed to be a flat surface, and both yield satisfactory results over the comparatively short distances usually encountered in piloting. The calculator greatly facilitates the solution of problems in either sailing.

In plane sailing we are concerned with only two locations, a point of departure and a destination. Traverse sailing applies particularly to sailing vessels which, when beating to windward, must tack from time to time; in this latter case, it is necessary to determine position after sailing on two or more different courses, and for differing distances.

Plane Sailing

In plane sailing the figure formed by the meridian passing through the point of departure, the

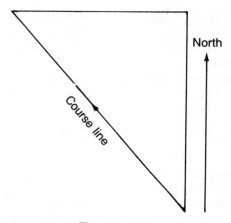

Figure 16-4.

parallel of latitude passing through the destination, and the course line, is considered to be a plane right triangle, as shown in figure 16-4. As in any right triangle, if a second angle and the length of any side are known, the remaining angle and the length of either other side can be determined using the formulas given below.

In the triangle in figure 16-5, P_1 represents the point of departure and P_2 represents the point of arrival. The side p represents the "departure," or distance in nautical miles, east or west, made good in proceeding to the destination. The side l is a portion of the meridian drawn from the point of departure to the parallel of latitude of the destination; it represents the difference of latitude between the two points. It is measured in nautical miles; a nautical mile is equal to one minute of latitude. The side D represents the distance in nautical miles separating P_1 and P_2. The angle C is the course angle from P_1 to P_2. Note that in

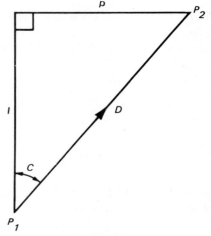

Figure 16-5.

plane sailing course is reckoned as course angle, figured from north or south to 90° east or west. A course of 283° is, therefore, written as N 77° W, and one of 147° becomes S 33° E.

The formulas for plane sailing are:

given C and D, to find l, $I = \cos C \times D$ (1)

given C and D, to find p, $p = \sin C \times D$ (2)

given l and p, to find C, $\tan C = p/l$ (3)

given C and p, to find D, $D = p/\sin C$ (4)

given C and l, to find D, $D = p/\cos C$ (5)

When it is desired to convert p to difference of longitude in minutes of arc, the formula is:

$$DL_o = p/\cos L \qquad (6)$$

in which L, for the greatest accuracy, should be the mid-latitude between P_1 and P_2.

Conversely, knowing DL_o,

$$p = DL_o \times \cos L \qquad (7)$$

The effect of an estimated current, for which allowance is to be made, in effect constitutes a traverse sailing problem, as the set is treated as a second course, and the drift multiplied by the number of hours involved is used as the distance.

Traverse Sailing

Traverse sailing permits the determination of a single course and distance, after a vessel has sailed on a number of different courses for differing distances. Essentially, it consists of making a tabulation of a series of plane-sailing problems; if allowance is to be made for current, it is handled as described above, in the section on plane sailing. All values in each column, N, S, E and W, are then totaled and combined to yield two values, such as miles N and E, or S and W, etc.

With calculators having the ability to convert polar to rectangular coordinates, and vice versa, the solution of plane-sailing problems is extremely simple. For example, with calculators using the reverse Polish notation, it is only necessary to key in the course, press the "Enter" key, then key in the distance and, finally, press the key that converts the entries to rectangular coordinates. The distance moved north will then appear as a positive value; if the distance is southerly, it will be preceded by a minus sign. The key exchanging the contents of the x and y registers is then pressed. If it is easterly, the distance will appear as a positive value; if the distance is westerly, it will be preceded by a minus sign. For algebraic notation calculators, the keying process will differ somewhat, but the process is essentially the same.

In traverse sailing, having calculated the distance sailed north or south on the first leg, this value is stored in an addressable memory; having obtained the distance east or west, it is stored in a second memory.

Having calculated the distance north or south on the second leg, the first distance N or S is recalled, and the new value is added to it, and the sum is stored in the same memory. The distance E or W is next obtained, added to the first distance E or W, and again stored in that memory. This process is repeated for each leg; after the process is completed, the total distances N or S and E or W will appear as single values when recalled from their respective memory slots.

Example: We sail 33.7 miles on $C\,135°$, then 16.1 miles on $C\,259°$, and finally 39.0 miles on $C\,293°$. We desire to know our change in latitude and departure. Without the polar-rectangular conversion feature, we would tabulate the results as follows:

$C\,135°$,	$D\,33.7$,	$l\,(-)$ 23.83 (S)	,p	23.83	(E)
259°	16.1	$(-)$ 3.07 (S)		$(-)$15.80	(W)
293°	39.0	$+$ 15.24 (N)		$(-)$35.90	(W)
		$l\,(-)$ 11.66 (S)	p	$(-)$27.87	(W)

When using the polar-rectangular conversion capability, and the memory storages, after adding the final l and p factors for the last leg to the sums of the previous values stored in their respective memories, it would only be necessary to read the two respective sums, l $(-)$ 11.66, and p $(-)$ 27.87; no tabulation of intermediate results would be required, and no addition of the various values.

chapter seventeen

Navigation Publications

A great number of charts, tables, and texts are published by various government agencies for the use of mariners. Those of interest to navigators of small craft, operating primarily in U.S. waters, are listed below.

Two texts warrant special attention. The first of these is the *American Practical Navigator,* usually called *Bowditch* after its original author. We have referred repeatedly to *Bowditch* in the course of this text; it is an encyclopedic compendium of navigational information and useful tables and warrants inclusion in every nautical library. It is published by the Defense Mapping Agency Hydrographic/Topographic Center (DMAHTC) as *Pub. No. 9. Bowditch* may be obtained through the DMAHTC or the Government Printing Office, Washington, D.C.

The second text is *Dutton's Navigation and Piloting* published by the U.S. Naval Institute, Annapolis, Maryland. This is one of the Navy's and Coast Guard's main references on navigation and is in general use throughout both services. It is recommended to all students who wish to obtain a good background in all aspects of marine navigation. *Dutton's* may be purchased from the U.S. Naval Institute or from bookstores.

NATIONAL OCEAN SERVICE PUBLICATIONS

The National Ocean Service* is charged with preparing charts of all of the United States waters, as well as with issuing various publications connected with navigation in these waters. These include the *U.S. Coast Pilots, Tide Tables, Tidal Current Tables,* and *Tidal Current Charts.* The *Coast Pilots* contain much helpful information which cannot be conveniently presented on charts, such as navigation regulations, outstanding landmarks, dangers, weather, and port facilities. The

* Prior to 1 December 1982, called the National Ocean Survey.

tidal data publications we have discussed in detail in previous chapters.

Particular attention is directed to NOS *Chart No. 1,* which lists all the symbols and abbreviations used on all U.S. charts, without regard to source; all chart-issuing authorities have standardized the same symbols and abbreviations. An understanding of these symbols and abbreviations is necessary to interpret correctly the information presented on charts. This information is reproduced on the reverse side of chart TR 1210. National Ocean Service charts are listed by number and the areas they cover in NOS *Nautical Chart Catalogs Nos. 1, 2, 3,* and *4,* which may be obtained without cost. *Catalog No. 1* lists the charts for the Atlantic and Gulf Coasts, including Puerto Rico and the Virgin Islands. *No. 2* covers the Pacific Coast, including Hawaii, Guam, and the Samoan Islands. *No. 3* takes in Alaska and the Aleutian Islands. *No. 4* covers the Great Lakes and adjacent waterways.

These catalogs also list the names and addresses of authorized sales agents for National Ocean Service charts and publications. Catalogs may be obtained gratis by application to the Distribution Division, National Ocean Service, Riverdale, Maryland 20840.

Importance of Up-to-date Charts

It seems appropriate at this point again to call attention to the necessity for keeping all charts up to date. National Ocean Service has the following to say on this subject:

> The date of a chart is of vital importance to the navigator. When charted information becomes obsolete, *further use of the chart for navigation may be dangerous.* Natural and artificial changes, many of them critical, are occuring constantly, and it is important that navigators obtain up-to-date charts at regular intervals, or hand correct their copies

for changes published in the *Notice to Mariners*.

Charts are revised at regular intervals. Users should consult the Dates of Latest Editions for date of current edition.

Any defects found in National Ocean Service charts should be reported to the Director, National Ocean Service, National Oceanic and Atmospheric Administration, Rockville, Maryland 20852.

A list of publications issued by the National Ocean Service and dealing with navigational matters follows.

United States Coast Pilots

Coast Pilots are published in a series of volumes covering the following areas:

ATLANTIC COAST
No. 1 Eastport to Cape Cod
No. 2 Cape Cod to Sandy Hook
No. 3 Sandy Hook to Cape Henry
No. 4 Cape Henry to Key West
No. 5 Gulf of Mexico, Puerto Rico, and Virgin Islands
No. 6 Great Lakes and St. Lawrence River

PACIFIC COAST
No. 7 California, Oregon, Washington, and Hawaii

ALASKA
No. 8 Dixon Entrance to Cape Spencer
No. 9 Cape Spencer to Beaufort Sea

Cumulative supplements to each volume, containing changes reported since the dates of the editions, are published early each year and are distributed free.

Tide Tables

The *Tide Tables* are published in four volumes covering the following areas:

East Coast, North and South America;
West Coast, North and South America;
Europe and West Coast of Africa;
Central and Western Pacific, and Indian Ocean.

Tidal Current Tables

The *Tidal Current Tables* are published in two volumes as follows:

Atlantic Coast of North America;
Pacific Coast of North America and Asia.

Tidal Current Charts

The *Tidal Current Charts* are published in a series of volumes, each consisting of a set of 12 charts which depict, by means of arrows and figures, the direction and velocity of the tidal current for each hour of the tidal cycle. They cover the following areas:

Boston Harbor
Narragansett Bay
Narragansett Bay to Nantucket Sound
Long Island Sound and Block Island Sound
New York Harbor
Delaware Bay and River
Chesapeake Bay (upper)
Charleston Harbor, South Carolina
San Francisco Bay
Puget Sound—Northern Part
Puget Sound—Southern Part

The Narragansett Bay and the New York Harbor tidal current charts are to be used with the annual tide tables. The other charts require the annual current tables.

U.S. COAST GUARD PUBLICATIONS

The primary publication of the Coast Guard is the *Light List*, which may be obtained through the National Ocean Service sales agents or the Superintendent of Documents, U.S. Government Printing Office, Washington, D.C. The *Light List* is intended to furnish more complete information concerning aids to navigation than can be conveniently shown on charts. It is not intended to be used in navigation in the place of charts, and *Coast Pilots* should not be so used. The *Light List* is published in five volumes as follows:

Volume I   Atlantic Coast from St. Croix River, Maine, to Little River, South Carolina
Volume II   Atlantic and Gulf Coasts from Little River, South Carolina, to Rio Grande, Texas
Volume III   Pacific Coast and Pacific Islands
Volume IV   Great Lakes
Volume V   Mississippi River System

U.S. ARMY ENGINEER DIVISION PUBLICATIONS

The U.S. Army Engineer Division is responsible for charts of the inland rivers. The areas of coverage and the appropriate offices from which charts may be obtained are listed below. Charts of the Great Lakes are now published by and available from the National Ocean Service.

> *Charts and maps of the Lower Mississippi River from the Gulf of Mexico to the Ohio River;* St. Francis River; White River; Big Sunflower River; and Atchafalaya River
>> U.S. ARMY ENGINEER DIVISION
>> *Lower Mississippi Valley*
>> P.O. Box 60
>> Vicksburg, Mississippi 39180

> *Charts of the Middle and Upper Mississippi River and Illinois Waterway to Lake Michigan*
>> U.S. ARMY ENGINEER DIVISION
>> 219 S. Dearbon St.
>> Chicago, Illinois 60604

> *Charts of the Missouri River*
>> U.S. ARMY ENGINEER DIVISION
>> 6014 U.S. Post Office
>> Omaha, Nebraska 68102

> *Charts of the Ohio River*
>> U.S. ARMY ENGINEER DIVISION
>> *Ohio River*
>> P.O. Box 1159
>> Cincinnati, Ohio 45201

DEFENSE MAPPING AGENCY HYDROGRAPHIC/ TOPOGRAPHIC CENTER

This office was formerly the U.S. Naval Oceanographic Office and is still sometimes referred to as the Oceanographic Office. It is charged with preparing charts, lists of lights, sailing directions (similar to the NOS *Coast Pilots*), etc., for all areas other than United States inland and coastal waters. Additionally, the Center publishes much other material of interest to the navigator, such as tables for the reduction of celestial observations, azimuth tables for checking the compass, etc.

In addition to *Bowditch,* referred to previously, the Center publishes *Pub. No. 117, Radio Navigational Aids.* This publication gives the necessary information on a world-wide basis to permit use of all available radio aids, such as nondirectional radio beacons, time signals, etc.

Other publications of wide interest include the monthly Pilot Charts for the North Atlantic and North Pacific Oceans. These can be of great help to anyone going offshore or making coastwise passages, as the Pilot Charts show on a monthly basis the direction and force of the winds normally encountered, the percentage of days when gales and fog may be expected, the average flow of ocean currents, normal temperatures and barometric pressure, as well as much other useful information.

DMAHTC publications can be obtained through many of the National Ocean Service sales agents, most of whom are also agents for the Hydrographic/Topographic Center.

U.S. NAVAL OBSERVATORY

The *Nautical Almanac* is published by the U.S. Naval Observatory. It is for sale by the Superintendent of Documents, U.S. Government Printing Office, Washington, D.C. 20402. The *Nautical Almanac* is a must for everyone interested in celestial navigation.

THE NATIONAL WEATHER SERVICE OF THE U.S. DEPARTMENT OF COMMERCE

The National Weather Service annually publishes a series of small charts called *Marine Weather Services Charts.* These charts show the locations of all points where visual storm warnings are displayed. In addition, they list the various National Weather Service Offices together with their telephone numbers and the hours when forecasts and warnings are available.

Also listed are the radio stations located in the area covered by each chart which broadcast weather data. The call letters of each station are given, together with the station's frequency, and the times of the weather broadcasts.

These charts also list the exact geographic location of the antenna of each station. This can be of great assistance to anyone using these stations to obtain RDF bearings.

Each chart covers a considerable stretch of the coast; the easternmost, for example, covers the area from Eastport, Maine, to Montauk Point, New York. The next extends from Montauk Point to Manasquan, New Jersey; the next from Manasquan to Cape Hatteras, North Carolina, etc. The latter-mentioned chart includes stations serving the Delaware and Chesapeake Bays.

These charts are available from the National Ocean Survey.

Notices to Mariners

The *Weekly Notice to Mariners* presents information affecting charts as well as *Coast Pilots, Sailing Directions, Fleet Guides,* Catalogues of Nautical Charts, *Light Lists, Radio Navigation Aids* and such other publications as may from time to time require updating. *Local Notices to Mariners* are issued by each Coast Guard district and should be used instead of the weekly notices by mariners operating within one Coast Guard district, the Intracoastal Waterway, and other waterways and small harbors not normally used by oceangoing vessels.

The *Weekly Notice to Mariners* may be obtained from the Commander, DMA Hydrographic/Topographic Center. *Local Notices to Mariners* may be obtained from the commanders of the local Coast Guard districts listed below:

First Coast Guard District
150 Causeway St.
Boston, Mass. 02114

Second Coast Guard District
1430 Olive St.
St. Louis, Mo. 63103

Third Coast Guard District
Governors Island
New York, N.Y. 10004

Fifth Coast Guard District
Federal Building
431 Crawford St.
Portsmouth, Va. 23705

Seventh Coast Guard District
Room 1018
Federal Building
51 Southwest First Ave.
Miami, Fla. 33130

Eighth Coast Guard District
Hale Boggs Federal Building
500 Camp St.
New Orleans, La. 70130

Ninth Coast Guard District
Federal Office Building
1240 East 9th St.
Cleveland, Ohio 44199

Eleventh Coast Guard District
Union Bank Building
1400 Oceangate
Long Beach, Calif. 90822

Twelfth Coast Guard District
Appraisers Building
630 Sansome St.
San Francisco, Calif. 94126

Thirteenth Coast Guard District
915 Second Ave.
Seattle, Wash. 98174

Fourteenth Coast Guard District
300 Ala Moana Blvd.
Honolulu, Hawaii 96850

Seventeenth Coast Guard District
Box 3-5000
Community Building
Juneau, Alaska 99802

Canadian Charts

Charts of Canadian coastal and Great Lakes waters may be obtained from:

Hydrographic Chart Dist. Office
P.O. Box 8080
1675 Russel Rd.
Ottawa, Ontario, K1G 3H6
Canada

Appendix

ABBREVIATIONS

ADF	Automatic Direction Finder
AM	Amplitude Modulation
AVC	Automatic Volume Control
B	Bearing
BFO	Beat Frequency Oscillator
C	Course
CC	Compass Course
CE	Compass Error
CHU	Canadian Radio Time Signal
CW	Continuous Wave
D	Drift
DLO	Difference of Longitude
DR	Dead Reckoning
E	Ebb
EP	Estimated Position
ETA	Estimated Time of Arrival
ETD	Estimated Time of Departure
F	Flood
FM	Frequency Modulation
GMT	Greenwich Mean Time
Hdg	Heading
HW	High Water
Hz	Hertz
ITR	Intended Track
kHz	Kilohertz
KT	Knot

L	Latitude
λ	Longitude
Lo	Longitude
LOP	Line of Position
LW	Low Water
MAG	Magnetic
MC	Magnetic Course
MH	Magnetic Heading
MHz	Megahertz
MPH	Miles per Hour
NOAA	National Oceanographic and Atmospheric Administration
NOS	National Ocean Service
RB	Relative Bearing
RDF	Radio Direction Finder
RFIX	Running Fix
S	Speed
SH	Ship's Head
SMG	Speed Made Good
SOA	Speed of Advance
SOG	Speed Over Ground
TB	True Bearing
TC	True Course
TH	True Heading
TR	Track
VHF	Very High Frequency
WWV	Radio Time Signal Station, Ft. Collins, Colo.
WWVH	Radio Time Signal Station, Hawaii

Conversion Table for Meters, Feet, and Fathoms

Meters	Feet	Fathoms	Meters	Feet	Fathoms	Feet	Meters	Feet	Meters	Fathoms	Meters	Fathoms	Meters
1	3. 28	0. 55	61	200. 13	33. 36	1	0. 30	61	18. 59	1	1. 83	61	111. 56
2	6. 56	1. 09	62	203. 41	33. 90	2	0. 61	62	18. 90	2	3. 66	62	113. 39
3	9. 84	1. 64	63	206. 69	34. 45	3	0. 91	63	19. 20	3	5. 49	63	115. 21
4	13. 12	2. 19	64	209. 97	35. 00	4	1. 22	64	19. 51	4	7. 32	64	117. 04
5	16. 40	2. 73	65	213. 25	35. 54	5	1. 52	65	19. 81	5	9. 14	65	118. 87
6	19. 68	3. 28	66	216. 54	36. 09	6	1. 83	66	20. 12	6	10. 97	66	120. 70
7	22. 97	3. 83	67	219. 82	36. 64	7	2. 13	67	20. 42	7	12. 80	67	122. 53
8	26. 25	4. 37	68	223. 10	37. 18	8	2. 44	68	20. 73	8	14. 63	68	124. 36
9	29. 53	4. 92	69	226. 38	37. 73	9	2. 74	69	21. 03	9	16. 46	69	126. 19
10	32. 81	5. 47	70	229. 66	38. 28	10	3. 05	70	21. 34	10	18. 29	70	128. 02
11	36. 09	6. 01	71	232. 94	38. 82	11	3. 35	71	21. 64	11	20. 12	71	129. 85
12	39. 37	6. 56	72	236. 22	39. 37	12	3. 66	72	21. 95	12	21. 95	72	131. 67
13	42. 65	7. 11	73	239. 50	39. 92	13	3. 96	73	22. 25	13	23. 77	73	133. 50
14	45. 93	7. 66	74	242. 78	40. 46	14	4. 27	74	22. 56	14	25. 60	74	135. 33
15	49. 21	8. 20	75	246. 06	41. 01	15	4. 57	75	22. 86	15	27. 43	75	137. 16
16	52. 49	8. 75	76	249. 34	41. 56	16	4. 88	76	23. 16	16	29. 26	76	138. 99
17	55. 77	9. 30	77	252. 62	42. 10	17	5. 18	77	23. 47	17	31. 09	77	140. 82
18	59. 06	9. 84	78	255. 90	42. 65	18	5. 49	78	23. 77	18	32. 92	78	142. 65
19	62. 34	10. 39	79	259. 19	43. 20	19	5. 79	79	24. 08	19	34. 75	79	144. 48
20	65. 62	10. 94	80	262. 47	43. 74	20	6. 10	80	24. 38	20	36. 58	80	146. 30
21	68. 90	11. 48	81	265. 75	44. 29	21	6. 40	81	24. 69	21	38. 40	81	148. 13
22	72. 18	12. 03	82	269. 03	44. 84	22	6. 71	82	24. 99	22	40. 23	82	149. 96
23	75. 46	12. 58	83	272. 31	45. 38	23	7. 01	83	25. 30	23	42. 06	83	151. 79
24	78. 74	13. 12	84	275. 59	45. 93	24	7. 32	84	25. 60	24	43. 89	84	153. 62
25	82. 02	13. 67	85	278. 87	46. 48	25	7. 62	85	25. 91	25	45. 72	85	155. 45
26	85. 30	14. 22	86	282. 15	47. 03	26	7. 92	86	26. 21	26	47. 55	86	157. 28
27	88. 58	14. 76	87	285. 43	47. 57	27	8. 23	87	26. 52	27	49. 38	87	159. 11
28	91. 86	15. 31	88	288. 71	48. 12	28	8. 53	88	26. 82	28	51. 21	88	160. 93
29	95. 14	15. 86	89	291. 99	48. 67	29	8. 84	89	27. 13	29	53. 04	89	162. 76
30	98. 42	16. 40	90	295. 28	49. 21	30	9. 14	90	27. 43	30	54. 86	90	164. 59
31	101. 71	16. 95	91	298. 56	49. 76	31	9. 45	91	27. 74	31	56. 69	91	166. 42
32	104. 99	17. 50	92	301. 84	50. 31	32	9. 75	92	28. 04	32	58. 52	92	168. 25
33	108. 27	18. 04	93	305. 12	50. 85	33	10. 06	93	28. 35	33	60. 35	93	170. 08
34	111. 55	18. 59	94	308. 40	51. 40	34	10. 36	94	28. 65	34	62. 18	94	171. 91
35	114. 83	19. 14	95	311. 68	51. 95	35	10. 67	95	28. 96	35	64. 01	95	173. 74
36	118. 11	19. 68	96	314. 96	52. 49	36	10. 97	96	29. 26	36	65. 84	96	175. 57
37	121. 39	20. 23	97	318. 24	53. 04	37	11. 28	97	29. 57	37	67. 67	97	177. 39
38	124. 67	20. 78	98	321. 52	53. 59	38	11. 58	98	29. 87	38	69. 49	98	179. 22
39	127. 95	21. 33	99	324. 80	54. 13	39	11. 89	99	30. 18	39	71. 32	99	181. 05
40	131. 23	21. 87	100	328. 08	54. 68	40	12. 19	100	30. 48	40	73. 15	100	182. 88
41	134. 51	22. 42	101	331. 36	55. 23	41	12. 50	101	30. 78	41	74. 98	101	184. 71
42	137. 80	22. 97	102	334. 64	55. 77	42	12. 80	102	31. 09	42	76. 81	102	186. 54
43	141. 08	23. 51	103	337. 93	56. 32	43	13. 11	103	31. 39	43	78. 64	103	188. 37
44	144. 36	24. 06	104	341. 21	56. 87	44	13. 41	104	31. 70	44	80. 47	104	190. 20
45	147. 64	24. 61	105	344. 49	57. 41	45	13. 72	105	32. 00	45	82. 30	105	192. 02
46	150. 92	25. 15	106	347. 77	57. 96	46	14. 02	106	32. 31	46	84. 12	106	193. 85
47	154. 20	25. 70	107	351. 05	58. 51	47	14. 33	107	32. 61	47	85. 95	107	195. 68
48	157. 48	26. 25	108	354. 33	59. 06	48	14. 63	108	32. 92	48	87. 78	108	197. 51
49	160. 76	26. 79	109	357. 61	59. 60	49	14. 94	109	33. 22	49	89. 61	109	199. 34
50	164. 04	27. 34	110	360. 89	60. 15	50	15. 24	110	33. 53	50	91. 44	110	201. 17
51	167. 32	27. 89	111	364. 17	60. 70	51	15. 54	111	33. 83	51	93. 27	111	203. 00
52	170. 60	28. 43	112	367. 45	61. 24	52	15. 85	112	34. 14	52	95. 10	112	204. 83
53	173. 88	28. 98	113	370. 73	61. 79	53	16. 15	113	34. 44	53	96. 93	113	206. 65
54	177. 16	29. 53	114	374. 02	62. 34	54	16. 46	114	34. 75	54	98. 76	114	208. 48
55	180. 45	30. 07	115	377. 30	62. 88	55	16. 76	115	35. 05	55	100. 58	115	210. 31
56	183. 73	30. 62	116	380. 58	63. 43	56	17. 07	116	35. 36	56	102. 41	116	212. 14
57	187. 01	31. 17	117	383. 86	63. 98	57	17. 37	117	35. 66	57	104. 24	117	213. 97
58	190. 29	31. 71	118	387. 14	64. 52	58	17. 68	118	35. 97	58	106. 07	118	215. 80
59	193. 57	32. 26	119	390. 42	65. 07	59	17. 98	119	36. 27	59	107. 90	119	217. 63
60	196. 85	32. 81	120	393. 70	65. 62	60	18. 29	120	36. 58	60	109. 73	120	219. 46

Index